Fred Herr

S0-AFC-028

TEILHARD
de
CHARDIN

TEILHARD de CHARDIN

Reconciliation in Christ

selected spiritual writings

introduced and edited by
Jean Maalouf

New City Press

I dedicate this book to all those who are or will be engaged in reconciling what seems irreconcilable, and especially to all those whose eyes perceive the inter-connection of all things, in the one earth, one universe, one God.

Published in the United States by New City Press
202 Cardinal Rd., Hyde Park, NY 12538
©2002 Jean Maalouf

Cover design by Nick Cianfarani

Library of Congress Cataloging-in-Publication Data:

Teilhard de Chardin, Pierre.
  [Selections. English. 2001]
  Reconciliation in Christ : selected spiritual writings / Teilhard de Chardin ; introduced and edited by Jean Maalouf.
    p. cm.
  Includes bibliographical references (p.)
  Contents: Reconciling the two faiths--Reconciling spirit and matter--Reconciling the within and the without--Reconciling science and religion--Convergence--Union--Unification through love--Synthesis--Reconciliation in Christ--Communion.
    1. Spiritual life--Catholic Church. 2. Reconciliation--Religious aspects--Catholic Church. I. Maalouf, Jean. II. Title.

  BX2350.3 .T4513 2001
  248.4'82--dc21   2001052143

Printed in Canada

Contents

Abbreviations

Introduction

Deep down, in the very core of the human heart, there is a huge hole of limitless dissatisfaction. It is the kind of hole that can never be filled with things we possess or do. This is why we keep running toward a new house, a new job, a new relationship, a new lifestyle, a new liturgy, a new church, a new spirituality, etc. . . . , thinking that each new step we make might be the answer to our dissatisfaction.

At an even deeper level, we suffer from the general conditions of our existence. We feel overwhelmed by the infinitely small in the constitution of matter, by the infinitely large in the structure of the universe, and by the infinite number of years going back in time and the unknown number of years stretching ahead. We are, perhaps unconsciously, crushed by the space-time factor. We realize our fragility in the face of wars and diseases. We are intimidated by the merciless hostility of the huge masses and of large, impersonal institutions. We fear the blind alley, the closed universe, our own death, and the death of humankind. We are afraid.[1]

The truth is that, underlying this fear, anxiety, unrest, and agitation, there seems to be a hidden quest for genuineness and a sincere search for a proper way out.

Indeed, we are looking for the Infinite and we don't know where to find it.

Where *is* God? How do we *experience* God? What is our *relationship* to God? Is Christ just in the books, in the caves, and in the deserts and remote places? Is Christ a *real* person? Can Christ be in the events of the day? Is Christ part of our endeavor of building the secular city, the new century, the new millennium? Could God have taken our flesh and become one of us if matter was bad? Is matter really separate from spirit? Is a general reconciliation between opposites possible?

7

To these questions, hundreds of answers have been given. They range from complete withdrawal from "matter" to complete withdrawal from "spirit," and the many possibilities in between. The truth is that Jesus Christ was fully divine and fully human. He was and is all in all. A synthesis was required to interpret the process of the universe and the unity of humankind, and of all things.

Many spiritual writers tried to make this synthesis. In modern times, only one, Pierre Teilhard de Chardin (1881-1955), was to be the champion of this school of thought. Indeed, he tried his best to reconcile faith and science, spirit and matter, soul and body, and heaven and earth. He saw that "The root source of the spiritual troubles in which mankind is struggling today is what may be called 'the conflict of the two faiths.' "[2] He wanted to prove that the "revealed God" is not opposed to the "world-God." He wanted "a communion . . . with God through the world."[3] He wanted to reach "to heaven through fulfilment of earth."[4] He wanted to see Christ as "principle of synthesis."[5] He wanted to give a face and a heart to the world, so that we can find rest for our unceasing dissatisfaction and continuous longing for the Infinite by finding Christ *where he is*—in the becoming of others and of the world, and in fuller being, for "fuller being is closer union."[6] He even defines being in terms of union. For him, "to be" means "to unite" or "to be united."[7]

In this union, there is zest and meaning for life. Then, we are passionate for reconciliation and peace because we are one in Christ. And by collaborating, in faith and adoration, with God, in the progressive realization of the cosmic Christ and of the "Thy Kingdom come," we contribute to the realization of Jesus' prayer that all may be one. Indeed, our world is meant to be one world. Why have we made it more than one?

Teilhard's World of Synthesis

Teilhard lived in, and was nourished by, two worlds. He lived in and by the world of Christian tradition, and he cherished the world of science and progress. He was a child of heaven as well as a "child of the earth."[8] He was totally engaged in both of them, although he knew the discrepancies that existed between the two.

Teilhard was a Jesuit priest and a profound mystic, but he lived in a scientific environment and in a non-Christian world; he spent much of his life in China. He knew how to master the two languages of religion and science. Except in some rare cases, his spiritual vocabulary was permeated with scientific terms and metaphors, and his scientific concepts had metaphysical connotations and implications. The project of his life, one can say, was to synthesize what he could synthesize in both worlds. His synthesis, unlike Hegel's synthesis that was based on the inner contradiction of each phenomenon (thesis/antithesis/synthesis), was based on the movement of convergence that presses ahead, toward centralization. This is a synthesis by way of totalization, without eliminating any of the phenomena. The secret of his success was what he called his "two passions." He was

> certain . . . of the inter-relations and quasi-reconciliations possible between two passions I really believe to be to some degree united in me, and which in any case I certainly experience—a passion for the world, and a passion for God.[9]

In most of his writings, Teilhard tried to reconcile two opposing attractions. He would speak of two egos (one pagan and one Christian), of two centers, two suns, two worlds, two communions, two religions, two faiths, two principles, two mysticisms, two stars, two influences, two currents, spirit and matter, within and without, upward and forward, sacred and profane, religion and science, cosmic and human, divine and human, Creator and creature, grace and nature, transcendent and immanent, the one and the many, the element and the whole, activities and passivities, attachment and detachment, development and renunciation, creation and evolution, adoration and intellect, supernatural and natural, personal and impersonal, freedom and determinism, growth and diminishment, convergence and divergence, love of God and love of the world. But each time he mentions the opposition, he immediately suggests that the two can be brought together, and he can experience "a communion with God through earth,"[10] and "a communion . . . with God through the world."[11] In 1934, he wrote:

I have allowed two apparent conflicting influences full
freedom to react upon one another deep within me. And
now, at the end of that operation, after thirty years
devoted to the pursuit of interior unity, I have the feeling
that a synthesis has been effected naturally between the
two currents that claim my allegiance. The one has not
destroyed, but has reinforced, the other. Today I believe
probably more profoundly than ever in God, and certainly more than ever in the world.[12]

This text and many similar ones throughout Teilhard's abundant
works raise the critical question of the relationship between Christ
and the world, and the implications that this relationship has for the
follower of Christ.

At a time when Marx's social doctrine was presenting a popular,
and seemingly viable, alternative to faith in God—in fact many of
his writings are either directly or indirectly addressing Marxism—Teilhard found it necessary to ask hard, yet timely, questions.
What is the relationship between the Christian life and the engage-
ment in the progress of the world? Can a good Christian be
immersed in business, politics, entertainment, science, and
high-tech discoveries? What does Christian perfection mean? What
about the renunciation that has been a basic element in our traditional spirituality? Is our Christianity more authentic when we dis-
connect ourselves from our many milieux? Can we be saints while
fully involved in the world?

Teilhard was certainly aware of all these questions and of the
spiritual dualism confronting Christianity. He described the
dilemma this way:

'Perfection consists in detachment; the world around us
is vanity and ashes.' The believer is constantly reading or
hearing these austere words. How can he reconcile them
with that other counsel, usually coming from the same
master and in any case written in his heart by nature,
that he must be an example unto the Gentiles in devotion to duty, in energy, and even in leadership in all the
spheres opened up by man's activity?[13]

But for him, an emphasis on the involvement in the world requires actually a true love of the world and a true dedication to it, in the very name of the Christ who is at its center. Then any Christian can devoutly pray: "Lord, grant that I may see, that I may see You, that I may see and feel You *present in all things and animating all things.*"[14] Teilhard also wrote:

> Without making the smallest concession to 'nature' but with a thirst for greater perfection, we can reconcile, and provide mutual nourishment for, the love of God and the healthy love of the world, a striving towards detachment and a striving towards the enrichment of our human lives. . . .[15]

It is obvious that when Teilhard used the word "world," he did not mean the world of sinful greed, pride, and selfishness, but the world that is created by God and directed ahead toward Christ, and at the same time whose center is Christ. Teilhard intended to unite with Christ through the world, and wanted to contribute to the completion of the world in participation with Christ at work in the world.

The milestones that help to understand Teilhard's vision of the world seem clearly marked in an equation found in the last page of his journal, three days before his death. It reads:

> Cosmos = Cosmogenesis—Biogenesis—Noogenesis—Christogenesis.
> (The Universe is centred—
> Christ is its Centre).[16]

And this echoes what he wrote 36 years before:

> We know from what St Paul and St John tell us that Christ is the Centre of Creation, the Force that can subject all things to itself, the term by which all things are informed.[17]

Teilhard saw evolution in stages of growth. Biogenesis expresses the beginning of life, while noogenesis, from the Greek *noos* which means mind, is the point in life where consciousness develops, where thought is born.

With this in mind, it becomes much easier to understand the "forward" approach which is a humanist mysticism, and the "upward" approach which is the Christian mysticism. These two approaches should not be in conflict. Instead, they are the two essential components of a true mysticism. A vertically moving faith in God and a horizontally moving faith in the world should go hand in hand. We cannot succeed in this unless Christ is at the center.

To reach this unified Christian vision, three steps are simultaneously at work. The first is a physics of evolution. Teilhard finds that evolution, based on scientific data, has a direction and is converging toward a center that is personal. Secondly, this personal center is identified with Christ. Thirdly, since Christ is the summit, and everything is converging toward Christ, it becomes clear that human efforts, carried out in Christ, are precious and important. Also, it becomes clear that the process of creation that is pointed toward Christ is a process of unification and reconciliation. Indeed, by the process of the centro-complexification-consciousness, the individual is more and more reconciled with the unified whole.

There is a logic of unity in the evolution of the universe. The process of successive phases of unifications characterized the continuous act of creation. Teilhard wanted to witness the constant presence of God in the created world and, at the same time, affirm the principle of the evolution of this world. The expression he used, "creative union," describes the essence of this delicate process. He also used the word "diaphany" to indicate how God is seen in and through the world, and how this very vision can transform everything and make all things shine anew.

Teilhard's theology of creation is built around a keystone that is Christ-omega, who is the center of everything and attracts everything. "The ultimate solution to all of Teilhard's problems," wrote Beatrice Bruteau, "is found with the passing of natural evolutionary 'cosmogenesis' into the supremely mystical 'christogenesis. . . .' The world is an evolution toward divinity, and the cosmic Christ is its Evolver."[18]

The entire process of the communion with God through the world—the great synthesis—should not be seen "as a single combination of two attractions," Ursula King reminds us, "but as something of a new order altogether." It is, King continues, our "attempt to relate God and the world in the most intimate manner, elsewhere expressed through [Teilhard's] efforts in seeing science and religion as part of the same quest for ultimate unity, and in relating mystical spirituality to effort and action."[19]

It is also important to note here that this process of synthesis is not in fact an abstract concept that scholars can work out. It is rather a real work of integration which is lived in concrete existence. We need people who, wrote Teilhard,

> will be passionately and *simultaneously* animated by both types of faith and so effect in themselves, *in one heart*, the junction of the two mystical forces and display, to those they move among, the *realisation* of the synthesis. We need men who are all the more convinced of the sacred value of human effort in that they are primarily interested in God.[20]

The Driving Forces of Teilhard's Spirituality

It is fair to say that perhaps the most concise way to detect and summarize Teilhard's spirituality is found in his prayers. Although his mind was searching to reconcile what seemed to be opposite in a scientific, theological, and philosophical manner, it was in his mystical experience rather than in his mental speculations, that the true reconciliation was going to take place. "There is a prayer," he wrote to his cousin Marguerite, "I'm fond of saying now, because it sums up what I mean: '*Jesu, sis mihi mundus verus.*' May all that is elect in the world, Jesus, be to me a channel for your influence, and be increasingly transformed through my efforts into you."[21]

Throughout all his life and work, Teilhard faced the traditional contemplation-action tension, and he tried to ease it. His deep conviction was to deflate that tension that existed for centuries before him, between "the two rival stars . . . : God and the world."[22] This is why we can perhaps say that his spirituality can be summarized in one sentence he wrote in 1933: "There is a communion (the true communion) with God through the world; and to surrender oneself to it is not to take the impossible step of trying to serve two masters."[23]

"Through the world" means being engaged totally in it and transforming it. Spirituality, then, is to live and grow in the marketplace and in every corner of ordinary life. Spiritual life should not be the monopoly of hermits, monks, nuns, and bishops, but a leavening agent that gives meaning to, and transforms, our everyday ordinary activities. This is a mysticism-in-action. It encourages involvement in the factory, the classroom, the workshop, the laboratory, the marketplace, and the places of leisure and entertainment.

Teilhard, by trying to put an end to the dichotomies that existed between heaven and earth, mind and body, spirit and matter, wanted to engage with the development of the world and the dynamics of an ever-changing society. He realized that spirituality could no longer be pursued in isolation from the environmental context and social action. Spirituality is concerned with, and engaged in, vital areas of ecology, politics, economics, and all that is related to the development of a given society. Spirituality should lead us into the world rather than out of it. In this sense, the more open to God and to the world, the more spiritual we are, and the more unified we become. Then our movement is "a movement of convergence in which races, peoples and nations consolidate one another and complete one another by mutual fecundation."[24] Then, all life is a "spiritual" life or it is meaningless, futile, worthless, and dissatisfying. Teilhard wrote: "In virtue of the fundamental unity of our being in the world, we may already say of every upright man that everything he does on earth is ordered, more or less directly, to the spiritualization of the universe,"[25] and: "*It is through the fulfilment of the world* that we reach Christ."[26]

What allowed and inspired Teilhard to think this way? His mysticism. The essence of mysticism is unification with God. Unification means neither fusion nor identification, nor even simple union of two given terms. Rather it means an ongoing process of successive centerings. It involves the unification of human beings as well as of the entire surroundings of nature and works. And more precisely, it is a complete surrender of love.

Love is the universal power that evolves the entire universe toward the Divine Center. It is the manifestation of God in creation. Love of God, love of neighbor, and love of all creation must be the answer to our anxieties, worries, distress, and fear. Teilhard wrote: "Under the persistent pressure of Christian thought, the infinitely distressing vastness of the world is gradually converging upward, to the point where it is transfigured into a focus of loving energy."[27]

This love, which is "the most universal, most tremendous and most mysterious of the cosmic forces,"[28] is a unifying principle that holds the universe together. "Driven by the forces of love, the fragments of the world seek each other so that the world may come to being."[29] Love breaks down isolationism and mutual repulsion, and pulls people to work together, and to unite: "Love alone is capable of uniting living beings in such a way as to complete and fulfil them, for it alone takes them and joins them by what is deepest in themselves."[30]

When Teilhard talks about the evolution of consciousness, he sometimes uses the term "amorization" to indicate that the love-energy should form a world of persons where individual and collective values are achieved, and the driving force of history is, according to him, love that unifies. This love is especially the total manifestation of God. It is Christ. The natural-supernatural polarity of love finds its foundation in the immanent-transcendent Omega—Jesus Christ—as the pole of attraction in the cosmogenesis and the christogenesis. The world is evolving toward divinity, and the cosmic Christ is its Evolver.

Teilhard's life was a communion with God through the Eucharist and prayer as well as through people and beings, with whom he sought an uninterrupted unity. This unity which is the fruit of love has its source in the heart of the Word incarnate which is the cause and the purpose of the world, and from whom all energies emerge.

The mystery of the Incarnation, of which Teilhard wrote: "The essence of Christianity is neither more nor less than a belief in the unification of the world in God by the Incarnation,"[31] was the very foundation of his Christian faith, his life, and his work. It is also an ongoing universal process. While it is linked to the historical Jesus, the Incarnation of Christ is extended to the entire cosmos. Every created reality needs to be completed, fulfilled, and redeemed. God is present in all things, and "everything around me," he wrote, "is the body and blood of the Word."[32] He also wrote: "The presence of the Incarnate Word penetrates everything, as universal element."[33] Then everything is sacred, for nothing is profane anymore. Teilhard was also clear on this when he wrote: "By virtue of the Creation and, still more, of the Incarnation, *nothing* here below is *profane* for those who know how to see."[34]

Incarnation and Redemption can no longer be considered as simple events completed once and for all. No. In fact, they must be considered ongoing processes that lead to what Teilhard called "divinization," or "deification" as the Greek Fathers would say. With this approach, Teilhard distanced himself for good from any remaining dualistic points of views.

Teilhard wasn't convinced that nature was a static reality. Nature, for him, was essentially dynamic and developing, and humankind was still in the making. Nature and humankind are interacting and becoming. A Christian must bring together into synthesis this order of nature with the order of grace. Unlike the medieval concept that wanted to separate nature and grace and make of the fleeing from the world a condition for holiness, Teilhard, by seeing the reconciliation of all things in Christ, saw the synthesis of nature and grace, and made of the Incarnation in the natural and the material, a way for holiness and a responsibility. The Christian, in imitation of Christ who descended into the heart of the world, must also descend into this world and be completely involved in it. Teilhard wrote:

> As we now see it, spiritualization can no longer be effected in a breakaway from matter or out of tune with matter: it must be effected by passing through and emerging from matter. *'Descendit, assendit, ut repleret omnia,'* 'He descended, and he ascended, that he might fill all things' (Cf. Ephesians 4:9-10)—there you have the very economy of the Incarnation.[35]

In this sense, even though the distinction between spirit and matter is maintained, the dichotomy between them no longer exists. "There is," Teilhard wrote, "neither spirit nor matter in the world; the 'stuff of the universe' is *spirit-matter*."[36]

Christian holiness becomes a personal relationship with Jesus Christ in and through matter, and "a communion . . . with God through the world."[37] Teilhard's objective is to see nature and human endeavor incorporated into the Kingdom of God by *christifying* them.

A Note of Caution

It must be noted that Teilhard's ideas and writings have not always been enthusiastically espoused by all. To the contrary, his innovative approach, or perhaps the fact that he never really wrote wholly as a theologian or wholly as a scientist, opened him up to inevitable criticism and rejection. In his own lifetime, the Catholic Church, already wary of developing scientific thought's impact on faith, questioned the orthodoxy of some of his work. These suspicions found justification in 1922 when a work he had written on original sin especially was judged to be unacceptable. Teilhard was subsequently asked to leave his teaching post at L'Institut Catholique de Paris. The Jesuit Order shortly thereafter transferred him to China where he was to remain, for all practical purposes, in exile.

Although no further condemnations ensued, his writings remained with a certain air of suspicion. On June 30, 1962, the Sacred Congregation of the Holy Office issued a "Monitum Concerning the Writings of Fr. Teilhard de Chardin." It is a short and succinct admonition stating that in Teilhard's writings there are "ambiguities, and indeed even serious errors, as to offend Catholic doctrine." It cautioned bishops, superiors of religious institutes, as well as rectors of seminaries and presidents of universities about the dangers of Chardin's ideas. Then on July 11, 1981, the Holy See Press Office issued a statement referring to the Monitum, stating that it still had "reservations in various passages" of Chardin's writings.[38]

What could some of these ambiguities be? Although not spelled out in the Monitum, they are his thought on the doctrine of original sin, the place of evil in a world in evolution, the concepts of creation and the cosmic Christ, and the spirit/matter relationship. In *Catholicism* Richard McBrien says that, "Teilhard's thought runs counter to traditional Catholic doctrine on Original Sin."[39] The divergence possibly rests in his view that, "initially then there were two poles of being, God and Multitude."[40] In that light evil appears to exist to the degree in which unity has not been fully achieved: "true growth is effected in a progress toward unity, less being increases with fragmentation."[41]

His thought also does seem to blur the distinction between the natural and the supernatural, between nature and grace. It can sometimes seem to appear that he is of the opinion that nature, in and of itself, has the power to attain divinization without the need of a free act of God. For example, when he says that "the stuff of which grace is made is strictly biological"[42] is he espousing pantheism or merely reiterating Saint Thomas's, "Grace builds on nature"? In the context of his entire work, I am sure it must be the latter.

Yes, Teilhard is often contradictory and at times confusing, especially when what he says is taken out of context. However, it is not within the scope of this small sampler of his writings to sort this out. Neither is it to defend him. Instead it is simply to introduce Teilhard, the man and his thought, who has so affected who we are and how we think today.

The Need for Teilhard's Spirituality Today

Although Teilhard wrote for various audiences either outside the Church or for people who were searching for answers in modern life and a deeper meaning to human existence, or for people who were deeply rooted within the Christian faith, or for friends, or just for himself, he seemed to have struck a chord that resonates loudly in the hearts and souls of the people of our time. His insights could help us in solving our problems today, because these insights are anchored in God who is all in all and because they try to define our profound involvement in the world. Teilhard did not hesitate to write:

> Who . . . will be the *ideal Christian*, the Christian, at once
> new and old, who will solve in his soul the problem of
> this vital balance, by allowing all the life-sap of the world
> to pass into his effort towards the Divine Trinity? That
> Christian will be the man who has understood that if he
> is to be supremely the child of God, if he is to fulfill his
> holy Will in its entirety, he must show himself more
> assiduous in working for the earth than any servant of
> Mammon.[43]

It is therefore an imperative duty for the Christian to participate in "God's creative work."[44]

Teilhard did not believe in the kind of spirituality that is characterized by individualism, the exclusive preoccupation of personal salvation, or the "religious" belief that to reach the next world we are supposed to withdraw from the one we are in and avoid the sins and the forbidden things listed in the moral code, and nothing else. Teilhard was a major figure among those who wanted the Christian to utilize all of his or her potential for the transformation of the world in Christ, and to materialize, here and now, the Kingdom of God and the Mystical Body of Christ. Consequently, the top priority is no longer just personal salvation, but the realization of the "total" Christ. Saints, then, would shift from what is just negative to what is certainly positive. They would strive to collaborate with all those who do something good and beautiful not only for the world after, but also for this very world. Then, they would reach their fulfillment as co-workers with each other and with Christ, and bring evolution to completion. In a more concrete way, they would accomplish, as perfectly as possible, their tasks in this world. Teilhard wrote:

> May the time come when men, having been awakened to a sense of close bond linking all the movements of this world in the single, all-embracing work of the Incarnation, shall be unable to give themselves to any one of their tasks without illuminating it with the clear vision that their work—however elementary it may be—is received and put to good use by a Centre of the universe.[45]

This is also what the Second Vatican Council recommended. *Gaudium et Spes. The pastoral Constitution on the Church in the Modern World* tells us that "by his incarnation the Son of God has united Himself in some fashion with every man" (No. 22). In the *Decree on the Apostolate of the Laity*, we are called on in a very special way: "The laity, too, share in the priestly, prophetic, and royal office of Christ and therefore have their own role to play in the mission of the whole People of God in the Church and in the world" (No. 2).

William Johnson, S.J., wrote: "The Second Vatican Council was indeed a conversion to the material world—the world of art and poetry and science, to the afflicted bodies of the poor and sick, to the whole world of matter."[46]

In his turn, Thomas M. King, S.J., affirmed that: "Teilhard has had considerable influence. He is probably the nontheologian of the 20th century with the greatest impact on what theology is doing . . . Teilhard was central to the change in Catholic spirituality. For Thomas Merton, 'the real importance of Teilhard is his affirmation of the "holiness of matter." ' Merton has said of page 79 of the Divine Milieu: 'No finer and more contemplative page has been written in our century.' "[47]

Although Teilhard was a modern scientist, he also was a radical Christian. His God was neither an aloof Being, nor an abstract concept. His God was the God of the Gospels and of Saint Paul. God was an incarnate God who animated every atom. Because of the Incarnation, one is led to a valuing of the world and to a respect of individuals and their fulfillment in becoming their own selves and in transforming their own milieux. Modern Christianity calls everyone to holiness,[48] and emphasizes the role of the laity—men and women—and their participation in Christian life as a whole. Everyone has a special calling to holiness and to making holy the world of Christ, in Christ.

No wonder Teilhard wanted to see the Divine and the human overlapping, interweaving, interacting, and interbeing organically. He was convinced that faith makes us more human and more passionate for all that makes us more human. Is there anything more urgent than this kind of participation in the progress of the human condition while, at the same time, maintaining a total fidelity to the Lord of all things, who is in all things? Christopher F. Mooney, S.J., wrote unambiguously:

> Today what motivates people is "the world." Christians want to feel they can reach God through the world, through the whole scientific, technological, humanist enterprise. But not until Teilhard appears on the scene has anyone succeeded in showing them how. He is the only one who has given this vivid image of modern man a completely Christian explanation.[49]

It is not necessarily Teilhard's great vision of the future of the Omega Point that makes an impact on our lives today. It is rather his invitation to, and insistence on, the actual involvement in the here and now, that makes a difference in our lives and our society. "God," wrote Teilhard, "in all that is most living and incarnate in him, is not far away from us, altogether apart from the world we see, touch, hear, smell and taste about us. Rather he awaits us every instant in our action, in the work of the moment."[50]

Thomas Corbishley, in concluding his book on Teilhard's spirituality, wrote: "Just as, in the fifth century, Ambrose and Augustine interpreted Christian truth in terms of contemporary philosophical systems, just as in the thirteenth Aquinas reinterpreted that same truth in the light of Aristotelian metaphysics, so Teilhard in the twentieth century drew on the vast wealth of scientific lore to open men's minds still wider to the majesty of God and the appeal of Christ."[51]

If, in the past, we had the spirituality of asceticism of the Fathers and Mothers of the Deserts, and the spirituality of cultures and contemplatives of the Middle Ages, then, in more recent times, the spirituality of "conquering" new nations for Christ, we are witnessing in these modern times, due to an evolution in consciousness, a new type of spirituality and of sanctity. Our spirituality today tends to make of the Christian an engaged person who is involved in research, in progress, in social and global issues, in the environment, in reconciling what it seems irreconcilable, in ecumenism, in love and peace, in building the earth, each other, and the Kingdom of God. Teilhard was a pioneer in creating this kind of spirituality. He lived, and worked, a mysticism of co-creative union. He showed how God is *alive* in our world—daring even to talk about the "sacrament of the world"[52]—how we *experience* God, and how we let God work and shine through us. He was a true prophetic figure for a true new age.

Teilhard's call to "communion . . . with God through the world"[53] takes the form of personal and social responsibility of a Christian ethics of building the earth and the future, and reconciling oneself and all things in Christ. What we do must have a religious value indeed. It is a cooperation with God in the creating act. Perhaps we can call this approach the third way—the first being the search for God beyond this world, the second being the search for God only in this world. The diagonal approach that synthesizes the vertical and the horizontal—finding God through a creative transformation of the world—could be the most adequate one for today.

Teilhard also supported the closer coming together of different religious traditions. He wrote: "A general convergence of religions upon a universal Christ who fundamentally satisfies them all: that seems to me the only possible conversion of the world, and the only form in which a religion of the future can be conceived."[54] He advocated new modes of thinking and feeling that lead to new forms of unity and community both more complex and more differentiated. He heralded the birth of a new consciousness that sees in the various religious experiences of the world a global spiritual fellowship, and in the numerous nations, ethnic groups and cultures, a global network and a single planetized community. Such a vision certainly has the potential to overcome opposition and separation at all levels of life. Indeed, the opposite to unity is not diversity. The opposite to unity is division and separation.

At a more personal level, Teilhard can speak to us through his uncompromising faithfulness to his vows as a priest who remained totally loyal[55] to his order and to his Church, in spite of all the doubts, temptations, and difficulties he found himself subjected to. His unshakable Christian faith and his "intelligent piety," as his friend and collaborator Pierre Leroy called it, can be a source of inspiration for many of us.

However, Teilhard did not finish his work. He himself admitted that others should complete what he had started. True team work is now needed. A group of expert theologians, philosophers, and scientists should be able to elaborate upon what he suggested, in detail and with more clarity, according to their respective disciplines, and deal with the important, and sometimes very delicate and difficult questions he raised.

Evolution and human endeavor do not always go in the direction of higher consciousness. Along the way there is evil. Teilhard was aware of this fact. Even though he was known for his "excessive" optimism, the problem of evil was always in the background of his thought,[56] but he did not set forth in great detail the concrete steps we must take to overcome it. And we can also say that even if his vision has captured and stimulated the souls and minds of many generations by awakening their faith in sacred and secular values, and by promoting the dreams of unity, peace, and development as the result of an inevitable evolution, he has not indicated concretely how to overcome all insecurities, and how our free will would necessarily choose to move in a good direction.

Teilhard has certainly set forth an extraordinary project for humankind. He pointed out the direction of the Promised Land. But we still have to accept, and head in, that direction. A convergence of souls, minds, hearts, and energies is required. It is through the universal Element—Christ—that "it becomes possible to use all life's forces to produce one and the same real thing."[57] Indeed, he also wrote:

> Mankind, the spirit of the earth, the synthesis of individuals and peoples, the paradoxical conciliation of the element with the whole, and of unity with multitude—all these are called Utopian and yet they are biologically necessary. And for them to be incarnated in the world all we may well need is to imagine our power of loving developing until it embraces the total of men and of the earth.[58]

Then, we will experience fullness of life. For fullness of life does not mean getting the most *out* of life, but putting the most *into* life. Christ, the Universal Element, by unifying our life's forces, makes us create reality. He pours life into our life. He makes us new, free, and genuine. He is our real satisfaction.

Selections and Translations

To make selections from Teilhard de Chardin's voluminous writings is not an easy task. First, because his work is very extensive, complex, and multi-faceted, and secondly, because there are a lot of materials to choose from, on a same specific subject. One cannot insert them all, and one does not want to miss any of them either. Besides this, even though Teilhard is an extraordinary thinker, one of the giants of the twentieth century, and perhaps because he is so, he is not an easy author.

In order to reduce these difficulties to a certain minimum and help especially the readers who are not very familiar with his thoughts, I have inserted headings and subheadings of my own, when I couldn't use his or when there was no heading for that particular excerpt, adding the abbreviations that indicate the sources from where that particular excerpt is taken. I used brackets [ ] to indicate that I added the heading. I also thought that because it could be important for some readers to know the exact date when Teilhard wrote that particular page, I added a special section at the end of the book called "Chronology of the Writings of Teilhard de Chardin," and I indicated in which volume in both French and English, where this particular essay can be found.

Most of Teilhard's writings have been translated into English, following their publication in French between 1955 and 1976. The credit for the French publication should go to Jeanne Mortier, Teilhard's literary executrix. It was she who took the initiative to do this immense publishing work, mainly with the Editions du Seuil, Paris. Details on the translations can be found in the bibliography at the end of this book.

I have chosen not to make any changes in the texts used here. For the sake of accuracy, I have retained the translators and publishers' way of the language use, both in the spelling of certain words (for example: humanisation instead of humanization, civilisation instead of civilization, reflexions instead of reflections, centre instead of centers, etc. . . .), and in the use of a non-inclusive language. Please note that when Teilhard used, for example, the word "l'homme" that was translated as "man" in English, he was obviously speaking inclusively about human beings of both sexes. The same thing can be said when "mankind" is used instead of "humankind" or "humanity," generally used today. These words and the pronouns referring to them were always intended to have, in Teilhard's mind as well as in the translators' minds and our minds, an inclusive meaning. I am sure the reader will understand my concern for accuracy and respect for the very words used by Teilhard himself and by his translators. I thought that any attempt to change this language would be awkward and artificial.

Furthermore, the notes found at the end of each chapter correspond to Teilhard's actual notes in his books.

* * *

I hope that these pages will be a contribution in shaping the spirituality and lifestyle of the new century and the new millennium. With the fire of Teilhard's words and his pressing invitation to live in the "divine milieu," we are invited, by the very fact of the Incarnation, to effect a radical reconciliation between faith and science, spirit and matter, soul and body, within and without, religion and religion, nation and nation, the one and the many, love of God and love of the world, and the Divine and the human. A general synthesis of this kind is possible, real, and realistic, if we convince ourselves existentially that we are one world, that we are its co-creators, that Christ is its Center, and that "communion . . . with God through the world"[59] is the best way to make this world holy, and to be ourselves holy in the process.

Holiness is not an escape from the life in the world, but from the life of the world. It requires a very solid basis in reality. The Incarnation is the synthesis of the Divine and the human. This is what fullness of life—and holiness—really is, and this is what Teilhard wanted to convey. Perhaps the supposed conflict between faith and nature has done more harm to Christianity than persecutions. Ultimately truth is one, life is whole, and reality is a unique Reality; the transcendence and the immanence of God are acting in the Word made flesh. In Christ, everything is in communion with everything else. "The universal Christ . . . is," wrote Teilhard, "a synthesis of Christ and the universe. He is not a new godhead—but an inevitable deployment of the mystery in which Christianity is summed up, the mystery of the Incarnation."[60]

To the temptations to regress, divide, or despair, Teilhard has offered, through his original way of synthesis and reconciliation, the Christian message of love and unity, progress and communion, and joy and zest for living. He taught us that human history has a direction and a goal. So does every one of us. He trained us to realize the sense of imminence, as if we are crossing the threshold of a new order. He singled out the particular role of Christians who have the responsibility, more than any other groups, to cooperate with God's plan to unite progressively and assiduously all things in Christ, for Christ is the true satisfaction for our human unrest. And he prayed:

> Lord Jesus Christ, . . . you are the Centre at which all things meet and which stretches out over all things so as to draw them back into itself: I love you for the extensions of your body and soul to the farthest corners of creation through grace, through life, and through matter. . . . Lord Jesus, you are the centre towards which all things are moving.[61]

Notes

1. See "A Phenomenon of Counter-Evolution in Human Biology or the Existential Fear" in AE, 181-195.

2. "Two Principles and a Corollary" in TF, 156.

3. "Christology and Evolution" in CE, 93.

4. "Research, Work, and Worships" in SC, 220.

5. Teilhard wrote: "Christ . . . is the plenitude of the universe, its principle of synthesis" ("Science and Christ" in SC, 33). He also wrote: "What is our Lord Jesus Christ if not the synthesis of the created universe and its Creator?" ("My Universe" in HM, 201).

6. PM, 31.

7. "My Fundamental Vision" in TF, 193.

8. "How I Believe" in CE, 96.

9. MM, 165.

10. Cosmic Life" in WTW, 14. See also "The Evolution of Chastity" in TF, 73.

11. "Christology and Evolution" in CE, 93.

12. "How I Believe" in CE, 97.

13. DM, 51.

14 Quoted in Henri de Lubac, *Teilhard de Chardin, the Man and His Meaning* (New York: Hawthorn Books, 1965), 28.

15. DM, 53.

16. See FM, 324.

17. "The Universal Element" in WTW, 297.

18. Beatrice Bruteau, *Evolution toward Divinity. Teilhard de Chardin and the Hindu Traditions* (Wheaton, IL: The Theosophical Publishing House, 1974), 7.

19. Ursula King, *Towards a New Mysticism. Teilhard de Chardin and Eastern Religions* (New York: The Seabury Press, 1981), 29-30.

20. "The Religious Value of Research" in SC, 204.

21. MM, 223

22. DM, 17.

23. "Christology and Evolution" in CE, 93.

24. PM, 242.

25. "Forma Christi" in WTW, 258.

26. "The Universal Element" in WTW, 300.

27. "Reflections on Happiness" in TF, 127-128.

28. "The Spirit of the Earth" in HE, 32.

29. PM, 264-265.

30. PM, 265.

31. "Sketch of a Personalistic Universe" in HE, 91.

32. "The Mass on the World" in HU, 28.

33. "My universe" in SC, 57.

34. DM, 66.

35. "A Note on the Concept of Christian Perfection" in TF, 106.

36. "Sketch of a Personalistic Universe" in HE, 57-58.

37. "Christology and Evolution" in CE, 93.

38. "Communique of Press Office of the Holy See," *L'Osservatore Romano,* 20 July, 1981, weekly English edition.

39. Richard P. McBrien, *Catholicism,* vol. I (Oak Grove, MN: Winston Press, Inc. 1980), 126.

40. WTW, 95.

41. Ibid.

42. CE, 153.

43. "Mastery of the World and the Kingdom of God" in WTW, 88.

44. Ibid., 89.

45. DM, 67.

46. William Johnson, *Being in Love* (London: Harper Collins Publishers, 1988), 31.

47. Thomas M. King, "The Milieux Teilhard Left behind" in *America*, March 30, 1985, 250-251.

48. *Lumen Gentium*, chap. V, "The Call of the Whole Church to Holiness," nos. 39-42; *Catechism of the Catholic Church*, nos. 2013-2014, 2028-2029.

49. Christopher F. Mooney, S.J., *The Making of Man* (New York: Paulist Press, 1971), 148.

50. DM, 64.

51. Thomas Corbishley, *The Spirituality of Teilhard de Chardin* (Paramus, NJ/New York, NY: Paulist Press, 1971), 126.

52. "The Evolution of Chastity" in TF, 73.

53. "Christology and Evolution" in CE, 93.

54. "How I Believe" in CE, 130.

55. Cf. LZ, 87; Pierre Leroy, S.J., *Pierre Teilhard de Chardin, tel que, je l'ai Connu* (Paris: Plon, 1958), 57-58; H. de Lubac, *Teilhard et notre temps* (Paris: Aubier, 1971), 110-126.

56. For more details, please see my book, *Le Mystère du Mal dans. l'Oeuvre de Teilhard de Chardin* (France: Editions du Cerf, 1986).

57. "The Universal Element" in WTW, 301.

58. PM, 266.

59. "Christology and Evolution" in CE, 93.

60. "How I Believe" in CE, 126.

61. "Cosmic Life" in WTW, 70.

Reconciling the Two Faiths

[Heaven and Earth]

The originality of my belief lies in its being rooted in two domains of life which are commonly regarded as antagonistic. By upbringing and intellectual training, I belong to the 'children of heaven'; but by temperament, and by my professional studies, I am a 'child of the earth.' Situated thus by life at the heart of two worlds with whose theory, idiom and feelings, intimate experience has made me familiar, I have not erected any watertight bulkhead inside myself. On the contrary, I have allowed two apparently conflicting influences full freedom to react upon one another deep within me. And now, at the end of that operation, after thirty years devoted to the pursuit of interior unity, I have the feeling that a synthesis has been effected naturally between the two currents that claim my allegiance. The one has not destroyed, but has reinforced, the other. Today I believe probably more profoundly than ever in God, and certainly more than ever in the world.

("How I Believe" in CE, 96-97)

It seems to me clear above all else, setting aside the countless minor divergences, and ignoring the dull, inert mass of those who believe in nothing at all, that the spiritual conflict afflicting Mankind today arises out of the division of minds and hearts into the two profoundly separated categories of:

a   Those whose hopes are directed towards a spiritual state or an absolute finality situated beyond and outside this world;   *b*   Those who hope for the perfection of the tangible Universe within itself.

The first of these groups, by far the older, is preeminently represented in these days by the Christians, protagonists of a transcendent and personal God.

The second group, comprising those who for a variety of reasons
have dedicated their lives to the service of a Universe which they
conceive as eventually culminating in some form of impersonal and
immanent Reality, is of very recent origin. Throughout human history this conflict between the 'servants of Heaven' and the 'servants
of earth' has gone on; but only since the birth of the idea of Evolution (in some sort divinising the Universe) have the devotees of
earth bestirred themselves and made of their worship a true form of
religion, charged with limitless hope, striving and renunciation.

Are we to disdain the world and put it behind us, or live in it in
order to master and perfect it? Mankind is rent asunder at this
moment by these two concepts or rival mysticisms; and in consequence its vital power of adoration is disastrously weakened.

Such in my view is the nature of the crisis, more profound than
any economic, political or social struggle, through which we are
passing.

("Some Reflections on Progress" in FM, 79-80)

[Faith in God and Faith in the World]

Any two forces, provided both are positive, must *a priori* be capable of growth by merging together. Faith in God and faith in the
World: these two springs of energy, each the source of a magnificent
spiritual impulse, must certainly be capable of effectively uniting in
such a way as to produce a resulting upward movement. But in practical terms where are we to look for the principle and the generative
medium which will bring about this most desirable evolutionary
step?

I believe that the principle and the medium are to be found in the
idea, duly 'realised', that there is in progress, within us and around
us, a continual heightening of consciousness in the Universe.

For a century and a half the science of physics, preoccupied with
analytical researches, was dominated by the idea of the dissipation
of energy and the disintegration of matter. Being now called upon
by biology to consider the effects of synthesis, it is beginning to

perceive that, parallel with the phenomenon of corpuscular disintegration, the Universe historically displays a second process as generalised and fundamental as the first. I mean that of the gradual concentration of its physico-chemical elements in nuclei of increasing complexity, each succeeding stage of material concentration and differentiation being accompanied by a more advanced form of spontaneity and spiritual energy.

The outflowing flood of Entropy equalled and offset by the rising tide of a Noogenesis! . . .

The greater and more revolutionary an idea, the more does it encounter resistance at its inception. Despite the number and importance of the facts that it explains, the theory of Noogenesis is still far from having established itself as a stronghold in the scientific field. However, let us assume that, as all the observable evidence suggests, it will succeed before long in gaining in one form or another the place it deserves at the head of the structural laws of our Universe. Plainly the first result will be precisely to bring about the *rapprochement* and automatic convergence of the two opposed forms of worship into which, as I said, the religious impulse of Mankind is at present divided. Once he has been brought to accept the reality of a Noogenesis, the believer in this World will find himself compelled to allow increasing room, in his vision of the future, for the values of personalisation and transcendency. Of Personalisation, because a Universe in process of psychic concentration is *identical* with a Universe that is acquiring a personality. And a transcendency because the ultimate stage of 'cosmic' personalisation, if it is to be supremely consistent and unifying, cannot be conceived otherwise than as having emerged by its summit from the elements it super-personalises as it unites them to itself.

On the other hand, the believer in Heaven, accepting this same reality of a cosmic genesis of the Spirit, must perceive that the mystical evolution of which he dreams presupposes and consecrates all the tangible realities and all the arduous conditions of human progress. If it is to be super-spiritualised in God, must not Mankind first be born and grow *in conformity with the entire system* of what we call 'evolution'? Whence, for the Christian in particular, there follows a radical incorporation of terrestrial values in the most fundamental concepts of his Faith, those of Divine Omnipotence, detachment and charity. First, Divine Omnipotence: God creates and shapes us

through the process of evolution: how can we suppose, or fear, that
He will arbitrarily interfere with the very means whereby He fulfils
His purpose? Then, detachment: God awaits us when the evolutionary process is complete: to rise above the World, therefore, does not
mean to despise or reject it, but to pass through it and sublime it.
Finally, charity: the love of God expresses and crowns the basic
affinity which, from the beginnings of Time and Space, has drawn
together and concentrated the spiritualisable elements of the Universe. To love God and our neighbour is therefore not merely an act
of worship and compassion superimposed on our other individual
preoccupations. For the Christian, if he be truly Christian, it is Life
itself, Life in the integrity of its aspirations, its struggles and its conquests, that he must embrace in a spirit of togetherness and personalising unification with all things.

The sense of the earth opening and exploding upwards into God;
and the sense of God taking root and finding nourishment down-
wards into Earth. A personal, transcendent God and an evolving
Universe no longer forming two hostile centres of attraction, but
entering into hierarchic conjunction to raise the human mass on a
single tide. Such is the sublime transformation which we may with
justice foresee, and which *in fact is* beginning to have its effect upon a
growing number of minds, free-thinkers as well as believers: the
idea of a spiritual evolution of the Universe. The very transformation
we have been seeking!

. . . From this standpoint it is at once apparent that, to unify the
living forces of humanity, at present so painfully at odds, the direct
and effective method is simply to sound the call-to-arms and form a
solid block of all those, whether of the right or the left, who believe
that the principal business of present-day Mankind is to achieve a
breakthrough straight ahead by forcing its way over the threshold of
some higher level of consciousness. Whether Christian or
non-Christian, the people inspired by this particular conviction constitute a homogeneous category. Though they may be situated at the
two extreme wings of Mankind on the march, they can advance
unequivocally side by side because their attitudes, far from being
mutually exclusive, are virtually an extension one of the other and
ask only to be completed. What more do they need that they may
know and love one another? The *union sacrée,* the Common Front of
all those who believe that the World is still advancing, what is this

but the active minority, the solid core around which the unanimity of tomorrow must harden?

Despite the wave of scepticism which seems to have swept away the hopes (too ingenuous, no doubt, and too materialistic) on which the nineteenth century lived, faith in the future is not dead in our hearts. Indeed, it is this faith, deepened and purified, which must save us. Not only does the idea of a possible raising of our conscious- ness to a state of super-consciousness show itself daily, in the light of scientific experience, to be better founded and psychologically more necessary for preserving in Man his will to act; but further- more this idea, carried to its logical extreme, appears to be the only one capable of paving the way for the great event we look for—the manifestation of a unified impulse of worship in which will be joined and mutually exalted both a passionate desire to conquer the World and a passionate longing to be united with God: the vital act, specifically new, corresponding to a new age in the history of Earth.

I am convinced that finally it is upon the idea of progress, and faith in progress, that Mankind, today so divided, must rely and can reshape itself.

("Some Reflections on Progress" in FM, 80-84)

The psychological situation of the world today is as follows: On one side there is an innate, tumultuous upsurge of cosmic and humanist aspirations; they emerge from the unsounded depths of human consciousness; they are irresistible in their rise but danger- ously ill-defined, and, what is even more dangerous, they are still 'impersonal' in their expression. That upsurge is the new faith in the world. And on the other side there are the vision and the anticipa- tion of a transcendent and loving pole of the universe; it is unswerv- ingly upheld by Christian dogma but, to all appearances, more and more abandoned by the main stream of religion; and this is the ancient faith in God. As for the meaning of this conflict and as for deciding how it is going to develop, that problem, to my mind, is solved by the very way in which we have just presented it. Surely the two terms—faith in the world and faith in God—so far from being antagonistic, are structurally complementary? On one side, repre- sented by modern humanism, we have a sort of neo-paganism, bursting with life, but still 'acephalous'—headless. On the other, in the form of Christianity, we have a head in which the blood no longer circulates at the necessary speed. On one, the fantastically enlarged stratified surfaces of a cone which are nevertheless incapable of closing up on themselves: a cone that has no apex. On the other, an apex which has lost its base: two detached parts, it is plain, that clamour to be joined together.

To put it briefly, Christianity has now enjoyed two thousand years of existence; it must obey an organic rhythm to which everything in nature would appear to be subject, and, precisely because it is immortal, the time has come when it cannot continue to exist without being rejuvenated and refashioned—and not by a change in its structure but by the assimilation of new elements. In other words what we must recognize in this present crisis, in which we can see and feel the confrontation between the traditional Christian forces and the modern forces of evolution, is simply the permutations of a providential and indispensable inter-fertilization. I am sure that this is so; but in that case it is clear that if the synthesis is to be effected Christianity must, without modifying the position of its peak, open up its axes to include in its totality the new surge of religious energy which is rising from below in its effort to be sublimated.

We must consider, then, how it may be possible, in the dual domain of theology and mysticism, for the guiding principles of Christianity to be expanded, without being distorted, to the dimensions of a universe which has been fantastically enlarged and integrated by modern scientific thought.

("Suggestions for a New Theology" in CE, 175-176)

Ever since my childhood an enigmatic force had been impelling me, apparently in conflict with the 'Supernatural,' towards some Ultra-human; and in trying to pin it down I had become accustomed to regard it as emanating not from God but from some rival Star. All I had to do, then, was to bring that Star into conjunction with God and dependence upon Him.

The time had now come when I could see one thing: that, from the depths of the cosmic future as well as from the heights of Heaven, it was still God, it was *always the same* God, who was calling me. It was a *God of the Ahead* who had suddenly appeared athwart *the traditional God of the Above,* so that henceforth we can no longer *worship fully* unless we superimpose those two images so that they form *one.*

A new Faith in which the ascensional Faith that rises up towards
a Transcendent, and the propulsive Faith that drives towards an
Immanent, form a single compound—a new Charity in which all the
Earth's dynamic passions combine as they are divinized: it is this, I
now see with a vision that will never leave me, that the World is des-
perately in need of at this very moment, if it is not to collapse.

("The Heart of Matter" in HM, 53)

It is generally agreed that the drama of the present religious conflict lies in the apparent irreconcilability of two opposed kinds of
faith—Christian faith, which disdains the primacy of the
ultra-human and the Earth, and 'natural' faith, which is founded
upon it. But is it certain that these two forces, neither of which, as
we have seen, can achieve its full development without the other,
are really so mutually exclusive (the one so anti-progressive and the
other so wholly atheist) as we assume? Is this so if we look to the
very heart of the matter? Only a little reflection and psychological
insight is required to see that it is not.

On the one hand, neo-human faith in the World to the extent
that it is truly a Faith (that is to say, entailing sacrifice and the final
abandonment of self for something greater) necessarily implies an
element of worship, the acceptance of something 'divine.'[1] Every
conversation I have ever had with communist intellectuals has left
me with a decided impression that Marxist atheism is not absolute,
but that it simply rejects an 'extrinsicist' form of God, a *deus ex
machina* whose existence can only undermine the dignity of the Universe and weaken the springs of human endeavour—a 'pseudo
God,' in short, whom no one in these days any longer wants, least of
all the Christians.

And on the other hand Christian faith (I stress the word Christian, as opposed to those 'oriental' faiths for which spiritual ascension often expressly signifies the negation or condemnation of the
Phenomenon), by the very fact that it is rooted in the idea of Incarnation, has always based a large part of its tenets on the tangible values of the World and of Matter. A too humble and subordinate part,
it may seem to us now (but was not this inevitable in the days when
Man, not having become aware of the genesis of the Universe in
progress, could not apprehend the spiritual possibilities still buried
in the entrails of the Earth?) yet still a part so intimately linked with

the essence of Christian dogma that, like a living bud, it needed only a sign, a ray of light, to cause it to break into flower. To clarify our ideas let us consider a single case, one which sums up everything. We continue from force of habit to think of the Parousia, whereby the Kingdom of God is to be consummated on Earth, as an event of a purely catastrophic nature that is to say, liable to come about at any moment in history, irrespective of any definite state of Mankind. This is one way of looking at the matter. But why should we not assume, in accordance with the latest scientific view of Mankind in an actual state of anthropogenesis[2] that the parousiac spark can, of physical and organic necessity, only be kindled between Heaven and a Mankind which has biologically reached a certain critical evolutionary point of collective maturity?

For my own part I can see no reason at all, theological or traditional, why this 'revised' approach should give rise to any serious difficulty. And it seems to me certain, on the other hand, that by the very fact of making this simple readjustment in our 'eschatological' vision we shall have performed a psychic operation having incalculable consequences. For if truly, in order that the Kingdom of God may come (in order that the Pleroma may close in upon its fullness), it is necessary, as an essential physical condition[3], that the human Earth should already have attained the natural completion of its evolutionary growth, then it must mean that the ultra-human perfection which neo-humanism envisages for Evolution will coincide in concrete terms with the crowning of the Incarnation awaited by all Christians. The two vectors, or components as they are better called, veer and draw together until they give a possible resultant. The super-naturalising Christian Above is incorporated (not immersed) in the human Ahead! And at the same time Faith in God, in the very degree in which it assimilates and sublimates within its own spirit the spirit of Faith in the World, regains all its power to attract and convert!

I said at the beginning of this paper that the human world of today has not grown cold, but that it is ardently searching for a God proportionate to the new dimensions of a Universe whose appearance has completely revolutionised the scale of our faculty of worship. And it is because the total Unity of which we dream still seems to beckon in two different directions, towards the zenith and towards the horizon, that we see the dramatic growth of a whole

race of the 'spiritually stateless' human beings torn between a
Marxism whose depersonalising effect revolts them and a Christianity so lukewarm in human terms that it sickens them.

But let there be revealed to us the possibility of believing *at the
same time and wholly* in God *and* the World, the one through the
other;[4] let this belief burst forth, as it is ineluctably in process of
doing under the pressure of these seemingly opposed forces, and
then, we may be sure of it, a great flame will illumine all things: for a
Faith will have been born (or re-born) containing and embracing all
others—and, inevitably, it is the strongest Faith which sooner or
later must possess the Earth.

("The Heart of the Problem" in FM, 278-281)

. . . The conflict is not between Christianity and atheism, but
between the old and traditional faith in a celestial escape *upward* and
another new faith, in an evolutionary escape *forward;* and the capital
thing to see is that between *upward* and *forward* there is no contradiction but essential complementarity.

(LTF, 186)

Let us not doubt it, and let us awaken to that light: the world is
full of God. For if it were empty, the world would long ago have died
of disgust.

(LTF, 57)

[The Two Fundamental Loves]

The whole problem of my interior life—and all, too, that gives it
value and delight—has consisted, and still consists, in knitting
together in myself the influences that radiate from each of the two
Centres (God and the World)—or, to put it more exactly, in making
them coincide.

I shall describe later at what particular, explicit, solution to the
problem I came to rest, after more than twenty years of feeling my
way and experimenting within myself.—What I wish to draw the
attention of my guides to above all is that, before seriously reflected

considerations came into play, the reconciliation and fusion of the two fundamental loves (love of God and love of the World) was realized in me, intellectually and affectively, by itself alone, *vitally.*

Without any effort, through a sort of natural expansion of creation, I came to see God as an extension of the attributes (magnitude, intimacy, unity) in the Universe which had made so vivid an appeal to me. In some way he was revealed to me through those attributes (shining through them, reaching me through them—impregnated with them, if I may so express what I mean), fulfilling them, going beyond them, and yet *not destroying them.*

Through dilation of the World's charms—and also, I may add, through the need to find an absolute principle for the World's successful issue and for its unity (*a remedy for its contingence*)—knowledge and love of the Universe developed *spontaneously* for me (with great clarity, but in a way that is difficult to express) into knowledge and love of God.

Today I can, I believe, see and feel how the two Centres of all human love insist on their need for one another and complete one another in an astonishing way: God using the World so that he may be attained by us and himself attain us (that is to say, receiving from the World, in relation to us, a sort of *esse tangibile);* and the World, in turn, relying on God in order to overcome its contingence and plurality (that is to say, receiving from God, by participation, a sort of *esse absolutum*—the consecration of its reality).

What is Our Lord Jesus Christ if not this synthesis of the created Universe and its Creator?

("My Universe" in HM, 200-201)

. . . And do believe me. Between my way of thinking and the really "orthodox" (I do not say "official" but "practical") Christian vision of the World, there is not such a big gulf as you think. The proof is the way in which the best of the Catholics are jumping on my poor essays. As I wrote a few days ago to a Superior, a good friend of mine, I do not know whether my bread is well baked: anyhow, the way the people eat it is a pathetic proof how much they are starving for a food in which Love of God does not exclude, but include, Love of the World. And that's that.

(LTF, 198)

Your Body, Jesus, is not only the Centre of all final repose; it is also the bond that holds together all fruitful effort. In you, side by side with *Him who is,* I can passionately love *Him who is becoming.* What more do I need for final peace to spread through my soul, in a way for which I could never have hoped, satisfying even its most apparently impossible aspirations for cosmic life?

There is one thing more, Lord: just one thing, but it is the most difficult of all, and, what is worse, it is a thing that you, perhaps, have condemned. It is this: if I am to have a share in your kingdom, I must on no account reject this radiant world in the ecstatic delight of which I opened my eyes.

("Cosmic Life" in WTW, 52-53)

Stage by stage, my initial faith in the world has taken a definite shape. What was at first a vague intuition of universal unity has become a rational and well-defined awareness of a presence. I know now that I belong to the world and that I shall return to it, not simply in the ashes of my body, but in all the developed powers of my mind and heart. I *can love the world.*

("How I Believe" in CE, 117)

[Christianity and the World]

Every man who is anxious to introduce unity into his life must squarely face, and openly proclaim, these two facts: first, that a too 'detached' Christianity or an exclusively secular cult of the world, is incapable of giving the heart of man all the nourishment it requires, or of existing in isolation; and secondly, that both, on the other hand, are manifestly well fitted to complete one another, and so enable our action to put out its full effort in carrying out its logical purpose.

I wish to prove that the proper balance of man's development is not to be found exclusively either in obedience to terrestrial laws and impulses, or in adhering to dogmas and a spirit revealed to us by our Heavenly Father, but in an effort towards God that forces the blood through every single vein in the universe without exception. It is in order to prove this that I am undertaking this study, for the glory of God, for peace, unity, and the freedom of minds of good will.

("Mastery of the World and The Kingdom of God"
in WTW, 75-76)

God has not seen fit to create in us a new and distinct centre of affection, through which we might love him. In accordance with the particular ordering of our world, in which *everything is made by the transformation of a pre-existing analogue,* it seems evident that, initially, divine Charity exists in us simply as the flame, supernaturalized and purified, that is kindled at the prospect of the Earth's promises. It could never possibly persist in a heart that had ceased to be fired by the quickening contact of tangible realities. Great love of God normally presupposes the maintenance of a strong natural passion. If the tree that is deprived of the soil that nourishes it withers and dies, are we justified in hoping that grace will make it grow green again in order to graft itself onto it?

Theoretically—biologically, one might go so far as to say—there would be nothing surprising in the idea of a rupture—of a blessed divorce—between Christianity and the world. Since life is a perpetual wrenching of itself out of its state of rest, nothing would be more 'natural' than to meet a sacrifice, a supreme immolation, on the threshold of the new and definitive life. Unhappily, the facts will not allow it. Man cannot yet so abandon himself to God, so live in heaven, as to relieve himself of his connatural task; *nevertheless,* since the heavens have lain open, that task *may well seem to him irreparably tainted.*

Like an unfinished pyramid that remains hanging in emptiness from its apex, so life, if accepted in accordance with a certain absolute way of understanding Revelation, seems to lack any real base.

Does this mean—if we can conceive such an impossibility—that by making man have no stomach for a task that is essential to him, the divine illumination has introduced a contradiction into the heart of the masterpiece its power has created?

. . . Historically, through seeking each in isolation to govern the behaviour of men, the two halves of truth have come into conflict. But it was some time before this happened.

For many centuries after the apostolic age—practically until the Renaissance—the duality of the two currents of life, the current that runs within the earth and that which comes down from heaven, remained blurred. *To all appearances, they ran in one stream;* for at that time man's evolution was going through a religious phase, and the Christian religion, for its part, had, as it happened, monopolized thought, the sciences and the arts, so completely that one might have said that they had become immobilized in its light.

Nevertheless, the time came when the autonomous pressure of natural aspirations made itself felt, and threatened to shatter the containing walls in which it was thought to be imprisoned. Heaven and earth had been blended together, human growth and religious perfection had been identified. The two specific movements could not be made to form one: an internal discord became apparent. This was *the break.*

Reacting against what it held to be an enslavement, the earth reviled the Church, and claimed the right to develop without any need of heaven, of its counsels or its help. This took the form first of naturalism and later of secularism. The Church, in turn, anathematized the world, and appeared to regard the work of Progress as diabolical.

And in consequence each of these two powers suffers cruelly from its isolation.[5]

For a moment, *the earth* believed that it could *forget* or *deny* the essential need for the infinite presupposed by the quest for truth or its practice. It was so absorbed by and took such delight in its earliest conquests, that at first it could only relax in amazement and feel that it lacked nothing more. When, however, its first enthusiasm for these new joys and for its own independence had worn off, the earth turned a critical eye on its works and sought to assess its hopes. It was then that the yawning void, deep within it, that calls out for the Absolute, seemed blacker than ever, and that it tried to *forge for itself some Divinity,* born or still to be born, whose glory would crown and illuminate the endless slope of evolution: omnipotent science, mankind, the superman. Idols all—and who, even among their most ardent devotees, would be so bold as to draw the exact features of any of them or wholeheartedly worship them?

In the domain of practical action and moral conduct, the disappointment and confusion are even more extreme. Not only does *reason find it impossible to choose* between the kindly doctrine of *charity,* that has compassion for the portionless, and the stern school of *might* that picks out the victors, not only can it not impress on men *the eminent value of virginity,* nor convince them of the *duty of fecundity*—but, what is more, it realizes that it is incapable of finding a natural basis for morality itself. The Imperative pronounced by its exponents is always an absolutely unqualified statement, or an expression of economic necessity. Man's autonomy then revolts against a duty that cannot justify itself rationally, and abandons itself to enjoyment and the line of least effort, or, perhaps, to violence and anarchy. The whole work of human development, the object of such wide adulation, seems as if it must disintegrate in a corruption for which there is no remedy.

At the same time religion, too, is bitterly aware of its impotence and defencelessness. Since it appeared to reject nature, it feels an alien body in mankind: it no longer enjoys the confidence of that lower, but so persuasive, life that continues to dominate the bodies and souls of its baptized children. Religion seeks to sanctify them and guard them jealously for itself alone, but they hear *another voice*, a winning voice that casts its spell over them, the voice of their first mother, the earth that suckled them. Religion is dimly conscious of this voice, and can even hear it; but because it *cannot understand* its language and its appeal, it mistrusts it and condemns it. Since it cannot silence the enchantress it would like, at least, to take her place and speak for her. But what can it say with any truth or insight about a world that does not belong to it? The Church (since she did not need it) was not given a special sense of terrestrial life: and that is why, when her rulers have sought to monopolize the *whole* control of mankind and the *whole* of human knowledge, they have been obliged, deeply humiliating and mortifying though it be, to remain silent, or make mistakes, or drag unwillingly behind.

Too often, Christians have seemed to behave as though the universe around them were immobile.

'*E si muove.*'

Think of all the infantile maledictions pronounced by Churchmen against new ideas!

Think of all the avenues of enquiry that have at first been forbidden and later found to be rich in results!

Think of all the futile subterfuges designed to make people believe that the Church was directing a movement by which it was, in fact, being forcibly dragged along!

In the field of evolution the Church certainly gives the impression of lagging behind, of allowing herself to be towed. And, in order to live the life of their own times, her bewildered children seem almost to be begging in the streets for crumbs of truth and practical knowledge.

When Christ's ardent disciples see this, they are overcome by a woeful amazement. And even when they are not spiritually impoverished and attenuated by an over-scrupulous isolation, their hearts suffer mortal agony at seeing their loved and admirable Mother so unjustly belittled and misunderstood.

. . . *The time has come,* as we can all see, at last to put together the broken pieces, to re-unite the complementary properties, to weld the apex of the pyramid to the base. Religion and evolution should neither be confused nor divorced. They are destined to form one single continuous organism, in which their respective lives prolong, are dependent on, and complete one another, without being identified or lost: the one offering an infinite ideal and immutable laws, and the other providing a focus of activity and a stuff that is essential to the transformation of beings in process of growth. Since it is in our age that the duality has become so markedly apparent, it is for us to effect the synthesis.

There can be no doubt about it: human progress cannot (on the ground of its autonomy, indisputable and legitimate though it is) be suspected of being a dangerous force—what force, indeed, is without its danger?—nor can it properly be condemned as a manifestation of evil and an incitement to it. It holds its essential place in the designs of providence. Does it not come to us winged and haloed like an angel, the humble brother of Revelation and, with Revelation, the messenger sent to guide us as we advance along the road of life?

The Church, then, must do more than tolerate it, and accept it, as an inevitable compulsion or a necessary stimulus. She must, as we anxiously wait for her to do, recognize it officially; she must adopt it in its principle (if not in all its methods); she must unreservedly encourage bold experiments and attempts made to open new roads. So long as she neglects to include, among the Christian's essential obligations, *the sacred duty* of *research,* in other words his being bound, under pain of sin, to assist in the specific and temporal betterment of the earth—it will be a waste of time for her apologists to put forward the illustrious names of scientists who have also been men of prayer. She will still have to prove that if science flourishes in her wake, too, it is by *right* that this is so, and *under her influence* and not in spite of her or through a happy chance.

Who then, at last, will be the *ideal Christian,* the Christian, at once new and old, who WILL SOLVE IN HIS SOUL THE PROBLEM OF THIS VITAL BALANCE, BY ALLOWING ALL THE LIFE-SAP OF THE WORLD to pass into HIS EFFORT TOWARDS THE DIVINE TRINITY?

That Christian will be the man who has understood that if he is to be supremely the child of God, if he is to fulfil his holy Will in its entirety, he must show himself more assiduous in working for the earth than any servant of Mammon. For some of the faithful, no doubt, this work will consist in spiritualizing the hearts and minds of men by the example of a life that is perfectly chaste and 'unmovingly' contemplative. These, we might say, will represent the *Christian component in the pure state*: but, quite apart from their being *separated from* the world through their *social* and *cosmic aim,* their vocation will still be exceptional. Even if the others, who will be the great majority, have devoted their lives to the practice of the evangelical counsels, their sacred task of sustaining natural life will rank among the most direct and effective factors in their sanctification.

For these latter, *not to seek,* not to plumb to its depths the domain of energies and of thought, not to strive to exhaust the Real, will be a grievous triple fault, a fault of infidelity to the Master who has placed man at the heart of things in order that he may see him, consciously and freely, prolong their immanent evolution and God's creative work.

A fault of presumption, that would make them *tempt God*, by hoping to obtain from indolent prayer, from Revelation or Miracle, what only natural toil can supply.

A fault, thirdly, of *intellectual intransigence*. They are invincibly convinced that if their adherence to their creed is to be beyond reproach, their assault upon the Real must be so constant and insistent that a Divinity other than Jehovah must make himself manifest, if, impossible though this be, he still lies hidden.

Nihil intentatum—nothing left untried—is their motto (the very motto, indeed, of evolution), which, in the fulfilment of nature's lofty destiny, *brings them into line with* the noblest spirit of Revelation.

The sincere and convinced artisan of progress is, in fact, a man of *great and endless renunciation*. He works; he is oblivious of self; he is even detached, because he loves causes better than himself, and he seeks for life's success much more than for his own selfish personal achievement. Even if, from his point of view, suffering is not seen directly as a punishment that expiates, nor exclusively as a factor or symptom of rupture with the earth, but rather as the condition of progress and the price that has to be paid for it—even so, he can at least still claim to be an authentic servant of the Cross.

In a very real sense, too, he can flatter himself that *he serves but one master*—the master of heaven and earth—in that he believes that his work of disclosing a new truth to men is of no less ultimate value and no less sacred than fighting for his country or administering a sacrament.

In so doing, he does not believe that he is transgressing the gospel precept that we must *contemn and hate the world*. He does, indeed, despise the world and trample it under foot—but the world that is cultivated for its own sake, the world closed in on itself, the world of pleasure, the damned portion of the world that falls back and worships itself.

Moreover, he is not so concerned with the immediate and visible success of his work as to be deprived of joy and peace. *Victory* will come from God, in the form his providence decides, *gratuitously* in his own good time; for the worker whose trust is in God knows that no attempt, no aspiration, conceived in grace, is lost: they attain their end by passing through the living Centre of all useful activity.

There is no question, obviously, of the Church's *magisterium* indiscriminately extending its faith, or even its approval, to include the particular detail of every adventure undertaken by mankind. To do that would be precisely to confuse once again the qualities proper to each current of life, and to reintroduce disorder; but the Church, for the sake of the faith and pride of her children, must finally decide to bless and encourage their undertakings, however turbulent and impetuous they may be at first. They must feel her look of approval and tender regard directed upon them, as well as the control of her vigilant hand, when they seek—both in virtue of their citizenship of the world and in the name of God's service—to head the movement that makes the universe follow a curve of progress that is governed by an incommunicable law. Never again, please God, may we be able to say of religion that its influence has made men more indolent, more unenterprising, *less human*; never again may its attitude lie open to the damning suspicion that it seeks to replace science by theology, effort by prayer, battle by resignation, and that its dogmas may well debase the value of the world by limiting in advance the scope of enquiry and the sphere of energy. Never again, I pray, may anyone dare to complain of Rome that it is afraid of anything that moves and thinks.

Even when it has become clear to all that religious faith is not hostile to progress but represents, rather, an additional force to be used by Christians, in the name of what they hold most sacred, to forward the common task of evolution, even then, I fear, we shall not have complete harmony between the children of Heaven and the sons of the earth. Too many will still prefer to turn away from the Gospel and worship the Golden Calf or look in the sky for some star other than Christ. The Parousia, we know, is promised as a dawn that will rise over a supreme onslaught of error . . . Life, at any rate, will neither openly approve nor find excuses for the lack of faith that will mark those last days: and this is because while the Church will be fighting in a continually more acute moral crisis and in a continually more stifling naturalist atmosphere, yet, wise with the experience of centuries, she will be able proudly to point out to life her finest children busy in *forwarding, side by side, mastery of the world and the Kingdom of God.*

("Mastery of the World and The Kingdom of God" in WTW, 83-91)

Whatever may be the corrections, more or less radical, that must be applied to the solution I have found for the 'problem of my life,' one point will remain indisputable: and that is the concern to *unify my interior vision,* of which I am so vividly aware that many others must, I am sure, feel it as strongly as I do.

The supernaturalization of the World does more than provide theologians with abstract difficulties.

It introduces into the heart of practical life an appearance *of duality* which, to my mind, it is important to express in definitively precise terms, and to reduce, so far as possible, by a complete, systematic, solution.

1. The man who really wishes to live his Christianity immediately finds himself confronted by a most perplexing dualism in *effort;* how is he to reconcile renunciation of the World (necessary to life in Christ) with ardour for the Earth (indispensable to man's effort)?

2. And this dualism in action has its source in (or extends into) a much more serious *dualism of religious feeling.* The soul feels itself

caught, in no metaphorical sense, *between two absolutes:* that of experience (the Universe) and that of Revelation (transcendent God).

Judging by my own case, I would say that the great temptation of this century (and of the present moment) is (and will increasingly be) that we find the World of nature, of life, and of mankind greater, closer, more mysterious, more alive, than the God of Scripture.

The tendency to pantheism is so universal and so persistent that there must be in it a soul (a naturally Christian soul) of truth which calls for 'baptism.'

I am convinced that the dogmas and practice of the Church have long provided us with all the elements required for this conquest.

For the glory of Our Lord and the triumph of his Truth, for the peace of many men of good will, I therefore cry out with all my strength for the moment when the age-old rules of Christian ascesis and direction (still, maybe, too empirical) will be brought together into a more organic and more rational code.

And I wish too—with all the longing I have to love God—that the elements of truth, universally believed and professed by the Church, relating to the action and universal presence of God and of Christ—that these may at last be examined as *one whole,* and *with no dilution.*

Then, perhaps, we shall be astonished to see how many of those considerations that have appeared in my writings to be forced, hazardous, or extravagant, derive quite naturally (they or their equivalents) from the most authentic and most practical beliefs of our faith—*once we take the trouble to bring those beliefs together,* not simply into an idiom, but into a coherent *reality.*

NOTE

It is not difficult to see how the tendency whose predominance I favour in Christian practice and in the interpretation of dogma, is exposed to a double danger:

1. So to magnify the Universe as to eclipse or 'materialize' God.

2. Cause the natural resources and affective powers of life to be used even to the point where we are allowed to profit from them and enjoy them, *in a merely pagan spirit.*

Both these mistakes would be *exaggerations* such as every truth is liable to suffer from.

Their avoidance is a matter of Catholic good sense and of Christian prudence.

("My Universe" in HM, 207-208)

You can convert only what you love: if the Christian is not fully in sympathy with the nascent world—if he does not *experience* in himself the anxieties and aspirations of the modern world—if he does not allow the sense of man to grow greater in his being, then he will never effect the emancipating synthesis between earth and heaven from which can emerge the Parousia of the universal Christ. He will continue to fear and condemn almost indiscriminately everything that is new, without seeing among the blemishes and evils the hallowed efforts of something that is being born.

To plunge into in order then to emerge and raise up. To share in order to sublimate. That is precisely the law of the incarnation. One day, already a thousand years ago, the Popes bade farewell to the world of Rome and decided to 'go over to the barbarians.' Is it not just such a gesture, but even more fundamental, that the present day looks for?

I believe that the world will never be converted to Christianity's hopes of heaven, unless first Christianity is converted (that so it may divinise them) to the hopes of the earth.

("Some Reflections on the Conversion of the World" in SC, 127)

Notes

1. As in the case of biological evolutionary theory which also bore a materialist and atheist aspect when it appeared a century ago, but of which this spiritual content is now becoming apparent.

2. And, it may be added, in perfect analogy with the mystery of the first Christmas which (as everyone agrees) could only have happened between Heaven and an Earth which was *prepared,* socially, politically and psychologically, to receive Jesus.

3. But not, of course, sufficient in itself!

4. In a Christ no longer seen only as the Saviour of individual souls, but (precisely because He is the Redeemer in the fullest sense) as the ultimate Mover of anthropogenesis.

5. This is, of course, only an extremely simplified version of the historical picture.

Reconciling Spirit and Matter

Relationship Between Spirit and Matter

In the first place, under the cosmos-system, a fatal dualism was inevitably introduced into the structure of the universe. On one side lay spirit, and on the other matter: and between the two there was nothing but the affirmation of some unexplained and inexplicable coupling together—in other words there was ultimately no more than a verbal inter-dependence, which too often was akin to a subjection of one to the other. And all this was because the two terms of the couple were halted and fixed and had lost all genetic connexion with one another. On the other hand, consider what happens when there comes a breath of wind both to bring them to birth and set them in opposition to one another; when what, only yesterday, was regarded as two *things,* becomes no more than two aspects or phases of a single 'interiorizing arrangement'. Then the current can pass from one extreme to the other of the cosmic spectrum—from the infra-unconscious to the ultra-reflective—and an ontological coherence is established. We no longer have matter the junior partner, matter the handmaid, but matter the mother—*Materia matrix.* Phenomenally speaking, the stuff of things passing from the simplified, pulverized, state to the unified state—in other words, matter becoming charged with spirit: surely, that is indeed the most general, the most all-embracing, and the most fruitful, expression, for our experience, of the universal operation in which we are involved.
("From Cosmos to Cosmogenesis" in AE, 258-259)

Ever since man reflected, and the more he reflected, the opposition between spirit and matter has constantly risen up as an ever higher barrier across the road that climbs up to a better awareness of the universe: and in this lies the deep-rooted origin of all our troubles. In physics and in metaphysics, as in morals, in social science and in religion, why are we constantly arguing with one another, why do we never seem to get any further? Surely the reason is that, being unable accurately to define the nature of the relationship that cosmically connects thought with the tangible, we cannot contrive to orientate ourselves in the labyrinth of things. Which is the top and which the bottom in our universe? Or are there even a top and a bottom?

("The Atomism of Spirit" in AE, 23)

In the system of creative union, moreover, it becomes impossible to continue crudely to contrast Spirit and matter. For those who have understood the law of 'spiritualisation by union,' there are no longer two compartments in the universe, the spiritual and the physical: there are only *two directions* along one and the same road (the direction of pernicious pluralisation, and that of beneficial unification). Every being in the world stands somewhere on the slope that rises up from the shadows towards the light. In front of it, lies the effort to master and simplify its own nature; behind, the abandonment of effort in the physical and moral disintegration of its powers. If it goes forward, it meets the good: everything is Spirit for it. If it falls back, it meets nothing on its road but evil and matter. Thus an infinite number of steps are spaced out between absolute evil (that is, nothingness, the total plurality to which everything reverts) and the Supreme Good (that is, the centre of universal convergence towards which everything tends); these steps are, no doubt, separated by a number of 'landings' (like that, for example, which marks off animal from man, or man from angel), but they nevertheless represent one general movement, and to each step there corresponds a particular distribution of good and evil, of Spirit and matter. What is evil, material, for me, is good, spiritual, for another advancing by my side. And the climber ahead of me on the mountain would be corrupted if he used what gives me unity.

Matter and Spirit are not opposed as two separate things, as two natures, but as two directions of evolution within the world.

("My Universe" in SC, 51)

If you ever read my "pious book," you will see that there is a paragraph devoted to Holy Matter. A matter that has nothing emaciated or Franciscan about it. You see, if you continue to be true to yourself, I think you will come to realize that Spirit is not the fleshless thing, the insubstantial specter, that is sometimes presented to us. True spirit must be formed of all the vitality and all the consistency of the body: it is an extension in the same direction. The spiritual life of all the great saints has been a richer and more intense life, not a restricted life. We live, in this respect, in a dim ambiguity. And it is my fundamental difficulty not to be able to voice as I would, by word and by example, my certitude that the Kingdom of God can only be established by a much more complete immersion of the Christian forces in the most powerful currents of the Earth. Ah, the great symbol of Baptism, in which ordinarily men see no more than the drop of water that cleanses, and miss the river that sweeps away! In everything that I have happened to read on the World, I seem never to have found an accent, a cry, that has not already escaped me. . . . Spirit is the most violent, the most incendiary of Matters.

(LTF, 55-56)

[Spirit—Matter's Synthesis]

As recently as yesterday Christianity represented the highest point attained by the consciousness of Mankind in its striving to humanise itself. But does it still hold this position, or at the best can it continue to hold it for long? Many people think not; and to account for this slackening impulse in the highest and most complete of human mystical beliefs they argue that the evangelical flowering is ill-adapted to the critical and materialist climate of the modern world. They hold that the time of Christianity is past, and that some other shoot must grow in the field of religion to take its place.

But if, as I maintain, the event that characterises our epoch is a growing awareness of the convergent nature of Space-Time, then nothing can be more ill-founded than this pessimism. Transferred within the cone of Time, and there transmuted, the Christian system is neither disorganised nor deformed. On the contrary, sustained by the new environment, it more than ever develops its main lines, acquiring an added coherence and clarity.

This is what, in conclusion, I wish to show.

What is finally the most revolutionary and fruitful aspect of our present age is the relationship it has brought to light between Matter and Spirit: spirit being no longer independent of matter, or in opposition to it,[1] but laboriously emerging from it under the attraction of God by way of synthesis and centration.

But what is the effect, for Christian faith and mysticism, of this redefinition of the Spirit? It is simply to confer absolute reality and absolute urgency upon the double dogma on which the whole of Christianity rests, and by which it is summed up: the physical primacy of Christ and the moral primacy of Charity.

("The New Spirit" in FM, 96-97)

All the great religions set out to raise man above matter, which means to spiritualize him, which again means to 'sanctify' him. Yet the definition of 'saint' or holy varies from one religion to another, as do the notions also of spirit and matter. What is the Christian position on this essential point?

In principle, and in a general way, we may say that the original characteristic of Christian ascesis has been from the outset a concern to respect the integrity, body and soul, of the 'human compound.' In the majority of Eastern religions matter, being regarded as evil, had to be gradually left behind in the course of sanctification; Christianity, on the other hand, maintains the value and rights of the flesh, which the Word assumed, and which he is going to raise to life again. At the same time as Christ saves spirit, he saves matter in which he immersed himself. Similarly, the Christian does not have to try to annihilate his body but to sanctify and sublimate it.

When we come to examine exactly what this sublimation consists in, we find that the Church's attitude is again in line with her living, progressive nature; she appears to be clarifying her views in an ascetical and mystical evolution which is closely linked with the elucidation of her dogmatic thought. Until quite recently (so long, that is, as matter and spirit could still be regarded as two heterogeneous elements statically coupled together in the world) the Christian saint was the man who was the most successful in introducing order into this dualist complex, by reducing physical energies to the position of being subservient to the aspirations of the spirit. Once again, as in the Eastern religions, this resulted in a predominant emphasis on mortification.

A different view now prevails: in a universe whose evolutive structure has finally been appreciated, matter and spirit are now seen as two terms mutually integrated in the unity of one and the same movement (spirit emerging experientially in the world only upon progressively more fully synthesized matter). In consequence of this, the question of ascesis assumes a different form. For the Christian of today it is no longer sufficient to introduce the reign of peace and silence into his body, so that his soul may be free to devote itself to the things of God. What matters to him, if he is to attain perfection, is above all to extract from his body all the *spiritual power* it contains—and not merely from this body strictly confined to its limbs of flesh, but from the whole immense 'cosmic' body which is made up for each of us by the enveloping mass of the *Weltstoff* in evolution.

As we now see things, with everything becoming sacred because capable of spiritualization, the gospel's 'Leave all and follow me' can ultimately only mean that it sends us back to 'all' seen in a higher perspective, in as much as this 'all' (we now realize) enables us to take hold of Christ and further his being in the universality of his incarnation. The emphasis now is not primarily on mortification—but on the perfecting of man's effort through mortification.

The saint, the Christian saint, as we now understand him and look for him, will not be the man who is the most successful in escaping from matter and mastering it completely; he will be the man who seeks to make all his powers—gold, love, or freedom—transcend themselves and co-operate in the consummation of Christ, and who so realizes for us the ideal of the faithful servant of evolution.

("Introduction to the Christian Life" in CE, 168-170)

God can only be defined as a *centre of centres.* In this complexity lies the perfection of His unity—the only final goal logically attributable to the developments of spirit-matter.

("Sketch of a Personalistic Universe" in HE, 68)

The Spiritual Power of Matter

The same beam of light which Christian spirituality, rightly and fully understood, directs upon the Cross to humanise it (without veiling it) is reflected on matter so as to spiritualise it.

In their struggle towards the mystical life, men have often succumbed to the illusion of crudely contrasting soul and body, spirit and flesh, as good and evil. But despite certain current expressions, this Manichean tendency has never had the Church's approval. And, in order to prepare the way for our final view of the divine *milieu*, perhaps we may be allowed to vindicate and exalt that aspect of it which the Lord came to put on, save and consecrate: *holy matter.*

From the mystical and ascetic point of view adopted in these pages, matter is not exactly any of the abstract entities defined under that name by science and philosophy. It is certainly the same *concrete* reality, for us, as it is for physics and metaphysics, having the same basic attributes of plurality, perceivability and inter-connection. But here we want to embrace that reality as a whole in its widest possible sense: to give it its full abundance as it reacts not only to our scientific or analytical investigations, but to all our practical activities. Matter, as far as we are concerned, is the assemblage of things, energies and creatures which surround us in so far as these are palpable, sensible and 'natural' (in the theological sense of the word). Matter is the common, universal, tangible setting, infinitely shifting and varied, in which we live.

How, then, does the thing thus defined present itself to us to be acted upon? Under the enigmatic features of a two-sided power.

On the one hand matter is the burden, the fetters, the pain, the sin and the threat to our lives. It weighs us down, suffers, wounds, tempts and grows old. Matter makes us heavy, paralysed, vulnerable, guilty. Who will deliver us from this body of death?

But at the same time matter is physical exuberance, ennobling contact, virile effort and the joy of growth. It attracts, renews, unites and flowers. By matter we are nourished, lifted up, linked to everything else, invaded by life. To be deprived of it is intolerable. *Non exui volumus sed superindui* (2 Cor. v, 4). Who will give us an immortal body?

Asceticism deliberately looks no further than the first aspect, the one which is turned towards death; and it recoils, exclaiming 'Flee!'

*But what would our spirits be, O God, if they did not have the bread of earthly
things to nourish them, the wine of created beauties to intoxicate them, and
the conflicts of human life to fortify them? What feeble powers and bloodless
hearts your creatures would bring you if they were to succeed in cutting themselves off* prematurely *from the providential setting in which you have
placed them! Teach us, Lord, how to contemplate the sphinx without suc-
cumbing to its spell; how to grasp the hidden mystery in the womb of death,
not by a refinement of human doctrine, but in the simple concrete act by
which you plunged yourself into matter in order to redeem it. By the virtue of
your suffering incarnation disclose to us, and then teach us to harness jealousy
for you, the spiritual power of matter.*

Let us take a comparison as our starting point. Imagine a deep-sea
diver trying to get back from the seabed to the clear light of day. Or
imagine a traveller on a fog-bound mountain-side climbing upward
towards the summit bathed in light. For each of these men space is
divided into two zones marked with opposing properties: the one
behind and beneath appears ever darker, while the one in front and
above becomes ever lighter. Both diver and climber can succeed in
making their way towards the second zone only if they use everything
around and about them as points of leverage. Moreover, in the course
of their task, the light above them grows brighter with each advance
made; and at the same time the area which has been traversed, as it is
traversed, ceases to hold the light and is engulfed in darkness. Let us
remember these stages, for they express symbolically all the elements
we need in order to understand how we should touch and handle
matter with a proper sense of reverence.

Above all matter is not just the weight that drags us down, the
mire that sucks us in, the bramble that bars our way. In itself, and
before we find ourselves where we are, and before we choose, it is
simply the slope on which we can go up just as well as go down, the
medium that can uphold or give way, the wind that can overthrow
or lift up. Of its nature, and as a result of original sin, it is true that it
represents a perpetual impulse towards failure. But by nature too,
and as a result of the Incarnation, it contains the spur or the allurement to be our accomplice towards heightened being, and this coun-
ter-balances and even dominates the *fomes peccati*. The full truth of
our situation is that, here below, and by virtue of our immersion in
the universe, we are each one of us placed within its layers or on its
slopes, at a specific point defined by the present moment in the

history of the world, the place of our birth, and our individual vocation. And *from that starting point,* variously situated at different levels,
the task assigned to us is to climb towards the light, passing
through, so as to attain God, *a given series of created things* which are
not exactly obstacles but rather foot-holds, intermediaries to be
made use of, nourishment to be taken, sap to be purified and elements to be associated with us and borne along with us.

That being so, and still as a result of our initial position among
things, and also as a result of each position we subsequently occupy in
matter, matter falls into two distinct zones, differentiated according
to our effort: the zone already left behind or arrived at, to which we
should not return, or at which we should not pause, lest we fall
back—this is the zone of matter *in the material and carnal sense;* and the
zone offered to our renewed efforts towards progress, search, conquest and 'divinisation', the zone of matter *taken in the spiritual sense;*
and the frontier between these two zones is essentially relative and
shifting. That which is good, sanctifying and spiritual for my brother
below or beside me on the mountainside, can be material, misleading
or bad for me. What I rightly allowed myself yesterday, I must perhaps deny myself today. And conversely, actions which would have
been a grave betrayal in a St. Aloysius Gonzaga or a St. Anthony, may
well be models for me if I am to follow in the footsteps of these saints.
In other words, the soul can only rejoin God after having traversed *a
specific path* through matter—which path can be seen as the distance
which separates, but it can also be seen as the road which links. Without certain possessions and certain victories, no man exists as God
wishes him to be. Each one of us has his Jacob's ladder, whose rungs
are formed of a series of objects. Thus it is not our business to withdraw from the world before our time; rather let us learn to orientate
our being in the flux of things; then, instead of the force of gravity
which drags us down to the abyss of self-indulgence and selfishness,
we shall feel a salutary 'component' emerge from created things
which, by a process we have already described, will enlarge our hori-
zons, will snatch us away from our pettinesses and impel us imperi-
ously towards a widening of our vision, towards the renunciation of
cherished pleasure, towards the desire for ever more spiritual beauty.
Matter, which at first seemed to counsel us towards the maximum
pleasure and the minimum effort, emerges as the principle of minimum pleasure and maximum effort.

In this case, too, the law which applies to the individual would seem to be a small-scale version of the law which applies to the whole. It would surely not be far wrong to suggest that, in its universality, the world too has a prescribed path to follow before attaining its consummation. There can really be no doubt of it. If the material totality of the world includes energies which cannot be made use of, and if, more unfortunately, it contains perverted energies and elements which are slowly separated from it, it is still more certain that it contains *a certain quantity of spiritual power* of which the progressive sublimation, *in Christo Jesu*, is, for the Creator, the fundamental operation taking place. At the present time this power is still diffused almost everywhere: nothing, however insignificant or crude it may appear, is without some trace of it. And the task of the body of Christ, living in his faithful, is patiently to sort out those heavenly forces—to extract, without letting any of it be lost, that chosen substance. Little by little, we may rest assured, the work is being done. Thanks to the multitude of individuals and vocations, the Spirit of God insinuates itself everywhere and is everywhere at work. It is the great tree we spoke of a moment ago, whose sunlit branches refine and turn to flowers the sap extracted by the humblest of its roots. As the work progresses, certain zones, no doubt, become worked out. Within each individual life, as we have noted, the frontier between spiritual matter and carnal matter is constantly moving upward. And in the same way, in proportion as humanity is Christianised, it feels less and less need for certain earthly nourishment. Contemplation and chastity should thus tend, quite legitimately, to gain mastery over anxious work and direct possession. This is the *general 'drift'* *of matter* towards spirit. This movement must have its term: one day the whole divinisable substance of matter will have passed into the souls of men; all the chosen dynamisms will have been recovered: and then our world will be ready for the Parousia.

Who can fail to perceive the great symbolic gesture of baptism in this general history of matter? Christ immerses himself in the waters of Jordan, symbol of the forces of the earth. These he sanctifies. And as he emerges, in the words of St. Gregory of Nyssa, with the water which runs off his body he elevates the whole world.

Immersion and emergence; participation in things and sublimation; possession and renunciation; crossing through and being borne onwards—that is the twofold yet single movement which answers the challenge of matter in order to save it.[2]

Matter, you in whom I find both seduction and strength, you in whom I find blandishment and virility, you who can enrich and destroy, I surrender myself to your mighty layers, with faith in the heavenly influences which have sweetened and purified your waters. The virtue of Christ has passed into you. *Let your attractions lead me forward, let your sap be the food that nourishes me; let your resistance give me toughness; let your robberies and inroads give me freedom. And finally, let your whole being lead me towards Godhead.*

(DM, 105-111)

Hymn to Matter

'Blessed be you, harsh matter, barren soil, stubborn rock: you who yield only to violence, you who force us to work if we would eat.

'Blessed be you, perilous matter, violent sea, untameable passion: you who unless we fetter you will devour us.

'Blessed be you, mighty matter, irresistible march of evolution, reality ever new-born; you who, by constantly shattering our mental categories, force us to go ever further and further in our pursuit of the truth.

'Blessed be you, universal matter, immeasurable time, boundless ether, triple abyss of stars and atoms and generations: you who by overflowing and dissolving our narrow standards or measurement reveal to us the dimensions of God.

'Blessed be you, impenetrable matter: you who, interposed between our minds and the world of essences, cause us to languish with the desire to pierce through the seamless veil of phenomena.

'Blessed be you, mortal matter: you who one day will undergo the process of dissolution within us and will thereby take us forcibly into the very heart of that which exists.

'Without you, without your onslaughts, without your uprootings of us, we should remain all our lives inert, stagnant, puerile, ignorant both of ourselves and of God. You who batter us and then dress our wounds, you who resist us and yield to us, you who wreck and build, you who shackle and liberate, the sap of our souls, the hand of God, the flesh of Christ: it is you, matter, that I bless.

'I bless you, matter, and you I acclaim: not as the pontiffs of science or the moralizing preachers depict you, debased, disfigured—a mass of brute forces and base appetites—but as you reveal yourself to me today, *in your totality and your true nature*.

'You I acclaim as the inexhaustible potentiality for existence and transformation wherein the predestined substance germinates and grows.

'I acclaim you as the universal power which brings together and unites, through which the multitudinous monads are bound together and in which they all converge on the way of the Spirit.

'I acclaim you as the melodious fountain of water whence spring the souls of men and as the limpid crystal whereof is fashioned the new Jerusalem.

'I acclaim you as the divine *milieu*, charged with creative power, as the ocean stirred by the Spirit, as the clay moulded and infused with life by the incarnate Word.

'Sometimes, thinking they are responding to your irresistible appeal, men will hurl themselves for love of you into the exterior abyss of selfish pleasure-seeking: they are deceived by a reflection or by an echo.

'This I now understand.

'If we are ever to reach you, matter, we must, having first established contact with the totality of all that lives and moves here below, come little by little to feel that the individual shapes of all we have laid hold on are melting away in our hands, until finally we are at grips with the *single essence* of all consistencies and all unions.

'If we are ever to possess you, having taken you rapturously in our arms, we must then go on to sublimate you through sorrow.

'Your realm comprises those serene heights where saints think to avoid you—but where your flesh is so transparent and so agile as to be no longer distinguishable from spirit.

'Raise me up then, matter, to those heights, through struggle and separation and death; raise me up until, at long last, it becomes possible for me in perfect chastity to embrace the universe.'

Down below on the desert sands, now tranquil again, someone was weeping and calling out: 'My Father, my Father! What wild wind can this be that has borne him away?'

And on the ground there lay a cloak.

("The Heart of Matter" in HM, 75-77)

Notes

1. Provided, of course, that we do not understand 'matter' in a 'reduplicative' and restricted sense to mean that portion of the Universe which 'redescends,' escaping the rising stream of Noogenisis.

2. The sensual mysticisms and certain neo-pelagianisms (such as Americanism), by paying too much attention to the first of these phases, have fallen into the error of seeking divine love and the divine kingdom *on the same level* as human affections and human progress. Conversely, by concentrating too much on the second phase, some exaggerated forms of Christianity conceive perfection as built upon the destruction of 'nature.' The true Christian supernatural, frequently defined by the Church, neither leaves the creature where he is, on his own plane, nor suppresses him: it 'sur-animates' him. It must surely be obvious that, however transcendent and creative they may be, God's love and ardour could only fall upon the *human* heart, that is to say upon an object prepared (from near or from afar) by means of all the nourishments of the earth. It is astonishing that so few minds should succeed, in this as in other cases, in grasping the notion of transformation. Sometimes the thing transformed seems to them to be the old thing unchanged; at other times they see in it only the entirely new. In the first case it is the spirit that eludes them; in the second case, it is the matter. Though not so crude as the first excess, the second is shown by experience to be no less destructive of the equilibrium of mankind.

Reconciling the Within and the Without

[The Within-Without's Interaction]

If there is one thing that has been clearly brought out by the latest advances in physics, it is that in our experience there are 'spheres' or 'levels' of different kinds in the unity of nature, each of them distinguished by the dominance of certain factors which are imperceptible or negligible in a neighbouring sphere or on an adjacent level. On the middle scale of our organisms and of our constructions velocity does not seem to change the nature of matter. Nonetheless, we now know that at the extreme values reached by atomic movements it profoundly modifies the mass of bodies. Among 'normal' chemical elements, stability and longevity appear to be the rule: but that illusion has been destroyed by the discovery of radio-active substances. By the standards of our human existence, the mountains and stars are a model of majestic changelessness. Now we discover that, observed over a sufficiently great duration of time, the earth's crust changes ceaselessly under our feet, while the heavens sweep us along in a cyclone of stars.

In all these instances, and in others like to them, there is no absolute appearance of a new dimension. *Every* mass is modified by it's velocity. *Every* body radiates. *Every* movement is veiled in immobility when sufficiently slowed down. But on a different scale, or at a different intensity, there will become visible some phenomenon that spreads over the horizon, blots out the other distinctions, and gives its own particular tonality to the whole picture.

It is the same with the *within* of things.

For a reason that will soon appear, objects in the realm of physico-chemistry are only made manifest by their outward determinisms.

In the eyes of the physicist, nothing exists legitimately, at least up to now, except the *without* of things. The same intellectual attitude is still permissible in the bacteriologist, whose cultures (apart from some substantial difficulties) are treated as laboratory reagents. But it is already more difficult in the realm of plants. It tends to become a gamble in the case of a biologist studying the behaviour of insects or coelenterates. It seems merely futile with regard to the vertebrates. Finally, it breaks down completely with man, in whom the existence of a *within* can no longer be evaded, because it is the object of a direct intuition and the substance of all knowledge.

The apparent restriction of the phenomenon of consciousness to the higher forms of life has long served science as an excuse for eliminating it from its models of the universe. A queer exception, an aberrant function, an epiphenomenon—thought was classed under one or other of these heads in order to get rid of it. But what would have happened to modern physics if radium had been classified as an 'abnormal substance' without further ado? Clearly, the activity of radium had not been neglected, and could not be neglected, because, being measurable, it forced its way into the external web of matter—whereas consciousness, in order to be integrated into a world-system, necessitates consideration of the existence of a new aspect or dimension in the stuff of the universe. We shrink from the attempt, but which of us does not in both cases see an identical problem facing research workers, which have to be solved by the same method, namely, *to discover the universal hidden beneath the exceptional?*

Latterly we have experienced it too often to admit of any further doubt: an irregularity in nature is only the sharp exacerbation, to the point of perceptible disclosure, of a property of things diffused throughout the universe, in a state which eludes our recognition of its presence. Properly observed, even if only in one spot, a phenomenon necessarily has an omnipresent value and roots by reason of the fundamental unity of the world. Whither does thus rule lead us if we apply it to the instance of human 'self-knowledge'?

'Consciousness is completely evident only in man,' we are tempted to say, 'therefore it is an isolated instance of no interest to science.'

'Consciousness is evident in man,' we must continue, correcting ourselves, 'therefore, half-seen in this one flash of light, it has a cosmic extension, and as such is surrounded by an aura of indefinite spatial and temporal extensions.'

The conclusion is pregnant with consequences, and yet I cannot see how, by sound analogy with all the rest of science, we can escape from it.

It is impossible to deny that, deep within ourselves, an 'interior' appears at the heart of beings, as it were seen through a rent. This is enough to ensure that, in one degree or another, this 'interior' should obtrude itself as existing everywhere in nature from all time. Since the stuff of the universe has an inner aspect at one point of itself, there is necessarily a *double aspect to its structure,* that is to say in every region of space and time—in the same way, for instance, as it is granular: *co-extensive with their Without, there is a Within to things.*

The consequent picture of the world daunts our imagination, but it is in fact the only one acceptable to our reason. Taken at its lowest point, exactly where we put ourselves at the beginning of these pages, primitive matter is something more than the particulate swarming so marvellously analysed by modern physics. Beneath this mechanical layer we must think of a 'biological' layer that is attenuated to the uttermost, but yet is absolutely necessary to explain the cosmos in succeeding ages. The *within, consciousness*[1] and then *spontaneity*—three expressions for the same thing. It is no more legitimate for us experimentally to fix an absolute beginning to these three expressions of one and the same thing than to any other lines of the universe.

In a coherent perspective of the world: life inevitably assumes a 'pre-life' for as far back before it as the eye can see.[2]

In that case—and the objection will come from materialists and upholders of spirituality alike—if everything in nature is basically living, or at least pre-living, how is it possible for a mechanistic science of matter to be built up and to triumph?

Determinate *without,* and 'free' *within*—would the two aspects of things be irreducible and incommensurable? If so, where is your solution?

The answer to this difficulty is already implicit in what we have said above about the diversity of 'spheres of experience' superposed in the interior of the world. It will appear more clearly when we have discerned the qualitative laws that govern in their growth and variation the manifestations of what we have just called the *within* of things. . . .

Considered in its pre-vital state, the *within* of things, whose reality even in the nascent forms of matter we have just admitted, must not be thought of as forming a continuous film, but as assuming the same granulation as matter itself.

Soon we shall have to return to this essential point. As far back as we began to descry them, *the first living things* reveal themselves to our experience as kinds of 'mega-' or ' ultra-' molecules, both in size and in number: a bewildering multitude of microscopic nuclei. Which means that for reasons of homogeneity and continuity, the pre-living can be divined, below the horizon, as an object sharing in the *corpuscular* structure and properties of the world. Looked at from *within,* as well as observed from *without,* the stuff of the universe thus tends likewise to be resolved backwardly into a dust of particles that are (i) perfectly alike among themselves (at least if they are observed from a great distance); (ii) each co-extensive with the whole of the cosmic realm; (iii) mysteriously connected among themselves, finally, by a global energy. In these depths the world's two aspects, external and internal, correspond point by point. So much is this so that one may pass from the one to the other on the sole condition that (mechanical interaction) in the definition of the partial centres of the universe given above is replaced by 'consciousness.'

Atomicity is a common property of the Within and the Without of things.

(*PM, 54-59*)

There is no concept more familiar to us than that of spiritual energy, yet there is none that is more opaque scientifically. On the one hand the objective reality of psychical effort and work is so well established that the whole of ethics rests on it and, on the other hand, the nature of this inner power is so intangible that the whole description of the universe in mechanical terms has had no need to take account of it, but has been successfully completed in deliberate disregard of its reality.

The difficulties we still encounter in trying to hold together spirit and matter in a reasonable perspective are nowhere more harshly revealed. Nowhere either is the need more urgent of building a bridge between the two banks of our existence—the physical and the moral—if we wish the material and spiritual sides of our activities to be mutually enlivened.

To connect the two energies, of the body and the soul, in a coherent manner: science has provisionally decided to ignore the question, and it would be very convenient for us to do the same. Unfortunately, or fortunately, caught up as we are here in the logic of a system where the *within* of things has just as much or even more value than their *without*, we collide with the difficulty head on. It is impossible to avoid the clash: we must advance.

Naturally the following considerations do not pretend to be a truly satisfactory solution of the problem of spiritual energy. Their aim is merely to show by means of one example what, in my opinion, an integral science of nature should adopt as its line of research and the kind of interpretation it should follow.

A. The Problem of the Two Energies

Since the inner face of the world is manifest deep within our human consciousness, and there reflects upon itself, it would seem that we have only got to look at ourselves in order to understand the dynamic relationships existing between the *within* and the *without* of things at a given point in the universe.

In fact to do so is one of the most difficult of all things.

We are perfectly well aware in our concrete actions that the two opposite forces combine. The motor works, but we cannot make out the method, which seems to be contradictory. What makes the crux—and an irritating one at that—of the problem of spiritual energy for our reason is the heightened sense that we bear without ceasing in ourselves that our action seems at once to depend on, and yet to be independent of, material forces.

First of all, the dependence. This is depressingly and magnificently obvious. 'To think, we must eat.' That blunt statement expresses a whole economy, and reveals, according to the way we look at it, either the tyranny of matter or its spiritual power. The loftiest speculation, the most burning love are, as we know only too well, accompanied and paid for by an expenditure of physical energy. Sometimes we need bread, sometimes wine, sometimes a drug or a hormone injection, sometimes the stimulation of a colour, sometimes the magic of a sound which goes in at our ears as a vibration and reaches our brains in the form of inspiration.

Without the slightest doubt *there is something* through which material and spiritual energy hold together and are complementary.

In last analysis, *somehow or other,* there must be a single energy operating in the world. And the first idea that occurs to us is that the 'soul' must be as it were a focal point of transformation at which, from all the points of nature, the forces of bodies converge, to become interiorised and sublimated in beauty and truth.

Yet, seductive though it be, the idea of the *direct* transformation of one of these two energies into the other is no sooner glimpsed than it has to be abandoned. As soon as we try to couple them together, their mutual independence becomes clear as their interrelation.

Once again; 'To think, we must eat.' But what a variety of thoughts we get out of one slice of bread! Like the letters of alphabet, which can equally well be assembled into nonsense as into the most beautiful poem, the same calories seem as indifferent as they are necessary to the spiritual values they nourish.

The two energies—of mind and matter—spread respectively through the two layers of the world (the *within* and the *without)* have, taken as a whole, much the same demeanour. They are constantly associated and in some way pass into each other. But it seems impossible to establish a simple correspondence between their curves. On the one hand, only a minute fraction of 'physical' energy is used up in the highest exercise of spiritual energy; on the other, this minute fraction, once absorbed, results on the internal scale in the most extraordinary oscillations.

A quantitative disproportion of this kind is enough to make us reject the naive notion of 'change of form' (or direct transformation)—and hence all hope of discovering a 'mechanical equivalent' for will or thought. Between the *within* and the *without* of things, the interdependence of energy is incontestable. But it can in all probability only be expressed by a complex symbolism in which terms of a different order are employed.

B. A Line of Solution

To avoid a fundamental dualism, at once impossible and anti-scientific, and at the same time to safeguard the natural complexity of the stuff of the universe, I accordingly propose the following as a basis for all that is to emerge later.

We shall assume that, essentially, all energy is psychic in nature; but add that in each particular element this fundamental energy is divided into two distinct components: a *tangential energy* which links the element with all others of the same order (that is to say, of the same complexity and the same centricity) as itself in the universe; and a *radial energy* which draws it towards ever greater complexity and centricity—in other words forwards.[3]

From this initial state, and supposing that it disposes of a certain free tangential energy, the particle thus constituted must obviously be in a position to increase its internal complexity in association with neighboring particles, and thereupon (since its centricity is automatically increased) to augment its radial energy. The latter will then be able to react in its turn in the form of a new arrangement in the tangential field. And so on.

In this view, whereby tangential energy represents 'energy' as such, as generally understood by science, the only difficulty is to explain the interplay of tangential arrangements in terms of the laws of thermo-dynamics. As regards this we may remark the following:

a. First of all, since the variation of radial energy in function of tangential energy is effected, according to our hypotheses, *by the intervention of an arrangement,* it follows that as much as you like of the first may be linked with as little as you like of the second—for a highly perfected arrangement may only require an extremely small amount of work. This fits in with the facts noted in section A above.

b. Moreover, in the system here proposed, we are paradoxically led to admit that cosmic energy is constantly increasing, not only in its radial form, but—which is much more serious—in its tangential one (for the tension between elements increases with their centricity itself). This would seem to be in direct contradiction with the law of conservation of energy. It must be noted, however, that this increase of the tangential of the second kind (the only one troublesome for physics) only becomes appreciable with very high radial values (as in man, for instance, and social tensions). Below this level, and for an approximately constant number of initial particles in the universe, the sum of the cosmic tangential energies remains practically and statistically invariable in the course of transformations. And this is all that science requires.

c. Lastly, since according to our reading, the entire edifice of the universe is constantly supported at every phase of its progressive 'centration' by its primary arrangements, it is plain that its achievement will be conditioned up to the highest stages by a certain primordial quantum of free tangential energy, which will gradually exhaust itself, following the principle of entropy.

Looked at as a whole, this picture satisfies the requirements of reality.

(PM, 62-66)

By their very nature, and at every level of complexity, the elements of the world are able to influence and mutually to penetrate each other by their within, so as to combine their 'radial energies' in 'bundles.' While no more than conjecturable in atoms and molecules, this psychic interpenetrability grows and becomes directly perceptible in the case of organised beings. Finally in man, in whom the effects of consciousness attain the present maximum found in nature, it reaches a high degree everywhere. It is written all over the social phenomenon and is, of course, felt by us directly. But at the same time, in this case also, it operates only in virtue of the 'tangential energies' of arrangement and thus under certain conditions of spatial juxtaposition.

And here there intervenes a fact, commonplace at first sight, but through which in reality there transpires one of the most fundamental characteristics of the cosmic structure—the roundness of the earth. The geometrical limitation of a star closed, like a gigantic molecule, upon itself. We have already regarded this as a necessary feature at the origin of the first synthesis and polymerisations on the early earth. Implicitly, without our having to say so, it has constantly sustained all the differentiations and all the progress of the biosphere. But what are we to say of its function in the noosphere?

What would have become of humanity if, by some remote chance, it had been free to spread indefinitely on an unlimited surface, that is to say left only to the devices of its internal affinities? Something unimaginable, certainly something altogether different from the modern world. Perhaps even nothing at all, when we think of the extreme importance of the role played in its development by the forces of compression.

Originally and for centuries there was no serious obstacle to the human waves expanding over the surface of the globe; probably this is one of the reasons explaining the slowness of their social evolution. Then, from the Neolithic age onwards, these waves began, as we have seen, to recoil upon themselves. All available space being occupied, the occupiers had to pack in tighter. That is how, step by step, through the simple multiplying effect of generations, we have come to constitute, as we do at present, an almost solid mass of hominised substance.

Now, to the degree that—under the effect of this pressure and thanks to their psychic permeability—the human elements infiltrated more and more into each other, their minds (mysterious coincidence) were mutually stimulated by proximity. And as though dilated upon themselves, they each extended little by little the radius of their influence upon this earth which, by the same token, shrank steadily. What in fact do we see happening in the modern paroxysm? It has been stated over and over again. Through the discovery yesterday of the railway, the motor car and the aeroplane, the physical influence of each man, formerly restricted to a few miles, now extends to hundreds of leagues or more. Better still: thanks to the prodigious biological event represented by the discovery of electro-magnetic waves, each individual finds himself henceforth (actively and passively) simultaneously present, over land and sea, in every corner of the earth.

Thus, not only through the constant increase in the numbers of its members, but also through the continual augmentation of their area of individual activity, mankind—forced to develop as it is in a confined area—has found itself relentlessly subjected to an intense pressure, a self-accentuating pressure, because each advance in it caused a corresponding expansion in each element.

(PM, 239-240)

Notes

1. Here, and throughout this book [*The Phenomenon of Man*], the term 'consciousness' is taken in its widest sense to indicate every kind of psychicism, from the most rudimentary forms of interior perception imaginable to the human phenomenon of reflective thought.

2. These pages had been written for some time when I was surprised to find their substance in some masterly lines recently written by J. B. S. Haldane:

> 'We do not find obvious evidence of life or mind in so-called inert matter, and we naturally study them most easily where they are most completely manifested; but if the scientific point of view is correct, we shall ultimately find them, at least in rudimentary forms, all through the universe.'

And he goes on to add these words which my readers would do well to recall when I come to unveil (with all due reservations and corrections) the perspective of the 'Omega Point':

> 'Now, if the co-operation of some thousands of millions of cells in our brain can produce our consciousness, the idea becomes vastly more plausible that the co-operation of humanity, or some sections of it, may determine what Comte calls a Great Being' (Essay on Science and Ethics in *The Inequality of Man*, Chatto, 1932, p. 113.)

What I say is thus not absurd. Moreover, any metaphysician must rejoice to discover that even in the eyes of physics the idea of absolutely brute matter (that is to say, of a pure 'transient') is only a first very rough approximation of our experience.

3. Let it be noted in passing that the less an element is 'centred' (i.e. the feebler its radial energy) the more will its tangential energy reveal itself in powerful mechanical effects. Between strongly 'centred' particles (i.e. of high radial energy) the tangential seems to become 'interiorised' and to disappear from the physicist's view. Probably we have here an auxiliary principle which could help to explain the apparent conservation of energy in the universe (see para. *b.* below). We probably ought to recognise *two* sorts of tangential energy, one of *radiation* (at its maximum with the lowest radial values, as in the atom), the other of *arrangement* (only appreciable with the highest radial values, as in living creatures, man in particular).

Reconciling Science and Religion

The Conjunction of Science and Religion

To outward appearance, the modern world was born of an anti-religious movement: man becoming self-sufficient and reason supplanting belief. Our generation and the two that preceded it have heard little but talk of the conflict between science and faith; indeed it seemed at one moment a foregone conclusion that the former was destined to take the place of the latter.

But, as the tension is prolonged, the conflict visibly seems to need to be resolved in terms of an entirely different form of equilibrium—not in elimination, nor duality, but in synthesis. After close on two centuries of passionate struggles, neither science nor faith has succeeded in discrediting its adversary. On the contrary, it becomes obvious that neither can develop normally without the other. And the reason is simple: the same life animates both. Neither in its impetus nor its achievements can science go to its limits without becoming tinged with mysticism and charged with faith.

Firstly *in its impetus.* We touched on this point when dealing with the problem of action. Man will only continue to work and to research so long as he is prompted by a passionate interest. Now this interest is entirely dependent on the conviction, strictly undemonstrable to science, that the universe has a direction and that it could—indeed, if we are faithful, it *should*—result in some sort of irreversible perfection. Hence comes belief in progress.

Secondly *in its construction.* Scientifically we can envisage an almost indefinite improvement in the human organism and human society. But as soon as we try to put our dreams into practice, we realise that the problem remains indeterminate or even insoluble

70

unless, with some partially super-rational intuition, we admit the convergent properties of the world we belong to. Hence belief in unity.

Furthermore, if we decide, under the pressure of facts, in favour of an optimism of unification, we run into the technical necessity of discovering—in addition to the impetus required to push us forward and in addition to the particular objective which should determine our route—the special binder or cement which will associate our lives together, vitally, without diminishing or distorting them. Hence, belief in a supremely attractive centre which has personality.

In short, as soon as science outgrows the analytic investigations which constitute its lower and preliminary stages, and passes on to synthesis—synthesis which naturally culminates in the realisation of some superior state of humanity—it is at once led to foresee and place its stakes on the *future* and on the *all*. And with that it out-distances itself and emerges in terms of *option* and *adoration.*

Thus Renan and the nineteenth century were not wrong to speak of a Religion of Science. Their mistake was not to see that their cult of humanity implied the re-integration, in a renewed form, of those very spiritual forces they claimed to be getting rid of.

When, in the universe in movement to which we have just awakened, we look at the temporal and spatial series diverging and amplifying themselves around and behind us like the laminae of a cone, we are perhaps engaging in pure science. But when we turn towards the summit, towards the *totality* and the *future*, we cannot help engaging in religion.

Religion and science are the two conjugated faces or phases of one and the same complete act of knowledge—the only one which can embrace the past and future of evolution so as to contemplate, measure and fulfil them.

In the mutual reinforcement of these two still opposed powers, in the conjunction of reason and mysticism, the human spirit is destined, by the very nature of its development, to find the uttermost degree of its penetration with the maximum of its vital force.

(PM, 283-285)

[Christianity and Science]

Faced with a sort of spiritual revolution, the first result of which was to make man bow down before himself, it is easy to imagine that Christianity first thought of the Temptation in the Wilderness, and that it initially recoiled in an attitude of disquiet and defence. Accidentally, owing to its materialistic interpretation of the evolutionary movement it had just discovered in the universe, the religion of science took up a hostile attitude to the God of the Gospels. To this challenge believers in the Gospels had necessarily to reply by condemnation. In this way the only too familiar unhappy war between science and religion was born and continued throughout the nineteenth century. Some have chosen to see this war as a conflict between reason and faith, but it was rather a struggle between two rival mysticisms for the mastery of the human heart.

Now it will be seen on reflexion that this state of war required to be resolved in a higher synthesis. Psychologically it produced a situation of constraint, and so could not last. For this reason.

Since its first struggles with paganism the tendency of Christianity's enemies has always been to regard it as an enemy or at least a despiser of humanity. This is a false truth. By his faith, of course, the disciple of Christ is led to place the goal of his hopes higher and farther off than other men. But the vision of this higher goal does not tend to destroy but on the contrary is destined to recast and elevate the aspirations and progress of what Tertullian has called the 'naturally Christian soul.' The Christian—and here is one of the most certain and precious portions of his creed—does not become so by simply negating but by transcending the world to which he belongs. By definition, his religion, if true, can have no other effect than to perfect the humanity in him.

In that case, if there was, as we have agreed, a deeply humanizing intuition in the idea which unfolded in the eighteenth century that each one of us is a conscious and responsible unit in a universe in progress, it was inevitable that this intuition should sooner or later raise an amplified echo in the heart of Christian consciousness. At the first stage, Christianity may well have seemed to exclude the humanitarian aspirations of the modern world. At the second stage, its duty was to correct, assimilate and preserve them. Is this not the stage to which it is coming at present?

The degree to which Christianity teaches and offers a prospect of universal transformation can never be sufficiently stressed. By the Incarnation God descended into nature to 'super-animate' it and lead it back to Him: this is the substance of the Christian dogma. In itself, this dogma can be reconciled with many representations of the empirical world. So long, for example, as the human mind saw the universe only as a fixed arrangement of ready-made elements, the Christian had no serious difficulty in introducing the mysterious process of his sanctification into this static assemblage. But was not this, to some extent, a second best? Was a fundamental immobility of the cosmos the best imaginable framework for the spiritual meta-morphosis represented by the coming of the kingdom of God? Now that the dust of early battles is dying down, we are apparently begin-ning to perceive that a universe of evolutionary structure—provided that the direction of its movement is truly located—might well be, after all, the most favourable setting in which to develop a noble and homogeneous representation of the Incarnation. Christianity would have been stifled by a materialist doctrine of evolution. But does it not find its most appropriate climate in the broad and mounting prospect of a universe drawn towards the spirit? What could serve as a better background and base for the descending illumination of a Christogenesis than an ascending anthropogenesis?

I will not venture any further in this field of theology. But I can vouch for one thing: that for a Christian working in the field of research, scientific activities take on marvellous significance once he reverses the mechanistic point of view and places the principle of movement, which the nineteenth century believed it had discovered at the antipodes to God, in an upper pole of creative attraction. Pascal and his contemporaries could still regard research in physics as an inferior kind of occupation, for which the believer had almost to apologize, a sort of theft from prayer and worship. For the evolu-tionist who is now a Christian, the barrier which appeared to sepa-rate the sacred from the profane can now be overcome. In a universe in which everything makes for the gradual formation of the spirit which God raises to final union, every undertaking acquires, in its tangible reality, the sacred value of a communion. A work which consists in developing our consciousness of the world by means of knowledge partakes in a very real sense of the priestly functions, since it prepares an object for them: their task being to push on still further beneath the creative impulse a universe at whose heart God comes to take His place.

This viewpoint seems to offer contemporary science a complete solution of the intellectual and moral problem with which we are at present wrestling. Not only does a spiritual 'evolutionism' in fact escape the theoretical difficulties encountered by mechanists in the final explanation of matter and life. But in becoming Christian, it also brings to the efforts of human research itself, as it develops and calls for life before our eyes, the full plenitude of the soul it awaited and the mysticism it sought. On the one side those who accept it find their proud assurance preserved and justified, in its entirety: their belief, born of human consciousness, that even the palpable world has a future, and this future is partly in our hands. On the other, since the perfection of the universe coincides with the coming of individual souls to a higher and distinct centre of personality, the evils resulting which have produced the moral crisis of progress are swept aside: boundlessly encouraged in his exploratory efforts, man, if he will be faithful to the end to his urge for discovery, at the same time undergoes a complete readjustment of his inner life. No more fear of mechanization. The reign of brute force is over. No more amorality. Fundamentally no mysticism can live without love. The religion of science believed that it had found a faith, a hope. It has died by excluding Christian love.

I will resume and conclude.

In order to sustain and extend the huge, invincible and legitimate effort of research in which the vital weight of human activity is at present engaged, a faith, a mysticism is necessary. Whether it is a question of preserving the sacred hunger that impels man's efforts, or of giving him the altruism he needs for his increasingly indispensable collaboration with his fellows, religion is the soul biologically necessary for the future of science. Humanity is no longer imaginable without science. But no more is science possible without some religion to animate it. Christianity is an exemplary form of the religion of science. Must I add that it is the necessary form, since earth seems unable to follow the true progress of its activities to the end except by becoming converted? To judge by the repugnance and despair in the face of effort to which especially clear-sighted unbelievers confess today, one might be led to believe so. I would not venture a positive judgement. It remains (and this is the least one can say) that the Christian scientist seems to everyone the best situated and the best prepared to develop in himself and foster around him the new human type seemingly awaited at present for the further advancement of the earth: the seeker who devotes himself, ultimately through love, to the labours of discovery. No longer a worshipper of the world but of something greater than the world, through and beyond the world in progress. Not the proud and cold Titan, but Jacob passionately wrestling with God.

("The Mysticism of Science" in HE, 177-181)

. . . When evolutionism and Christianity are considered in their complementary values, all they call for is the fertilizing and *synthesizing* of one another. There are two great psychological currents which today divide the world between them—passion for the earth that has to be built up, and passion for the heaven that has to be gained. Cut off from one another these two currents run sluggish, and are the source of countless conflicts inside each one of us. By contrast, what a surge of energy there would be if Christ took his fitting and rightful place, now being restored to him (precisely in virtue of his most theological attributes), at the head of the universe in movement, and so at last the confluence were effected between the mysticism of human progress and the mysticism of charity.

The truth is that, far from running counter to modern forward-looking aspirations, the Christian faith stands as the only attitude in which a mind that is enamoured with the conquest of the world can find full and complete justification for its conviction.

Only to the Christian is it given to be able to locate at the summit of space-time not merely a vague, cold *something* but a warm and well-defined *someone*; and so *hic et nunc* only he in all the world is in a position to believe *utterly* in evolution—evolution that is no longer simply personalizing, but is personalized—and (what is psychologically even more important) to dedicate himself to it *with love.*

By its very structure Christianity is the religion made to measure for an earth that has awoken to a sense of its organic unity and its developments.

There, in short, we have the great proof of the truth of Christianity, the secret of its appeal, and the guarantee that it possesses a vitality which cannot but grow more intense as men become more conscious of their humanity.

("Introduction to the Christian Life" in CE, 156-157)

Catholicism and Science

It is always rash and taking too much upon oneself to speak in the name of a group, if the group as a whole is as homogeneous and vitally knit together as the Catholic Body. Rather, then, than try to make a general diagnosis of the Church's attitude to science, I shall confine myself, in answering *Esprit's* enquiry, to pointing out the recent appearance inside the body of Catholicism of a particularly lively and significant movement which (if God spares it) may be regarded as bringing a radical and constructive solution to the conflict that ever since the Renaissance has constantly brought science and faith into opposition.

First, let us examine the essential nature of this conflict.

During a first, and much the longest, phase, the hostility between experience and Revelation was seen almost entirely in local difficulties encountered by exegesis in its attempt to reconcile Biblical statements with the results of observation: the immobility of the earth, for example, and the seven days of Creation. Gradually, however, with progress in physics and natural sciences, a much more general and much deeper schism ultimately became apparent. By force of circumstances (in view of the date of its birth) the best that Christian dogma could do, originally, was to express itself in the dimensions and to the requirements of a universe that in many respects was still the Alexandrine cosmos: a universe harmoniously revolving upon itself, limited and divisible in extension and duration, made up of objects more or less arbitrarily transposable in space and time. At the time we are speaking of, this view, under the effort of human thought, was beginning to change. Space was becoming boundless. Time was being converted into organic duration. And within this vitalised domain the elements of the world were developing so close an interrelationship that the appearance of any one of them was inconceivable except as a function of the global history of the whole system. In man's eyes a universe *in genesis* was irresistibly taking the place of the static universe of the theologians. Inevitably again, a specific form of mysticism was emerging from this new intuition: faith, amounting practically to worship, in the terrestrial and cosmic future of evolution. Thus, from beneath exegetical difficulties in matters of detail, a fundamental religious antinomy ended by coming to the surface: the conflict that was involved (though this was not clearly realised) in the Galileo controversy. With the universe rescued from immobility, a kind of divinity, completely immanent in the world, was progressively tending to take the place in man's consciousness of the transcendent Christian God.

That was the fatal danger whose threat to the Catholic faith, in our era, was daily becoming more serious.

It is, then, at this critical point of a conflict which has now reached its full dimensions that the reaction of believers is beginning to crystallise. Hitherto, in their confrontation with the scientific neo-gospel, Catholics had simply remained on the defensive. Their over-all strategy was confined to showing that in spite of every new discovery their position was still tenable; to admit (if the worst came to the worst) that evolution was a plausible but nevertheless precarious hypothesis. Why did they show such timidity? I said earlier that Christian dogma, as it first emerged, had necessarily adapted itself to a cosmos of the static type. It could not do otherwise, because at that time human reason could not conceive the world in any other form. But consider what would happen if an attempt were made, following a line already suggested by the Greek Fathers long ago, to transpose the evidence of Revelation into a universe of the non-static type. It is to this that in our time a number (an ever-increasing number, I may say) of Catholic thinkers have turned their attention; and we have not had long to wait for the results of their attempt. Experience shows that traditional Christology can accept an evolutionary world-structure; but, what is even more, and what contradicts all predictions, it is within this new organic and unitary ambience, and by reason of this particular curve of linked Space-Time, that it can develop most freely and fully. It is there that Christology takes on its true form. The great cosmic attributes of Christ, those (more particularly in St Paul and St John) which accord to him a universal and final primacy over Creation—these had without difficulty been susceptible of a moral and juridical explanation. But it is only in the setting of an evolution that they take on their full dimensions: always subject to a condition which science itself in fact suggests in so far as it makes up its mind to allow man his rightful place in Nature—that this evolution be of the type that is both spiritual and convergent. With that reservation nothing is simpler or more tempting than to look to revealed

Christogenesis for an ultimate explanation of the Cosmogenesis of the scientists and to set the final seal upon it. Christianity and evolution: not two irreconcilable points of view, but two ways of looking at things that are designed to dovetail together, each completing the other. After all, has not this alliance for long been deeply enshrined in the instinctive felicity of the spoken language? Creation, Incarnation, Redemption—do not these very words, in their grammatical form, evoke the idea of a process rather than a local or instantaneous act?

Thus it is, I believe, that the incorporation and assimilation by Christian thought of modern evolutionary views is sufficient to break down the barrier that for four centuries has continually been rising between reason and faith. Once the immobilist obstacle has been removed there is nothing in future to prevent Catholics and non-Catholics from advancing together, hand in hand, along the highways of discovery. Today frank collaboration on both sides has become possible.

If, however, we ask whether all cause of divergence between yesterday's antagonists has been permanently removed we shall have to answer that it has not. Underlying the devotion to research which is common to both and identical in both, two contradictory mystical attitudes, two different 'spirits', can still be distinguished; and these are bound still, and for a long time to come, to find themselves in conflict. On one side there is the 'Faustian spirit' which attributes the secret of our destiny to a certain power inherent in mankind of fulfilling itself by its own energies, unaided; on the other side, the 'Christian spirit' whose tension, in its constructive effect, is towards union with a God who supports us and draws us to him through all the forces of a world in evolution.

Between these two spirits the ancient antagonism between science and religion is clearly re-appearing in an essential and subtle form; but by its very nature there is no longer anything sterile nor shameful in this new conflict. The old opposition between mobilists and immobilists has gone. Henceforth Catholics and non-Catholics meet as one through their basic faith in a progress of the earth. The whole problem between the two consists in knowing which will perceive and attain the higher peak.

In this noble rivalry, pure scientists seem on the whole still to favour the Faustian spirit; but the Christian already has no fundamental doubt but that he will have the last word. For, ultimately, only his 'Christic' vision of the world is capable of providing man's effort with two elements without which our action cannot continue its forward progress to the very end:

1. valorisation
2. amorisation

First, a divine guarantee that, in spite of all death, the fruit of our labour is *irreversible* and *cannot be lost.*

Secondly, the magnetic attraction of an objective that is capable, *because its nature is super-personal,* of releasing deep in our souls the forces of love, beside which other forms of spiritual energy fade into insignificance and are as nothing.

Evolution is the daughter of science; but when all is said and done, it may well, perhaps, be faith in Christ that tomorrow will preserve in us the zest for evolution.

("Catholicism and Science" in SC, 187-191)

Science and Christ

Many people believe, and you must often have heard it maintained, that 'science is strong enough to save us on its own'. Precisely because science has broken everything down, it holds the secret of putting it together again. Thus it has usurped the power that we used to regard as the prerogative of God. 'Look', we are told, 'at the results we have already achieved. We are able (or soon shall be able) to make the ether vibrate at our will, to construct extremely complex molecular structures that are well on the road to organic matter. One day, perhaps, we shall be able artificially to create such conditions that we shall cause life to germinate as and when we wish. Why should it not be possible to lay our hands on energies that are considered even more sacred? Medical and psychological science are still groping their way in the empirical, but they have not said their last word. May we not quite possibly succeed in mastering the energies of body and soul, and so methodically free ourselves from the restrictions of our organism and spiritualise ourselves scientifically?'

We have just met, and tried to overcome, the illusion or temptation that tried to make us believe that we were nothing but matter.

How are we to counter this new, spuriously scientific, view that we have become like gods? One would have to be very rash, I realise, to determine in advance a point beyond which scientific synthesis will never advance. I shall refrain, therefore, from relying on such predictions, which facts have too often belied. I shall even maintain that our duty as men is to act *as though there were no limit to our power*. Life has made us conscious collaborators in a Creation which is still going on in us, in order to lead us, it would appear, to a goal (even on earth) much more lofty and distant than we imagined. We must, therefore, help God with all our strength, and handle matter as though our salvation depended solely upon our industry.

Granting that, however, I shall add this observation, which, if properly understood, will suffice to acquit the scientific conquest of the world of any spirit of pride or insensitivity. For all the progress of science in the mastery of matter and in the art of releasing vital forces, we have no reason to fear that these advances will ever oblige us, logically, to slacken our effort; on the contrary, we may be certain that they will serve only to make the impetus of moral and religious effort assert itself in us more imperatively.

When you come to think about it, there is something impossible, and contradictory, in the attempt, like that of the Titans, to force the gates of fuller life without reference to, or contrary to, moral values. The effort towards organic unity is essentially (by structural necessity) complicated by an internal attitude of the heart and the will. *The scientific synthesis of man* (if I may put it so) *is continued just as necessarily in moral progress, as the chemical synthesis of proteins is continued in biological manifestations.* To act like Titans?—impossible. And why? (1) because synthesis that unifies *in se* = ∝ virtue. (2) because synthesis that unifies *inter se* = ∝ centre. We are always tempted to regard the moral governance of life, the mystical view of things, as superficial, subjective phenomena, as energies belonging to a lower physical 'stuff'. In reality, they both represent in us the direct continuation of the forces, that, under the creative influx, have built up the successive circles of the world. They are the index, the measure, the factors, of the true organic synthesis of Spirit.

The further we advance along the highways of matter towards the perfecting of our organism, the more imperative will it become for the unity our being has won to be expressed, and to be completed, in the fibres of our consciousness by the predominance of spirit over flesh, by the harmonisation and sublimation of our passions.

And the closer we come, through the diligent convergence of our efforts, to the common centre to which the elements of the world gravitate, the more will it become our duty, as conscious atoms of the universe, to submit ourselves 'constructively' to the more and more far-reaching ties, to the dominating, universal influence of this more fully known centre—and the more incumbent will be the duty of worship.

I would never dream, my friends, of deducing Christian dogmas solely from an examination of the properties our reason attributes to the structure of the world. Christ, we must add, is the plenitude of the universe, its principle of synthesis. He is therefore something more than all the elements of this world put together; in other words, although the world can justify our expectation of Christ, he cannot *be deduced from it.*

What is legitimate, and at the same time heartening, is to note, as we shall now do, how appropriately Christian views supply what we are looking for. Science, we saw, by the very impotence of its analytical efforts has taught us that in the direction in which things become complex in unity, there must lie a supreme centre of convergence and consistence, in which everything is knit together and holds together. We should be overcome with joy (which is not putting it too strongly) to note how admirably Jesus Christ, in virtue of his most fundamental moral teaching and his most certain attributes, fills this empty place which has been distinguished by the expectation of all Nature.

Christ preaches purity, charity and self-denial. But what is the specific effect of purity if it is not the concentration and sublimation of the manifold powers of the soul, the unification of man in himself? What, again, does charity effect, if not the fusion of multiple individuals in a single body and a single soul, the unification of men among themselves? And what, finally, does Christian self-denial represent, if not the deconcentration of every man in favour of a more perfect and more loved Being, the unification of all in one?

And then comes the question of Christ himself—who is he? Turn to the most weighty and most unmistakable passages in the Scriptures. Question the Church about her most essential beliefs; and this is what you will learn: Christ is not something added to the world as an extra, he is not an embellishment, a king as we now crown kings, the owner of a great estate . . . He is the alpha and the omega, the principle and the end, the foundation stone and the keystone, the Plenitude and the Plenifier. He is the one who consummates all things and gives them their consistence. It is towards him and through him, the inner life and light of the world, that the universal convergence of all created spirit is effected in sweat and tears. He is the single centre, precious and consistent, who glitters at the summit that is to crown the world, at the opposite pole from those dim and eternally shrinking regions into which our science ventures when it descends the road of matter and the past.

When we consider this profound harmony that for us Christians links and subordinates the zone of the multiple and the zone of unity, the essentially analytical domain of science and the ultra-synthetic domain of religion, then, my friends, I believe that we may draw the following conclusions: and they are the moral of this over-long address.

1. Above all, we Christians have no need to be afraid of, or to be unreasonably shocked by, the results of scientific research, whether in physics, in biology, or in history. Some Catholics are disconcerted when it is pointed out to them—either that the laws of providence may be reduced to determinisms and chance—or that under our most spiritual powers there lie hidden most complex material structures—or that the Christian religion has roots in a natural religious development of human consciousness—or that the human body presupposes a vast series of previous organic developments. Such Catholics either deny the facts or are afraid to face them. This is a huge mistake. The analyses of science and history are very often accurate; but they detract nothing from the almighty power of God nor from the spirituality of the soul, nor from the supernatural character of Christianity, nor from man's superiority to the animals. Providence, the soul, divine life, are synthetic realities. Since their function is to 'unify', they presuppose, outside and below them, a system of elements; but those elements do not constitute them; on the contrary it is to those higher realities that the elements look for their 'animation'.

2. Thus science should not disturb our faith by its analyses. Rather, it should help us to know God better, to understand and appreciate him more fully. Personally, I am convinced that there is

no more substantial nourishment for the religious life than contact with scientific realities, if they are properly understood. The man who habitually lives in the society of the elements of this world, who personally experiences the overwhelming immensity of things and their wretched dissociation, that man, I am certain, becomes more acutely conscious than anyone of the tremendous need for unity that continually drives the universe further ahead, and of the fantastic future that awaits it. No one understands so fully as the man who is absorbed in the study of matter, to what a degree Christ, through his Incarnation, is interior to the world, rooted in the world even in the heart of the tiniest atom. We compared the structure of the universe to that of a cone: only that man can fully appreciate the richness contained in the apex of the cone, who has first gauged the width and the power of the base.

3. It is useless, in consequence, and it is unfair, to oppose science and Christ, or to separate them as two domains alien to one another. By itself, science cannot discover Christ—but Christ satisfies the yearnings that are born in our hearts in the school of science. The cycle that sends man down to the bowels of matter in its full multiplicity, thence to climb back to the centre of spiritual unification, *is a natural cycle.* We could say that it is a *divine cycle,* since it was first followed by him who had to 'descend into Hell' before ascending into Heaven, that he might fill all things. 'Quis ascendit nisi qui descendit prius, ut impleret omnia.'[2]

("Science and Christ" in SC, 31-36)

Notes

1. The worker-priest's 'social' demand for *better-life* obscures the neo-humanistic aspiration for, *faith in, fuller-life.* But to my mind, that faith is always present, and constitutes the chief and most vital part of the 'worker-spirit.' (Cf. the repeated evidence provided by Paul Vaillant-Courturier, Dr Rivet, and others.)

2. After Ephesians 4.9, 10.

Convergence

[Convergence of the Universe and the Human]

The human 'species', like any other piece of living matter, has an organic tendency to multiply itself to the maximum. However, unlike what happens in a shoal of fish or a colony of bacteria (and for a number of reasons which will be apparent later), this multiplication does more than simply increase the number of elements that make up the population: in addition, it produces a system of ever more closely linked and more fully centred structures in the totality of the group that is in a state of expansion.

In itself, we should note, this phenomenon of concentration and organization is absolutely indisputable. It seems difficult in these days to deny that mankind, after having gradually covered the earth with a loosely socialized living fabric, is now coming to knit itself together (racially, economically and mentally) at a rapidly increasing speed. Before we attempt any explanation of the process, we must realize that the world of man is being irresistibly driven to form one single bloc. It is *converging* upon itself.

No one, I repeat, disputes this convergence because everyone is subject to it. On the other hand, it is an odd fact that no one seems to notice it (except to lament it); and no one seems to suspect that, beneath the complex of historical accidents into which the event may be reduced by analysis, a certain 'force' is undoubtedly at work: a force as primordial and general as nuclear forces or gravity, but one which tells us much more, perhaps, about the physical nature of the universe.

We have here the massive fact, which is nevertheless completely disregarded (precisely, it may be, because it is too vast and too obvious), of a gradual totalization of mankind on itself which nothing can stop.

("The Refection of Energy" in AE, 321)

. . . In spite of the quarrels, which it disturbs and saddens us to see, the idea that a concentration of humanity is taking place in the world and that, far from breaking up, we are increasingly coming together, is not an absurd one. Indeed, without it, I cannot find any explanation that can be applied without contradiction to the phenomenon of man as a whole. The hypothesis that a human concentration is taking place is satisfactory therefore because it is utterly coherent with itself and the facts. But it also possesses the second sign of all truth, that of being endlessly productive. To admit, in fact, that a combination of races and peoples is the event biologically awaited for a new and higher extension of consciousness to take place on earth, is at the same time to define, in its principal lines and internal dynamism, the thing that our action stands most in need of: an international ethic.

("The Natural Units of Humanity" in VP, 211)

A new tactic, one might say, invented by life in order to raise itself to higher states of complexity and consciousness, for the realization of which the old methods were no longer sufficient. Synthesis of groups after synthesis of individuals. A living construction of a type unknown in the past is taking place, all around us, although we are incapable of measuring it.

If this viewpoint is correct, we can expect that, having attained a certain maximum distance from one another, without having ever actually separated, the human branches are beginning to come close together rather than diverge, that is to say are beginning to *coalesce*. To coalesce, I said; not to fuse together, which would be very different. In all realms, organic union differentiates, but does not neutralize the elements it groups together. Applied to the case of races and peoples, this principle allows us to foresee a certain future growth in the uniformity of man's somatic and psychic characteristics; but in combination with a living richness in which the qualities belonging to each of the lines of convergence is recognizably carried to its maximum. The formation of a synthesized human type, on the basis of all the slight variations of humanity that have appeared and matured in the course of history; that, if my hypothesis holds, should be the process at present developing on this earth.

("The Natural Units of Humanity" in VP, 208)

[Convergence of Religions]

. . . The various creeds still commonly accepted have been primarily concerned to provide every man with an *individual* line of escape; this is because they were born and grew up in a time when problems of cosmic totalization and maturing *did not exist*. However universal their promises and visions of the beyond might be, they did not explicitly (and with good reason) allow any room to a global and controlled transformation of the whole of life and thought in their entirety. And yet, in the light of what we have already seen, is it not precisely an event of this order (an event that involves the expectation and the advent of some ultra-human) that we are asking them to include, to hallow, and to animate now, and for ever after?

No longer simply a religion of individuals and of heaven, but a religion of mankind and of the earth—that is what we are looking for at this moment, as the oxygen without which we cannot breathe.

In these circumstances, we are forced to recognize that nothing can subsist tomorrow—nothing has any chance of heading (as must be done) the general movement of planetary hominization—except those mystical currents which are able, through a synthesis of the traditional faith in the above and our generation's newborn faith in some issue towards the ahead, to make ready and provide a complete pabulum for our 'need to be.'

A SIFTING AND GENERAL CONVERGENCE OF RELIGIONS, GOVERNED BY AND BASED ON THEIR VALUE AS AN EVOLUTIONARY STIMULUS—THAT, IN SHORT, IS THE GREAT PHENOMENON OF WHICH WE WOULD APPEAR TO BE AT THIS MOMENT BOTH THE AGENTS AND THE WITNESSES.[1]

But, then, it will be said, if the great spiritual concern of our times is indeed a re-alignment and re-adjustment of old beliefs towards a new Godhead who has risen up at the anticipated pole of cosmic evolution—then why not simply slough off the old—why not, that is, regroup the whole of the earth's religious power directly and *a novo* upon some 'evolutionary sense' or 'sense of man'—and pay no attention to the ancient creeds? If we wish to satisfy the planetary need for faith and hope which is continually increasing with the world's technico-social organization, why not have a completely fresh faith, rather than a rejuvenation and confluence of 'old loves'?

Why not?—for two good reasons, is my answer: they have both a solid foundation in nature, and they may be set out as follows.

First of all, there can be no doubt that, in each of the great religious branches that cover the world at this moment, a certain spiritual attitude and vision which have been produced by centuries of experience are preserved and continued; these are as indispensable and irreplaceable for the integrity of a total terrestrial religious consciousness as the various 'racial' components which have successively been produced by the phylogenesis of our living group that may well be for the looked-for perfecting of a final human zoological type. In the matter of religion, just as in that of cerebration, the cosmic forces of complexification, it would seem, proceed not through individuals but through complete branches.

This, however, is not all. What is carried along by the various currents of faith that are still active on the earth, working in their incommunicable core, is no longer only the irreplaceable elements of a certain complete image of the universe. Very much more even than *fragments of vision*, it is *experiences of contact* with a supreme Inexpressible which they preserve and pass on. It is as though, from the final issue which evolution demands and towards which it hastens, a certain influx came down to illuminate and give warmth to our lives: a true 'trans-cosmic' radiation for which the organisms that have appeared in succession throughout the course of history would seem to be precisely the naturally provided receivers.

Beneath its apparent naïveté, this is an extraordinarily daring outlook; and, if it is justified, its effect is profoundly to re-cast the whole theory of the zest for life and its maintenance in the world.

To preserve and increase on earth the 'pressure of evolution' it is vitally important, I pointed out, that through the mutual buttressing provided by the reflection of religious ideas a progressively more real and more magnetic God be seen by us to stand out at the higher

pole of hominization. We now find another condition of cosmic animation and another possibility in it. It is that sustained and guided
by the tradition of the great human mystical systems, along the road
of contemplation and prayer, we succeed in entering directly into
receptive communication with the very source of all interior drive.

The vital charge of the world, maintained not simply by physiological artifices or by rational discovery of some objective or ideal,
bringing with it—but poured directly into the depths of our being, in
its higher, immediate, and most heightened form—love, as an effect
of 'grace' and 'revelation.'

The zest for life: the central and favoured ligament, indeed, in
which can be seen, within the economy of a supremely organic universe, a supremely intimate bond between mysticism, research, and
biology.

("The Zest for Living" in AE, 240-242)

[Ecumenism]

At this moment a form of ecumenism is trying to assert itself: it is
inevitably tied up with the psychic maturing of the earth, and therefore it will certainly come. About the conditions, however, in which
this ecumenism can exist and take practical form, I am still uncertain—or rather it seems to me continually more evident that, as for-
mulated at present (not, indeed in their basic aspiration, which is
identical) the great mystical currents of today are not immediately
reconcilable. In particular the eastern current (with its substra-
tum-God in whom the elements and determinations of the world
are dissolved as though within a sphere of infinite radius) seems to
me to flow in the opposite direction from the western-Christian current (in which a God of tension and love is seen as the consummation of all personalisation and all determination, as the centre of
universal concentration). Similarly, another fundamental psychological dualism seems to me to exist between Christians (or between
representatives of various other groups) according to whether they
accept or reject a certain faith in man at the root of their religious
faith. Similarly again, two incompatible attitudes are apparent in
the notion of a convergence of religions, so long as it is still not

decided whether it must be effected between lines of equal value (syncretism) or along a privileged central axis—around a Christ who is incommensurable (in cosmic dignity) with any prophet or any Buddha (which is the only possible Christian and biological concept).

In these conditions, I wonder whether the only two effective ways to ecumenism today may not be:

(summit-ecumenism) 1, between Christians, concerned to bring out an ultra-orthodox and ultra-human Christianity, on a truly 'cosmic' scale.

(basal-ecumenism) 2, between men in general, concerned to define and extend the foundations of a common human 'faith' in the future of mankind.

Combined, these two efforts would automatically lead us to the ecumenism we are waiting for; because faith in mankind, if carried as far as it can be taken, cannot, it would seem, be satisfied without a fully explicit Christ. Any other method, I fear, would lead to a failure to distinguish confusion from coherence, or to syncretisms without vigour or originality. What, in short, we need to achieve unity is the clear perception of a sharply defined (and real) 'type' of God, and an equally sharply defined 'type' of humanity.—If each group retains its own type of God and its own type of humanity (and if those types are heterogeneous) then no agreement can have serious value: it will be based only on ambiguities or pure sentimentality.

In these circumstances, a movement towards unity or an alliance between ecumenic movements that still retain these corrupting elements, would appear to me (apart from a general sympathy) still premature.

N.B. The options are not independent of one another. For example, to choose faith in man entails choosing the God of tension (and vice versa), and, in all probability, a universe that is cephalised (around a Christic nucleus).

("Ecumenism" in SC, 197-198)

[The Mystical Oneness]

1. The mystical sense is essentially a feeling for, a presentiment of, the total and final unity of the world, beyond its present sensibly apprehended multiplicity: it is a cosmic sense of 'oneness'. This holds good for the Hindu and the Sufi, no less than for the Christian. It enables us to appreciate the mystical 'tenor' of a piece of literature or of a man's life, but its expression varies greatly according to circumstances.

2. Both a priori and a posteriori, two principal ways (and only two—I wonder?) of realizing oneness suggest themselves and have been tried by mystics. (Two roads, or rather two *components*, that have hitherto to all intents and purposes been merged into one.)

a. The first road: to become one with all by co-extension 'with the sphere': that is to say, by suppression of all internal and external determinants, to come together with a sort of common stuff which *underlies* the variety of concrete beings. Access to Aldous Huxley's 'common ground'.

This procedure leads ultimately to an *identification* of each and all with the common ground—to an ineffable of de-differentiation and de-personalization.

Both by definition and by structure, this is mysticism WITHOUT LOVE.

b. The second road: to become one with all by access to the centre of the cosmic sphere, conceived as being in a state of (and possessing the power of) concentration upon itself with time. This access is no longer by 'dissolution' but through a peak of intensity arrived at by what is most incommunicable in each element.

This procedure leads ultimately to an ultra-personalizing, ultra-determining, and ultra-differentiating UNIFICATION of the elements within a *common focus*; the specific effect of LOVE.

In the first case, God (an impersonal 'God') was *all*. In the second, God (an ultra-personal, because 'centric', God) is 'all in all' (which is precisely as St Paul puts it).

3. It would appear that only the second road—a road not yet described in any 'book' (? !) (the 'road of the West', born from the Christianity-modern-world contact)—is the true path 'towards and for' oneness. Only this road of unification

a. respects the facts and history (science and history), which shows us consciousness (spirit) as a process of differentiation and synthesis;

b. and at the same time retains in 'spiritual' man that intensity, that ardour, that 'drive', which are, for us, inseparable from the idea of true mysticism.—The road of tension, not of relaxation.

4. Structurally (theology) and practically (primacy of charity), Christianity follows (*is*) road 2.

At the same time, we have to recognize that, as a result of a certain excess of anthropomorphism (or primitive nationalism) the Judeo-Christian mystical current has had some difficulty in getting rid of a point of view which sought oneness too exclusively in *singleness*, rather than in God's *synthetic power*. God loved above all things (rather than *in* and *through* all things). This accounts for a certain 'lack of richness' in the mysticism of the prophets and of many saints: it is too 'Jewish' or too 'human' in the narrow sense of the words—not sufficiently universalist and cosmic (there are exceptions, of course: Eckhart, Francis of Assisi, St John of the Cross . . .).

5. I need no more than mention one perverted way of seeking oneness:

'suppression of the multiple, in destruction and death, and so leaving only "God" subsisting.'

It is doubtful whether this morbid interpretation has ever fed a true religious and mystical current. But, in as much as it represents a distortion or perversion, it has to be guarded against; for it is a *constant potential danger (suffering of annihilation* being confused with *suffering of transformation*). Can we be quite certain that traces of this 'illusion' may not still be found in some interpretations of the meaning of the Cross? . . .

("Some Notes on the Mystical Sense" in TF, 209-211)

All of us, Lord, from the moment we are born feel within us this disturbing mixture of remoteness and nearness; and in our heritage of sorrow and hope, passed down to us through the ages, there is no yearning more desolate than that which makes us weep with vexation and desire as we stand in the midst of the Presence which hovers about us nameless and impalpable and is indwelling in all things. *Si forte attrectent eum.*

Now, Lord, through the consecration of the world the luminosity and fragrance which suffuse the universe take on for me the lineaments of a body and a face—in you. What my mind glimpsed through its hesitant explorations, what my heart craved with so little expectation of fulfilment, you now magnificently unfold for me: the fact that your creatures are not merely so linked together in solidarity that none can exist unless all the rest surround it, but that all are so dependent on a single central reality that a true life, borne in common by them all, gives them ultimately their consistence and their unity. . . .

. . . I thank you, my God, for having in a thousand different ways led my eyes to discover the immense simplicity of things. Little by little, through the irresistible development of those yearnings you implanted in me as a child, through the influence of gifted friends who entered my life at certain moments to bring light and strength to my mind, and through the awakenings of spirit I awe to the successive initiations, gentle and terrible, which you caused me to undergo: through all these I have been brought to the point where I can no longer see anything, nor any longer breathe, outside that *milieu* in which all is made one.

("The Mass on the World" in HM, 124-125)

32. What I mean here by mysticism is the need, the science and the art of attaining simultaneously, and each through the other, the universal and the spiritual. To become at the same time, and by the same act, one with All, through release from all multiplicity or material gravity: there you have, deeper than any ambition for pleasure, for wealth or power, the essential dream of the human soul—a dream which, as we shall see, is still incorrectly and incompletely expressed in the noosphere, but can be clearly recognized throughout the already lengthy history of holiness.

33. An effort to escape spiritually, through universalization, into the ineffable: mystics of all religions and of all times[2] are in complete agreement that it is this general direction that must be followed by the interior life as it seeks for perfection. Nevertheless, I have long been convinced that this superficial unanimity disguises a serious opposition (or even a fundamental incompatibility) which originates in a confusion between two symmetrical but 'antipodal' approaches to the understanding, and hence to the pursuit, of spirit.

a. If the first road, which for convenience I shall call 'the road of the East' is followed, spiritual unification is conceived as being effected through return to a common 'divine' basis *underlying*, and *more real than*, all the sensibly perceptible determinants of the universe. From this point of view, mystical unity appears and is acquired by direct suppression of the multiple: that is to say, by relaxing the cosmic effort towards differentiation in ourselves and around ourselves. It is pantheism of identification, the spirit of 'release of tension' unification by co-extension with the sphere through dissolution.

b. If the second road, however, is followed (the road of the West), it is impossible to become one with All unless we carry to their extreme limit, in their direction at once of differentiation and convergence, the dispersed elements which constitute us and surround us. From this second point of view, the 'common basis' of the Eastern road is mere illusion: all that exists is a central focus at which we can arrive only by extending to their meeting-point the countless guide-lines of the universe. Pantheism of union (and hence of love): spirit 'of tension'; unification by concentration and hyper-centration at the centre of the sphere.

Surprisingly, it would not appear that a clear distinction has yet been drawn between these two diametrically contrasted attitudes: and this accounts for the confusion which muddles together or identifies the ineffable of the Vedanta and that of, for example, St John of the Cross[3]—and so not only allows any number of excellent souls to become helpless victims of the most pernicious illusions produced in the East, but also (what is more serious) delays a task that is daily becoming more urgent—the individualization and the full flowering of a valid and powerful modern mysticism.

34. In this connection, the first point—and it is the decisive point—to bring out and fix in our minds is this: once our physics and metaphysics have been accepted, as expressed in the terms we agreed on earlier, then there can be no possible hesitation about the direction we must choose at this crossroads. In a universe of self-involution, the only homogeneous form of spiritualization, the only viable mysticism, must be—what, in fact, they are becoming more and more—a positive act not of relaxation, but of active convergence and concentration.

Now that we have realized this, let us try to define and describe the two modes—one simply rational, the other specifically Christian—in which the human swarm, by an instinctive and imperative choice, is adopting the road of the West: a mass movement which we can even now witness for ourselves.

35. At the psychological root of all mysticism there lies, if I am not mistaken, the more or less ill-defined need or magnetic power which urges each conscious element to become united with the surrounding whole. This *cosmic* sense is undoubtedly akin to and as primordial as the sense of sex; we find it sporadically very much alive in some poets or visionaries, but it has hitherto remained dormant, or at any rate localized (in an elementary and questionable form) in a number of Eastern centres. In recent times there has emerged in our interior vision a universe that has at last become knit together around itself and around us, in its passage through the immensity of time and space. As a result of this, it is quite evident that the passionate awareness of a universal quasi-presence is tending to be aroused, to become correctly adjusted and to be generalized in human consciousness. The sense of evolution, the sense of species, the sense of the earth, the sense of man: these are so many different and preliminary expressions of one and the same thirst for unification—and, it goes without saying, they all, by establishing a correct relation to the object that gives rise to them and stimulates them, conform to the Western type of spiritualization and worship. Contradicting the most obstinate of preconceived opinions, the light is on the point of appearing not from the East, but here at home, in the very heart of technology and research.

36. From this point of view, it is in the direction of a dynamic and progressive neo-humanism (one, that is, which is based on man's having become conscious of being the responsible axis of cosmic evolution) that a mysticism of tomorrow is beginning to assert itself as the answer to the new and constantly increasing needs of anthropogenesis. A common faith in a future of the earth is a frame of mind, perhaps even the only frame of mind, that can create the psychic atmosphere required for a spiritual convergence of all human consciousness: but can that common faith, in its merely natural form, constitute a religion that will be permanently satisfactory? . . . In other words, is not *something more* required to maintain the evolutive effort of hominization unimpaired and unfaltering to

its final term, and to love it: does it not call for the manifest appearance and explicit intervention of the ultimate focus of biological involution? I believe that it does; and it is here that Christic faith comes in to take over from and to consummate faith in man.

37. Twice already we have met this supreme crown to both the phenomenon of man and the metaphysics of union—the mysterious figure of the parousiac or risen Christ, in whom the two linked processes of involution and pleromization are simultaneously consummated. In 'Christ-Omega', the universal comes into exact focus and assumes a personal form. Biologically and ontologically speaking, there is nothing more consistent, and at the same time nothing bolder,[4] than this identification we envisage, at the upper limits of noogenesis, between the apparently contradictory properties of the whole and the element. And it follows necessarily that, psychologically, there is nothing more miraculously fruitful, because, in this anticipated centre to the total sphere, attitudes and 'passions' are able to meet and to be multiplied by one another, which in every other mental compass remain irreparably separate. 'To lose oneself in the cosmic'; 'to believe in and devote oneself to progress'; 'to love another being of the same sort as one's self'; such are the only relationships possible in a purely human ambience—and there they cannot but be independent of one another or even mutually exclusive. 'To love (with real love, with a true love) the universe in process of formation, in its totality and in its details', 'to love evolution'—that is the paradoxical interior act that can immediately be effected in the Christic ambience. For the man who has once thoroughly understood the nature of a world in which cosmogenesis, proceeding along the axis of anthropogenesis, culminates in a Christogenesis—for that man, everything, in every element and event of the universe, is bathed in light and warmth, everything becomes animate and a fit object for love and worship—not, indeed, directly in itself (as popular pantheism would have it) but at a deeper level than itself: that is, at the extreme and unique term of its development.

Once things are seen in this light, it is impossible to adhere to Christ without doing all one can to assist the whole forward drive. In that same light, too, communion becomes an impassioned participation in universal action; and expectation of the parousia merges exactly . . . with the coming of a maturity of man; and the upward movement towards the 'above' combines harmoniously with the drive 'ahead' . . . And from all this follows that Christian charity, generally presented as a mere soothing lotion poured over the world's suffering, is seen to be the most complete and the most active agent of hominization.

By Christian charity, in the first place, the reflected evolutive effort, whether considered in its individual parts or as one whole, is charged, as we have just said, with love: and that is the only way in which the full depths of its whole psychic reserves can be released.

By charity, again, the miseries of failure and vital diminishment—even these!—are transformed into factors of unitive excentration (by which I mean the gift to, and transition into, another greater than self): so that they cease to appear as a waste-product of creation and, by a miracle of spiritual super-dynamics, they become a positive factor of super-evolution: the true and supreme solution of the problem of evil (cf. above, n. 35).

Thereby, too, if the vast and formidably complex motor of evolution is to drive ahead under full power, without distorting a single working part, Christian mysticism, the higher and personalized form of the mysticism of the West, must be recognized by the thinking mind as the perfect energy for the purpose, the eminently appropriate energy.—And in that conclusion we have a most significant indication that nothing can prevent it from becoming the universal and essential mysticism of tomorrow.

38. A phenomenology of involution, leading up to the notion of super-reflection. A metaphysics of union, culminating in the figure of the universal-Christ. A mysticism of centration, summed up in the total and totalizing attitude of a love of evolution. Super-humanity crowned by a super-Christ, himself principle of super-charity. Such are the three coherent and complementary aspects under which the organic one-ness of a convergent universe is made manifest to us intellectually, emotionally, and in our practical activity.

("My Fundamental Vision" in TF, 199-206)

'The whole spiritual mass of the East once more under way': I would like to conclude the evidence offered here with that great possibility or even, I would say—if my judgement is correct—that great event.

An ever-increasing number of persons is concerned with this much canvassed question of a convergence of East and West; they are apt to picture it to themselves by the idea of two complementary blocs, or two conflicting principles, which are merging into one: another example of Chinese Tao's *yin* and *yang*. To my mind, if the meeting is effected—as sooner or later *must* happen—the phenomenon will come about as the result of a different mechanism, one much more akin to that by which a number of streams pour simultaneously through a breach opened by one of them in a common retaining barrier.

As it happens, and through a complex of historical factors which it would not be difficult to analyse, the honour and the opportunity of opening the road for a new surge of human consciousness have fallen, I repeat, to the West. But while there can no longer be any doubt about the correct approach, or even about whether the breach has been made, we are still a long way from the final target; nor can we be certain of success. In one sense, the real battle for spirit is only beginning in our world; and if we are to win it, all the available forces must be brought into action.

So far, as I have tried to show, the three main spiritual currents of the Far East have not yet found their point of confluence nor, in consequence, their complete expression. Their waters have been rising silently in enclosed lakes. Yet I am sure that the time is approaching when their massive reserves will pour through the gap made by Europe's penetrating tenacity and be incorporated in ours. For a long time now, the Eastern soul (Hindu, Chinese, or Japanese), each following its own specially favoured line and in its own special way, has had the answer to the religious aspirations whose pole of convergence and whose laws we, in the West, are now engaged in determining more exactly: that answer is no doubt less clear than ours and less of a synthesis, but it has, possibly, a deeper innate foundation, and greater vigour. And what results may we not expect when the confluence is at last effected? In the first place, there will be the quantitative influx of a vast human flood now waiting to be used; but, what is even more valuable, there will be the qualitative enrichment produced by the coming together of different psychic essences and different temperaments.

In every domain of thought, whether religious or scientific, it is only in union with all other men that each individual man can hope to reach what is most ultimate and profound in his own being. By this I do not mean that we have to be initiated into a higher form of spirit, but rather that, forming a new resonant whole, we must add volume and richness to the new (the humano-Christian) mystical note rising from the West. Such, in a word, I believe to be the indispensable role and the essential function at the present moment of the Far East.

("The Spiritual Contribution of the Far East" in TF, 145-147)

The Religion of Tomorrow

Fully to accept that Christianity is not only satisfying but true, is to believe not only that it directs our free activity in a direction that is biologically advantageous, but also that there is justification for its claim to bring us into relationship (anticipated or adumbrated) with the *actual* Centre of the world: and that, not in a symbolic but a trans-experiential way.

The classical apologists relied, to establish this prerogative, on miracles, whose appearance, if we are to believe them, was the 'specific' test appropriate to 'true' religion.

I would be most unwilling to deny the possibility, or indeed the likelihood, of the *true* religion being closely associated with an unexpected relaxation of determinisms, caused by some super-animation of Nature under the influence of a power radiating from God; nevertheless we have to recognise that, as a consideration, the miracle has ceased to have an effective impact on our minds. Its establishment involves such historical and physical difficulties that there are probably very many Christians who at the present moment are still believers not *because of* but *in spite of* the wonders related by Scripture.

What has more influence on our minds is the consideration of the astonishing harmony that is constantly to be found, as time goes on, between the Christian God and the most subtle developments of our human ideal. In the sciences, it is a recognised proof of the 'reality' of an object (even one, like an atom, that cannot be directly observed) that it can be distinguished, always in the same form, by a series of different methods; this complete consistency possessed by something that remains identical in a varied group of experiments defines a 'natural nucleus' as certainly as does touch or sight. It is the same, it would seem, with Christ. Millions of lives (among the best of lives) have been spent for the last two thousand years, and are still engaged, in applying to this mysterious Object the most subtle and most searching tests known to our psychological experience. Countless minds and hearts have asked this Christ to satisfy their most imperative and finest aspirations. *And he has never been found lacking.* On the contrary, he has always emerged from this test (such that probably no other reality in the world has had to face its like) with a greater capacity to stimulate around him a more wonderfully synthetic effort of all our faculties: an astonishing object, indeed, which can be apprehended as an experiential element, sought after as an ideal, cherished as a person, worshipped as a world. *This endless capacity of harmonising with the whole physical and psychological order of our universe* can have but one explanation: the Christ who gradually reveals himself to Christian thought is not a phantasy nor a symbol (*if that were so he would be found in some way wanting or would cease to satisfy us*); he is, or at least he introduces, the reality of what, through the whole structure of human activity, we are awaiting.

We can come to the same conclusion by following another road, which has the advantage of enabling us to take in those general analogies of the universe whose over-all harmony is often more effectively convincing than the restricted logic of any syllogism. The fact of religion, as we said earlier, is a biological phenomenon, directly associated with the increase in the release of the earth's psychic energy. *The curve it follows is therefore not individual, nor national, nor racial, but human.* Religion, like science or civilisation, has (if I may use the term) an 'ontogenesis' co-extensive with the history of mankind. Thus true religion (by which I mean the form of religion at which the general groping of reflective action on earth will one day arrive), like every other reality of the 'planetary' order, partakes of the nature of a 'phylum'. It must be possible to trace its origins back to the beginning of all time. That means that *at some particular moment* in human duration (and even more once the embryonic period had been left behind) a specially favoured current of religious thought must (as it still must) have represented in a relatively distinct form the living fibre of the faith in which the future will permanently develop. All the religious currents, therefore, are not at every moment on an equal footing—any more than in the past of the animal world all the phyla were destined to emerge into humanity. *On every page of the earth's history*, one of them (or at any rate one group of them) represents the place at which one must stand if one is to forward and experience more effectively the progress of the divinisation of the world. And we are no more free to alter this condition than we are to change the axes of a crystal or of a living body. If we apply this to our world today, we shall find, as we were saying earlier, that only one religious current can be seen at the present time which is capable of meeting the requirements and aspirations of modern thought; only one religion *is both possible and phyletic*: Christianity. There can be no shadow of a doubt. It is through Christianity that there runs the fibre which we are looking for, knowing that the fibre must exist. If Christianity is now the only factually possible religion, it is because it is the only one logically possible. The divine, with which mankind cannot do without if it is not to fall back into dust, will be found for us only if we adhere closely to the movement from which Christ is progressively emerging.

How, then, are we to envisage the coming developments of faith on earth?

In the form, we may be sure, of a slow concentration of man's power of worship around a Christianity that has gradually reached the stage of being *'religion for the sake of research and effort'*. The first great event to come about (and it is undoubtedly already happening) will be the schism between those who believe and those who do not believe in the future of the world: the non-believers, logically lost to every creed (which will have become to them without purpose or goal) and to every conquest (now without interest or value); the believers, biologically impelled to adhere to the only religious organism in which faith in the world retains the two characteristics that are proper to real things: indefinite coherence with facts, and co-extension with duration. The world must be converted in its whole mass, or it will, by physiological necessity, fall into decay. And, if it is converted, it will be by convergence around a *religion of action* that will gradually be seen to be identical with, and governed by, *Christianity faithfully extended to its utmost limit*.

From this a final conclusion can be drawn: Christianity does not represent in the world, as would sometimes appear, simply the religious side of a transient civilisation that flowered in the West. It is much more, like the Western ethos itself (whose mysticism it expresses and whose hopes it justifies) a phenomenon of universal embrace, which marks the appearance within the human stratum of a new vital order.

("Christianity in the World" in SC, 108-112)

Notes

1. I am, advisedly, adopting here a strictly neutral point of view. Were I speaking as a 'Catholic', I should have to add that if the Church is not to be false to herself, then (without any 'arrogance' but by structural necessity) she *cannot but* regard herself as the *very axis* upon which the looked-for movement of concentration and convergence can, and must, be effected.

2. See a selection of quotations from many different sources in Aldous Huxley's *Perennial Philosophy*.

3. When approached by the road of the East (identification) the ineffable is not such that it can be loved. By the road of the West (union) it is attained through a continuation of the direction of love. This very simple criterion makes it possible to distinguish and keep separate, as being antithetical, verbal expressions that are almost identical when used by Christian or Hindu.

4. Left to itself, biology would no doubt shrink from carrying the effects of socialization beyond a common reflection (unanimity), which combines and interlocks the thinking elements in a sort of vaulting—but without the appearance of a centre of common consciousness.

Union

[The Energies of Unification]

How depressing is the spectacle of the scattered human mass! A turbulent ant-hill of separate elements whose most evident characteristic, excepting certain limited cases of deep affinity (married couples, families, the team, the mother country) seems to be one of mutual repulsion, whether between individuals or groups. Yet we nurse in the depths of our minds and hearts the conviction that it could be otherwise, that such chaos and disorder are 'against nature' inasmuch as they prevent the realisation, or delay the coming, of a state of affairs which would multiply as though to infinity our human powers of thought, feeling and action.

Is the situation really desperate, or are there reasons for believing in view of certain definite indications, despite appearances to the contrary, that Mankind as a whole is not only capable of unanimity but is actually in process of becoming truly unanimised? Do there exist, in other words, certain planetary energies which, as a whole, overcoming the forces of repulsion that seem to be incurably opposed to universal human harmony, are tending inexorably to bring together and organise upon itself (unbelievable though this may seem) the terrifying multitude of thousands of millions of thinking consciousnesses which forms the 'reflective layer' of the earth?

My object here is to show that such energies do exist.

They are of two kinds: forces of compression, which by external and internal determinisms bring about a first stage of *enforced* unification; and subsequently forces of attraction, which through the action of internal affinity effect a genuine unanimisation by *free consent*.

("How We Conceive and Hope That Human Unanimisation
Will Be Realised on Earth?" in FM, 295-296)

Clearly no one can yet predict the exact nature of the world-group towards which events are leading us. But here and now one thing is certain, and it appears to me that its recognition in theory, and acceptance in practice, must be the *sine qua non* of any valid discussion and effective action affecting the political, economic and moral ordering of the present world: this is that nothing, absolutely nothing—we may as well make up our minds to it—can arrest the progress of social Man towards ever greater interdependence and cohesion. The reason is this. The human mass on the restricted surface of the earth, after a period of expansion covering all historic time, is now entering (following an abrupt but not accidental acceleration of its rate of reproduction) a phase of compression which we may seek to control but which there are no grounds for supposing will ever be reversed. What is the automatic reaction of human society to this process of compression? Experience supplies the answer (which theory can easily explain)—*it organises itself*. To adapt themselves to, and in some sort to escape from, the planetary grip which forces them ever closer together, individuals find themselves compelled (eventually they acquire a taste for it) to arrange their communal lives more adroitly; first in order to preserve, and later to increase their freedom of action. And since the compulsion is applied on a uniform and total scale to the whole mass of humanity the ultimate social organisation which it evokes must of necessity be unitary. I have said elsewhere and I repeat it here: it would be easier, at the stage of evolution we have reached, to prevent the earth from revolving than to prevent Mankind from becoming totalised.

("The Directions and Conditions of the Future" in FM, 237-238)

Present-day Mankind, as it becomes increasingly aware of its unity—not only past unity in the blood, but future unity in progress—is experiencing a vital need to close in upon itself. A tendency towards unification is everywhere manifest, and especially in the different branches of religion. We are looking for something that will draw us together, below or above the level of that which divides.

("Faith in Man" in FM, 196-197)

This is the truth. Not only *a priori*, that is to say by deducing the future of the world from a property which conditioned its past; but *a posteriori* by observing around us the creative effects of love, we are led to accept this paradoxical proposition, which contains the final secret of life: true union does not fuse the elements it brings together, by mutual fertilization and adaptation it gives them a renewal of vitality. It is egoism that hardens and neutralizes the human stuff. *Union differentiates.*

Thus the law of fundamental convergence reappears not only below but above us as well. Union made us men by organizing the confused powers of matter under the control of a thinking spirit. It will now transform us into supermen by making us into elements governed by some higher soul. Up to now inner union has personalized us. Now external union is going to 'superpersonalize' us.

("Sketch of a Personalistic Universe" in HE, 63)

The Organic Unity of Humanity

Such is, in fact, the distinctive and remarkable character of the envelope woven by humanity on the terrestrial globe that this envelope is not formed of elements coarsely juxtaposed or irregularly distributed, but tends to constitute a network informed by a common vitality.

Clearly, this conscious cohesion that we claim as peculiar to the human group does not represent a totally new phenomenon in the world. Humanity is not outside life but extends the line of life. Now just as the so-called physico-chemical matter seems incomprehensible without some deeper unity found by the corpuscular plurality in a common reality that we call sometimes ether, sometimes space-time; just as drops of water lost within the vast sheets of oceans participate in all sorts of common chemical, thermal or capillary relationships; so, at a higher degree of reality, no living mass (whether it is the whole biosphere or a fraction of it) is conceivable by science, except as permeated and animated by certain forces of solidarity which bring the particular forms into balance and control the unifying currents within the All. In the social insects especially, the collective forces acquire an extraordinary individuality and precision. Humanity, recognizably presents a unity of this type for us, when taken as a whole. Indeed it presents, as we shall repeat later on, *the same* fundamental unity. But in such unparalleled amplitude and in such detailed and increased perfection!

Humanity, one may say, is an anthill. But how can one fail to see that it differs from an anthill by two characteristics which profoundly affect its nature? First, it is universal, extending over the whole earth; and this totalitarian characteristic seems, as we shall see, to have a particular qualitative significance. Furthermore—and this is the point on which we should dwell—it is provided with special linking organs which not only assure rapid communication between the elements but little by little transform their aggregate into a sort of organism which it would be wrong to consider as simply metaphorical.

In fact, it must be repeated, our view of life is obscured and inhibited by the absolute division that we continually place between the natural and the artificial. It is, as we stated, because we have assumed in principle that the artificial has nothing natural about it (that is to say because we have not seen that artifice is *nature humanized*), that we fail to recognize vital analogies as clear as that of the bird and the aeroplane, the fish and the submarine. It is owing to this same fatal assumption that we have for years watched the astonishing system of earth, sea and air routes, postal channels, wires, cables, pulsations in the ether covering the face of the earth more closely every day without understanding. 'Merely communications for business or pleasure', they repeat, 'the setting up of useful commercial channels'. 'Not at all', we say; 'something much more profound than that: the creation of a true nervous system for humanity; the elaboration of a common consciousness, on a mass scale clearly in the psychological domain and without the suppression of individuals, for the whole of humanity.['] By developing roads, railways, aeroplanes, the press, the wireless, we think we are *only* amusing ourselves, or *only* developing our commerce, or *only* spreading ideas. In reality, as anyone can see who tries to put together the general design of human movements and of the movements of all physical organisms, we are quite simply continuing on a higher plane and by other means, the uninterrupted work of biological evolution.

It would be worthwhile to discover and define by means of a special study, the various organs, apparently artificial but really natural and profound, by which the true life of the human layer establishes itself and develops. One would then see that institutions as ordinary as our libraries, that forces as external to our bodies as education, come far closer than might be supposed to constituting a memory and heredity for humanity. Let us leave these developments aside, for it is as easy to exaggerate the analogies as it is wrong to under-estimate them and dangerous to deny them; and let us conclude our inventory of the known properties of humanity by remarking that they all emanate from two special psychic factors as observable scientifically as any other measurable energy: reflexion and (to use Edouard Le Roy's expression) 'conspiration'. Reflexion, from which has arisen the discovery of the artificial instrument and, consequently, the invasion of the world by the human species: this is the faculty possessed by every human consciousness of turning in on itself in order to recognize the conditions and mechanism of its activity. 'Conspiration', from which is born the entirely new form of connection that distinguishes the human layer from all other departments of earthly life, is the aptitude of different consciousnesses, taken in a group, to unite (by language and countless other, more obscure links) so as to constitute a single All, in which, by way of reflexion, each element is conscious of its aggregation to all the rest.

Reflexion, 'conspiration': on discerning these two essentially human properties, we reach the final, but also the upper limit of what we can learn from the look that we proposed to take at man and life, as pure natural scientists. We have never left the ground of facts. Yet we have found the best means of sharpening our perception of all that is special and unique in the phenomenon of man.

("Humanization" in VP, 58-61)

Until now, one might say, men were living both dispersed and at the same time closed in on themselves, like passengers in a ship who have met by chance below decks with no idea of its mobile character and its motion. They could, accordingly, think of nothing to do on the earth that brought them together but to quarrel or amuse themselves. And now, by chance, or rather as a normal effect of growing older, we have just opened our eyes. The boldest of us have found their way to the deck. They have seen the vessel that was carrying us along. They have marked the creaming of her bow wave. They have realized that there are boilers to be stoked and a wheel to be manned. And most important of all, they have seen the clouds floating overhead, they have savoured the sweet scent of the Western Isles, over the curve of the horizon: it ceases to be the restless human to-and-fro on the same spot, it is no longer a drifting—it is *the voyage*.

Another mankind must inevitably emerge from this vision, one of which we have as yet no idea, but one which I believe I can already feel stirring through the old mankind, whenever the chances of life bring me into contact with another man whom, however alien he may be to me by nationality, class, race or religion, I find closer to me than a brother, *because he, too, has seen the ship and he, too, feels that we are steaming ahead.*

The sense of a common venture, and in consequence of a common destiny: the sense of an evolution in common that we can see with ever increasing clarity to be a genesis (and even a 'noogenesis'): what forms of action, hitherto impossible to realize—what forms of association, hitherto utopian—what revelation from on high, hitherto misunderstood, may we not anticipate in the special richness of this new milieu and in its special curvature! If charity has so far failed to reign upon earth, may not the reason be simply that in order to establish itself it was necessary for the earth first to have become conscious of its spiritual cohesion and convergence? If we are to be able to love one another must we not first *effect a change of plane?*

Everything, in short, locks and knits together in our outlook provided the rising warmth of a sense of man can be distinguished, by certain signs, beneath the fever from which the world is suffering at this moment. This warmth is evidence of a coming together, a concentration, and in consequence of an ultra-centration of the earth's thinking molecules, and it enables us to recognize that the psychic synthesis of the universe is continuing to be effected through the human mass. That being so, there is undoubtedly no longer anything that should alarm us either in the increased pressure of number or in the growing bonds of collectivization: because, in this

instance, the irresistible rise of the other all around us, and its intru-
sion even into our individual lives, is without any possible doubt the
expression and the measure of our own ascent into the personal.
                              (*"The Rise of the Other" in AE, 73-75*)

Thus we are beginning to be too numerous to share the earth
between us. 'Living space' is running out.

And, in an instinctive reaction against this continual cropping-up
of the other on all sides, the first thing we do is to repel or liquidate
the intruders who are stifling us.

It is at this point that there appears a further, and at first sight
aggravating, effect of the multiplying force which is incessantly
being renewed from deep within the flesh of which we are made.

The more we struggle among ourselves to win free, the less we
succeed in standing alone. The more, instead, we become involved
in one another, and the more we realize, not without anxiety, that a
new order—not to say a new *being*—is striving invincibly to emerge
from our reciprocal bondage—animated by a sort of life proper to
itself, and tending, formed though it is entirely from our individual
consciousnesses, to absorb the latter, without assimilating them, in
a blind network of organic forces.

This is the collective.

For a long time—in fact, ever since the appearance of the first
Palaeolithic groupings—links had begun to be formed between men
who were brought closer together by the need to defend themselves,
to help one another, and to feel in common. Man benefited by and
appreciated this community of effort, and imagined that he could
control it. Now, however, and particularly since the rise of the industrial mega-civilizations, the force whose growth we had assisted is
tending to emancipate itself from us and take its stand in opposition
to us. There has been a reversal of mathematical sign, with the result
that society, which man thought he had made for his own personal
advantage, is now showing signs of preparing to round on the individual and devour him. *Relationships are becoming bonds.*

Confronted, then, by this irresistible rise around us of unitary
systems—itself a consequence of the irresistible rise of masses
—students of biology are coming to ask themselves whether we may
not be in this process the impotent actors and spectators of one of
life's oldest and most characteristic performances: for life, this

consists, once an organic type has been produced, in using it simply as a brick to be incorporated in what it then proceeds to construct. There has been much talk, and with good reason, of the birth, the development, senescence and death of living branches. What has attracted less attention in this life of the species is the tendency they all display, once they have attained maturity, to group themselves in various ways in large socialized units: as though, in colonies of polyps or in the fantastically differentiated associations formed by the insects, a sort of super-organism were trying to establish itself beyond the individual. The more, adopting this mental perspective, we try to interpret the progress of the phenomenon of man, the more the evidence builds up that under the cloak of 'totalitarian forces' that is now being spread over us it is exactly the same biological determinism at work as that from which the hive and the termitary emerged some millions of years ago.

We noted earlier that, looked at from outside, mankind, being now in contact with itself in every direction, is coming close to its 'setting-point' or solidification. It is beginning to form but one single bloc.

("The Rise of the Other" in AE, 64-65)

[Socialisation]

Prehistory teaches us that in the beginning Man must have lived in small, autonomous groups; after which links were established; first between families and then between tribes. These associations became more elaborate as time went on. In the phase of the 'neolithic revolution' they hardened and became fixed on a territorial basis. For thousands of years this principle remained essentially unchanged; it was the land, despite all social readjustments, which remained the symbol and the safeguard of individual liberty in its earliest form. But now a further transformation is taking place; it has been going on irresistibly for a century under our very eyes. In the totalitarian political systems, of which time will correct the excesses but will also, no doubt, accentuate the underlying tendencies or intuitions, the citizen finds his centre of gravity gradually transferred to, or at least aligned with, that of the national, or ethnic group to which he belongs. This is not a return to primitive and undifferentiated cultural forms, but the emergence of a defined social system in which a purposeful organisation orders the masses and tends to impose a specialised function on each individual. We can find many ways of accounting in part for this development, which is so important a characteristic of the modern world—the automatic complication of economic relations, the compression within the limits of the earth's surface of a living mass in process of continual expansion, and a great deal besides. External pressures of this sort undoubtedly play a part in what is happening. But taken as a whole and in its essentials the phenomenon can only be interpreted as a basic transformation, that is to say a change of major dimensions in the human state, of which comparative biology suggests the cause. The immense social disturbances which today so trouble the world appear to signify that Mankind in its turn has reached the stage, common to every species, when it must of biological necessity undergo the coordination of its elements. *In our time Mankind seems to be approaching its critical point of social organisation.*

. . . Our species, let us accept it, is entering its phase of socialisation; we cannot continue to exist without undergoing the transformation which in one way or another will forge our multiplicity into a whole.

("The Grand Option" in FM, 41-42)

[Totalisation]

In every sphere, physical no less than intellectual and moral, and whether it be a question of flowing water, a traveller on a journey, or a thinker or mystic engaged in the pursuit of truth, there inevitably comes a point in time and place when the necessity presents itself, to mechanical forces, or to our freedom of choice, of deciding once and for all which of two paths is the one to take. The enforced, irrevocable choice at a parting of the ways that will never occur again: which of us has not encountered that agonizing dilemma? But how many of us realise that it is precisely the situation in which social man finds himself, *here and now,* in face of the rising tide of socialisation?

Borne on a current of Totalisation that is taking shape and gathering speed around us, we cannot, as I have said, either stop or turn back. Indeed, how can we even contemplate escaping from a tide that is not only planetary but cosmic in its dimensions?

As I have also shown, two attitudes are theoretically possible in this situation, two forms of 'existentialism'. We can reject and resist the tide, seeking by every means to slow it down and even to escape individually (at the risk of perishing in stoical isolation) from what looks like a rush to the abyss; or we can yield to it and actively contribute to what we accept as a liberating and life-giving movement.

It remains for me to demonstrate the urgency of the problem; that is to say, to fulfil my purpose by showing that we have truly reached the parting of the ways, the point where the waters divide; and also to show that in this momentous hour we cannot continue physically to exist (to act) without deciding here and now which of the two attitudes we shall adopt: that of defiance or that of faith in the unification of mankind.

The urgency is due first and foremost to the state of deep-seated irresolution created by our seeming lack of choice in face of the immense problems which Mankind must solve without delay if it is to survive. We debate endlessly about Peace, Democracy, the Rights of Man, the conditions of racial and individual eugenics, the value and morality of scientific research pushed to the uttermost limit, and the true nature of the Kingdom of God; but here again, how can we fail to see that each of these inescapable questions has *two aspects*, and therefore *two answers,* according to whether we regard the human species as culminating in the individual or as pursuing a collective course towards higher levels of complexity and consciousness? Let such organisations as the UN and UNESCO continue to multiply and flourish; I for one shall always rejoice unreservedly in their existence. But we must realise that we shall be forever building on shifting sand so long as bodies of this kind are not agreed on the basic values and purpose underlying their projects and decisions—that is to say, on their attitude towards human totalisation. What good does it do to discuss the ripples on the surface while the under-tow is still uncontrolled?

("Does Mankind Move Biologically upon Itself?" in FM, 266-268)

[Planetisation]

To open any book treating scientifically, philosophically or socio-
logically of the future of the Earth (whether by a Bergson or a Jeans)
is to be struck at once by a presupposition common to most of their
authors, certain biologists excepted. Explicitly or by inference they
talk as though Man today had reached a final and supreme state of
humanity beyond which he cannot advance; or, in the language of
this lecture, that, Matter having attained in *Homo sapiens* its maximum of centro-complexity on Earth, the process of super-
moleculisation on the planet has for good and all come to a stop.

Nothing could be more depressing, but also, fortunately, more
arbitrary and even scientifically false, than this doctrine of immobility. No proof exists that Man has come to the end of his potentialities, that he has reached his highest point. On the contrary,
everything suggests that at the present time we are entering a pecu-
liarly critical phase of super-humanisation. This is what I hope to
persuade you of by drawing your attention to an altogether extraordinary and highly suggestive condition of the world around us, one
which we all see and are subject to, but without paying any attention to it, or at least without understanding it; I mean the increasingly rapid growth in the human world of the forces of
collectivisation.

The phenomenon calls for no detailed description. It takes the
form of the all-encompassing ascent of the masses; the constant
tightening of economic bonds; the spread of financial and intellectual associations; the totalisation of political regimes; the closer
physical contact of individuals as well as of nations; the increasing
impossibility of being or acting or thinking *alone*—in short, the rise,
in every form, of the *Other* around us. We are all constantly aware of
these tentacles of a social condition that is rapidly evolving to the
point of becoming monstrous. You feel them as I do, and probably
you also resent them. If I were to ask your views you would doubtless reply that, menaced by this unleashing of blind forces, there is
nothing we can do but evade them to the best of our ability, or else
submit, since we are the victims of a sort of natural catastrophe
against which we are powerless and in which there is no meaning to
be discerned.

But is it true that there is nothing to understand? Let us look more closely, once again by the light of our principle of complexity.

The first thing to give us pause, as we survey the progress of human collectivisation, is what I would call the inexorable nature of a phenomenon which arises directly and automatically out of the conjunction of two factors, both of a structural kind: first, the confined surface of the globe, and secondly, the incessant multiplication, within this restricted space, of human units endowed by ever-improving means of communication with a rapidly increasing scope for action; to which may be added the fact that their advanced psychic development makes them pre-eminently capable of influencing and inter-penetrating one another. Under the combined effect of these two natural pressures a sort of mass-concretion of Mankind upon itself comes of necessity into operation.

But, the second noteworthy point, the phenomenon of concretion, or cementing, turns out to be no sudden or unpredictable event. Looking at the picture as a whole we see that Life, from its lowest level, has never been able to effect its syntheses except through the progressively closer association of its elements, whether in the oceans or on land. Upon an imaginary earth of constantly increasing extent, living organisms, being only loosely associated, might well remain at the monocellular stage (if indeed they got so far); and certainly Man, if free to live in a scattered state, would never have reached even the neolithic stage and social development. The totalisation in progress in the modern world is in fact nothing but the natural climax and paroxysm of a process of grouping which is fundamental to the elaboration of organised matter. Matter does not vitalise or super-vitalise itself except by compression.

I do not think it is possible to reflect upon this twofold in-rooting, both structural arid evolutionary, which characterises the social events affecting us, without being at first led to the surmise, and finally overwhelmed by the evidence, that the collectivisation of the human race, at present accelerated, is nothing other than a higher form adopted by the process of moleculisation on the surface of our planet. The first phase was the formation of proteins up to the stage of the cell. In the second phase individual cellular complexes were formed, up to and including Man. We are now at the beginning of a third phase; the formation of an organico-social super-complex, which, as may easily be demonstrated, *can only occur* in the case of *reflective, personalised elements*. First the vitalisation of matter, associated with the grouping of molecules; then the hominisation of Life, associated with a super-grouping of cells; and finally the *planetisation* of Mankind, associated with a *closed* grouping of people: Mankind, born on this planet and spread over its entire surface, coming gradually to form around its earthly matrix a single, major organic unity, enclosed upon itself; a single, hyper-complex, hyper-centred, hyper-conscious arch-molecule, co-extensive with the heavenly body on which it was born. Is not this what is happening at the present time—the closing of this spherical, thinking circuit?

This idea of the planetary totalisation of human consciousness (with its unavoidable corollary, that wherever there are life-bearing planets in the Universe, they too will become encompassed, like the Earth, with some form of planetised spirit) may at first sight seem fantastic: but does it not exactly correspond to the facts, and does it not logically extend the cosmic curve of molecularisation? It may seem absurd, but in its very fantasy does it not heighten our vision of Life to the level of other and universally accepted fantasies, those of atomic physics and astronomy? However mad it may seem, the fact remains that great modern biologists, such as Julian Huxley and J. B. S. Haldane, are beginning to talk of Mankind, and to predict its future, as though they were dealing (all things being equal) with a brain of brains.

So why not?

Clearly this is a matter in which I cannot compel your assent. But I can assure you, of my own experience, that the acceptance of this organic and realistic view of the social phenomenon is both eminently satisfying to our reason and fortifying to our will.

Satisfying to the intelligence above all. For if it be true that at this moment Mankind is embarking upon what I have called its 'phase of planetisation', then everything is clarified, everything in our field of vision acquires a new sharpness of outline.

The tightening network of economic and psychic bonds in which we live and from which we suffer, the growing compulsion to act, to produce, to think collectively which so disquiets us—what do they become, seen in this way, except the first portents of the super-organism which, woven of the threads of individual men, is preparing (theory and fact are at one on this point) not to mechanise and submerge us, but to raise us, by way of increasing complexity, to a higher awareness of our own personality?

The increasing degree, intangible, and too little noted, in which present-day thought and activity are influenced by the passion for discovery; the progressive replacement of the workshop by the laboratory, of production by research, of the desire for well-being by the desire for *more*-being—what do these things betoken if not the growth in our souls of a great impulse towards super-evolution?

The profound cleavage in every kind of social group (families, countries, professions, creeds) which during the past century has become manifest in the form of two increasingly distinct and irreconcilable human types, those who believe in progress and those who do not—what does this portend except the separation and birth of a new stratum in the biosphere?

Finally, the present war; a war which for the first time in history is as widespread as the earth itself; a conflict in which human masses as great as continents clash together; a catastrophe in which we seem to be swept off our feet as individuals—what aspect can it wear to our awakened eyes except that of a crisis of birth, almost disproportionately small in relation to the vastness of what it is destined to bring forth?

Enlightenment, therefore, for our intelligence. And, let it be added, *sustenance and necessary reassurance for our power of will*. Through the centuries life has become an increasingly heavy burden for Man the Species, just as it does for Man the Individual as the years pass. The modern world, with its prodigious growth of complexity, weighs incomparably more heavily upon the shoulders of our generation than did the ancient world upon the shoulders of our forebears. Have you never felt that this added load needs to be compensated for by an added passion, a new sense of purpose? To my mind, this is what is 'providentially' arising to sustain our courage—the hope, the belief that some immense fulfilment lies ahead of us.

If Mankind were destined to achieve its apotheosis, if Evolution were to reach its highest point, in our small, separate lives, then indeed the enormous travail of terrestrial organisation into which we are born would be no more than a tragic irrelevance. We should all be dupes. We should do better in that case to stop, or at least to call a halt, destroy the machines, close the laboratories, and seek whatever way of escape we can find in pure pleasure or pure nirvana.

But if on the contrary Man sees a new door opening above him, a new stage for his development; if each of us can believe that he is working so that the Universe may be raised, in him and through him, to a higher level—then a new spring of energy will well forth in the heart of Earth's workers. The whole great human organism, overcoming a momentary hesitation, will draw its breath and press on with strength renewed.

Indeed, the idea, the hope of the planetisation of life is very much more than a mere matter of biological speculation. It is more of a necessity for our age than the discovery, which we so ardently pursue, of new sources of energy. It is this idea which can and must bring us the spiritual fire without which all material fires, so laboriously lighted, will presently die down on the surface of the thinking earth: the fire inspiring us with the joy of action and the love of life.

All this, you may say to me, sounds splendid: but is there not another side to the picture? You tell us that this new phase of human evolution will bring about an extension and deepening of terrestrial consciousness. But do not the facts contradict your argument? What is actually happening in the world today? Can we really detect any heightening of human consciousness even in the most highly collectivised nations? Does it not appear, on the contrary, that social totalisation leads directly to spiritual retrogression and greater materialism?

My answer is that I do not think we are yet in a position to judge recent totalitarian experiments fairly: that is to say, to decide whether, all things considered, they have produced a greater degree of enslavement or a higher level of spiritual energy. It is too early to say. But I believe this can be said, that in so far as these first attempts may seem to be tending dangerously towards the sub-human state of the ant-hill or the termitary, it is not the principle of totalisation that is at fault but the clumsy and incomplete way in which it has been applied.

We have to take into account what is required by the law of complexity if Mankind is to achieve spiritual growth through collectivisation. The first essential is that the human units involved in the process shall draw closer together, not merely under the pressure of *external* forces, or solely by the performance of material acts, but directly, centre to centre, through *internal* attraction. Not through coercion, or enslavement to a common task, but through *unanimity* in a common spirit. The construction of molecules ensues through atomic affinity. Similarly, on a higher level, it is through *sympathy,* and this alone, that the human elements in a personalised universe may hope to rise to the level of a higher synthesis.

It is a matter of common experience that within restricted groups (the pair, the team) unity, far from diminishing the individual, enhances, enriches and liberates him in terms of himself. True union, the union of heart and spirit, does not enslave, nor does it neutralise the individuals which it brings together. It *superpersonalises* them. Let us try to picture the phenomenon on a terrestrial scale. Imagine men awakening at last, under the influence of the ever-tightening planetary embrace, to a sense of universal solidarity based on their profound community, evolutionary in its nature and purpose. The nightmares of brutalisation and mechanisation which are conjured up to terrify us and prevent our advance are at once dispelled. It is not harshness or hatred but a new kind of love, not yet experienced by man, which we must learn to look for as it is borne to us on the rising tide of planetisation.

Reflecting, even briefly, on the state of affairs which might evoke this universal love in the human heart, a love so often vainly dreamed of, but which now leaves the fields of Utopia to reveal itself as both possible and necessary, we are brought to the following conclusion that for men upon earth, all the earth, to learn to love one another, it is not enough that they should know themselves to be members of one and the same *thing;* in 'planetising' themselves they must acquire the consciousness, without losing themselves, of becoming one and the same *person.* For (and this is writ large in the Gospel) there is no total love that does not proceed from, and exist within, that which is personal.

And what does this mean except, finally, that the planetisation of Mankind, if it is to come properly into effect, presupposes, in addition to the enclosing Earth, and to the organisation and condensation of human thought, yet another factor? I mean the rise on our inward horizon of a cosmic *spiritual* centre, a supreme pole of consciousness, upon which all the separate consciousnesses of the world may converge and within which they may love one another: the *rise of a God.*

("Life and the Planets" in FM, 117-125)

[The Philosophy and Properties of Union]

Having admitted that Christ coincides with the Universe, by virtue of being the *universal Centre* common to cosmic progress and gratuitous sanctification, we have now to discover whether we can go further in our elaboration of his divine co-extension with the World: in other words, we must form an idea of *the law of the transformation* of all things *in Ipso* and *per Ipsum.*

Such a formulation has seemed possible to me.

I have thought (cf. 'Creative Union') that the entire development of the supernaturalized World, seen through man's experience, might well assume the form of a vast movement of unification, converging towards Christ.

I have tried, accordingly, to show that the successive advances of created being, from its first appearance out of Non-being until the formation of rational soul, until the incorporation of the elect in the mystical Body of Our Lord, are *connected with* (if not due to) the progressive reduction of an initial plurality. On this hypothesis, the differentiation of beings (which is the immediate term of their individual perfection) is no more than the preliminary to an ever closer and more spiritual union of the elements of the Universe. The *unique attraction* of Christ animates this great effort towards self-concentration made by created Spirit.

The *advantages* of this theory (of creative Union) are as follows:

1. Firstly, *philosophically:*

a. it satisfies simultaneously the *monist* and *pluralist* tendencies which clash so distressingly, I believe, in every mind that is impressed by the REAL need to reach some small understanding of the World *(the unity* of the World is brought about by our fidelity in *individualizing ourselves);*

b. it also reconciles the postulates of *materialism* and (using the word in the wide sense) *spiritualism.* Although matter is not volatilized (a temptingly easy solution, but one contrary to dogma), it is dethroned by Spirit, to which, nevertheless, it serves as a support. The whole coherence and ontological value of the Universe depend, in fact, upon Spirit, which alone locks together in itself, and inter-locks, the elements that constitute the World . . . This perception of the soul's annexation of the attributes that most attracted me in Matter, has been, I believe, one of the last great advances in my thought.

2. Secondly, *mystically:* creative Union satisfies me (though I should rather say that 'I find satisfaction in it') because it reduces all the World's movement to a communion. *Communion* becomes the *unique and essential act* of the World; in other words, it takes on the qualities of universality and the absolute that I persist in trying to give to everything I love 'absolutely.' The fact is that the system of 'creative Union' was born in my mind from the need to *generalize,* and to *link indissolubly to the structure of the World,* what we know of the mystical Body and of union with Jesus.

For me, the *best philosophy* will always be that which allows me most fully *to feel Christ, necessarily,* and *everywhere.*

I can readily understand that the theory of creative Union calls for rectifications, if not in its central core (where it is close to Christ), at least in *its extension* to the initial creation and the formation of the soul.

Nevertheless, I must emphasize here:

In seeking to reduce everything to union, my aim has not been so much to find a metaphysical solution for the Universe as to discover an historical pattern, practically applied, in the developments of Creation.

Supposing it were proved that the creation and spiritualization of beings can in no way be reduced to the mechanism of a union:

It would even then be true that a progressive unification of things accompanies, and is the measure of, their entitative augmentations.

Union would still be the *apparent,* empirical, *law* that governs the perfection and sanctification of creatures.

That is all I ask.

("My Universe" in HM, 205-206)

Unity: an abstract term, maybe, in which philosophers delight; and yet it is primarily a very concrete quality with which we all dream of endowing our works and the world around us. To the apparent fragmentation of material elements, to nature's capricious movements, to the irregularity of colour and sound, to the busy confusion of the masses of mankind, and the undisciplined vacillations of our aspirations and thoughts—what is it that, through all that is best in our activities, we are trying to do, if not constantly to introduce a little more unity? Science, art, politics, ethics, thought, mysticism: these are so many different forms of one and the same impulse towards the creation of some harmony; and in that impulse is expressed, through the medium of our human activities, the destiny and, I would even say, the very essence of the universe. Happiness, power, wealth, wisdom, holiness: these are all synonyms for a victory over the many. At the heart of every being lies creation's dream of a principle which will one day give organic form to its fragmented treasures. God is unity.

("At the Wedding of M. and Mme de la Goublaye
de Ménorval" in, HM, 140)

Supposing, for example, we replace a metaphysics of *Esse* by a metaphysics of *Unire*—which comes to much the same thing as once again imitating physics in the substitution, forced upon it by experience, of motion for the mobile in phenomena. What happens? In the metaphysics of *Esse,* pure act, once posited, monopolizes all that is absolute and necessary in being; and, no matter what one does, nothing can then justify the existence of participated being. In a metaphysics of union, on the other hand, we can see that, when once immanent divine unity is complete, a degree of absolute *unification* is still possible: that which would restore to the divine centre an 'antipodial' aureole of pure multiplicity. Defined as being in tension towards a final state of maximum unification, the universal system contains an additional 'freedom'. The created, which is 'useless', superfluous, on the plane of being, becomes essential on the plane of union. Surely this is a profitable line to explore?[1]

("Christianity and Evolution: Suggestions
for a New Theology" in CE, 178)

Of every being we know it is true to say that the more it is divided, the less existence it has. To relax the tension of our spirit is to make it sink back towards matter. Disintegration of animal life reduces our bodies to crude substance. All the elements of the earth, without exception, lose their characteristic properties and cease to exist for us, as their mass is progressively reduced. By dispersing, a being is annihilated. It vanishes in plurality. If, along the line of its essential capacities and natural 'planes of cleavage,' the stuff of things were to become infinitely loose-textured, infinitely dissociated, it would be as though it had ceased to exist. Dissolved in non-activity and non-reaction, it would be indistinguishable from nothingness; it would be tantamount to, and so identical with nothingness. So true is this, that only the eye of the Creator could follow it in this tenuousness, in what we might call the blackness of its night, where it exists as an infinitely diffuse capacity to concentrate, condense, associate . . . *Physically speaking, to annihilate the world would be to reduce it to dust.*

Thus, while true growth is effected in a progress towards unity, less-being increases with fragmentation.

At their vanishing point, things present themselves to us in a state of division, that is to say in a state of supreme multiplicity. They then disappear in the direction of pure number. They founder in multitude. No-being coincides, and is one, with completely realized plurality. Pure nothingness is an empty concept, a pseudo-idea.

True nothingness, physical nothingness, the nothingness found on the threshold of being, that on which, at their lowest levels, all possible worlds converge, is pure *Multiple, is Multitude.*

Initially, then, there were two poles of being, God and Multitude. Nevertheless, God stood alone, since supremely dissociated Multitude had no existence. From all eternity God saw beneath his feet the scattered shadow of his Unity, and, while that shadow was an absolute capacity for producing something, it was not another God, since it did not exist of its own accord, had never existed, and would never have been able to exist—its essence being to be infinitely divided in itself, in other words to lie on the very verge of non-being. Infinitely vast and infinitely rarefied, the Multiple, made nothing by its very essence, slept at the opposite pole front Being, which was one and concentrated.

It was then that the superabundant unity of life engaged, through the creation, in battle with the non-existing Multiple that was opposed to it as a contrast and a challenge. *So far as we can see, to create is to condense,* concentrate, organize—*to unify.*

("*The Struggle against the Multitude*" in WTW, 94-95)

The Laws of Union

From one extreme to the other of evolution, as we have defined it, everything in the universe moves in the direction of unification: but this it does with a train of concrete modifications which correct or give particular accuracy to the theoretical ideas of union we might entertain.

a. In the first place, union (true, *physical* union) creates. Where there is complete disunity in the stuff of the cosmos (at an infinite distance from Omega), there is *nothing*. And when consciousness takes a step or a leap ahead (the appearance of life through association of fragments of centres, deepening of phyletic centres, emergence of reflective centres, birth of mankind, dawn of Omega) this progress is invariably linked with an increase of union. It is not, of course, that the coming together and ordered arrangement of the centres are *by themselves* sufficient to increase the world's being; there can be no doubt, however, that they succeed in doing so under the influence of the radiation of Omega.

b. Secondly, *union differentiates.* By that I mean that by reason of their association under the influence of a centre higher, in order $(n+1)$, the centres of the order n do not tend to become blurred and confused together: on the contrary, their own nature is reinforced: just like the working parts of a mechanism which can be adjusted to one another only if they are constructed in a large number of exactly determined shapes: Such are the multiple cells that make up a Metazoa, and such again the nervous fibres of a brain, and the various members of an insect colony. Organization not only presupposes but also produces the complexity upon which its unity flowers. This is a fact of universal experience.

c. In consequence, *union*, when operating in the eu-centric domain of the reflective, *personalizes.* Since personalization is a *creative differentiation* (*is* creative differentiation), this third law of union does no more than sum up, link together and clarify the other two. It does this not only in the sense that the grain of thought emerges from the perfect centration on itself of complexity, but in the further sense that through centre-to-centre (that is, personal) aggregation with other grains of thought, it is super-personalized. Such again, as experience shows, is indeed the result on our human consciousness of unanimity. Whether it is a matter of a team, or of a pair of lovers, or, even more, of a mystic absorbed in divine contemplation, the result is invariably the same. Far from tending to be confused together, the reflective centres intensify their ego the more, the more they concentrate together. They become progressively more super-centred as they come closer to one another in their convergence on Omega.[2] This, I insist, is a fact of experience: and at the same time a simple re-affirmation of the law of centro-complexity.

("Centrology" in AE, 115-117)

Fuller being is closer union: such is the kernel and conclusion of this book. [*The Phenomenon of Man*]. But let us emphasise the point: union increases only through an increase in consciousness, that is to say in vision.

(PM, 31)

Notes

1. From this point of view, we might say that for the discursive reason *two phases* can be distinguished in 'theogenesis'. In the first, God posits himself in his trinitarian structure ('fontal' being reflecting itself, self-sufficient, upon itself): 'Trinitization'. In the second phase, he envelops himself in participated being, by evolutive unification of pure multiple ('positive non-being') born (in a state of absolute potency) by antithesis to pre-posited trinitarian unity: *Creation*.

2. Hence the necessity and importance of not confusing the two notions, which are to some degree independent of one another, of *personal* and *individual*. What makes a centre 'individual' is that it is distinct from the other centres that surround it. What makes it 'personal' is being profoundly itself. We would instinctively be inclined to add to our *ego* by an increased separatism and isolation—which is an impoverishment to us. The laws of union show us that true and legitimate 'egoism' consists, on the contrary, in being united to others (provided the union be centre-to-centre, that is through love—cf. section 29); for it is only in that case that we succeed in realizing ourselves fully, without losing anything (but rather attaining the true maximum) of what makes us incommunicable. If individuality is understood in a restricted sense, as defining not the *distinction* between beings, but their *separateness*, it decreases with centrogenesis and ceases to exist (in Omega), when personality reaches its maximum.

Unification Through Love

[Love as Energy]

Love is the most universal, the most tremendous and the most mysterious of the cosmic forces. After centuries of tentative effort, social institutions have externally dyked and canalized it. Taking advantage of this situation, the moralists have tried to submit it to rules. But in constructing their theories they have never got beyond the level of an elementary empiricism influenced by out-of-date conceptions of matter and the relics of old taboos. Socially, in science, business and public affairs, men pretend not to know it, though under the surface it is everywhere. Huge, ubiquitous and always unsubdued—this wild force seems to have defeated all hopes of understanding and governing it. It is therefore allowed to run everywhere beneath our civilization. We are conscious of it, but all we ask of it is to amuse us, or not to harm us. Is it truly possible for humanity to continue to live and grow without asking itself how much truth and energy it is losing by neglecting its incredible power of love?

From the standpoint of spiritual evolution, which we here assume, it seems that we can give a name and value to this strange energy of love. Can we not say quite simply that in its essence it is the attraction exercised on each unit of consciousness by the centre of the universe in course of taking shape? It calls us to the great union, the realization of which is the only process at present taking place in nature. By this hypothesis, according to which (in agreement with the findings of psychological analysis) love is the primal and universal psychic energy, does not everything become clear around us, both for our minds and our actions? We may try to reconstruct the history of the world from outside by observing the play of atomic, molecular or cellular combinations in their various processes. We may attempt, still more efficaciously, this same task from within by following the progress made by conscious spontaneity and noting the successive stages achieved. The most telling and profound way of describing the evolution of the universe would undoubtedly be to trace the evolution of love.

In its most primitive forms, when life was scarcely individualized, love is hard to distinguish from molecular forces; one might think of it as a matter of chemisms or tactisms. Then little by little it becomes distinct, though still *confused* for a very long time with the simple function of reproduction. Not till hominization does it at last reveal the secret and manifold virtues of its violence. 'Hominized' love is distinct from all other love, because the 'spectrum' of its warm and penetrating light is marvellously enriched. No longer only a unique and periodic attraction for purposes of material fertility; but an unbounded and continuous possibility of contact between minds rather than bodies; the play of countless subtle antennae seeking one another in the light and darkness of the soul; the pull towards mutual sensibility and completion, in which preoccupation with preserving the species gradually dissolves in the greater intoxication of two people creating a world. It is fact, that through woman the universe advances towards man. The whole question (the vital question for the earth) is that they shall recognize one another.

If man fails to recognize the true nature, the true object of his love the confusion is vast and irremediable. Bent on assuaging a passion intended for the All on an object too small to satisfy it, he will strive to compensate a fundamental imbalance by materialism or an ever increasing multiplicity of experiments. His efforts will be fruitless—and in the eyes of one who can see the inestimable value of the 'spiritual quantum' of man, a terrible waste. But let us put aside any sentimental feelings or virtuous indignation. Let us look very coolly, as biologists or engineers, at the lurid atmosphere of our great towns at evening. There and everywhere else as well, the earth is continually dissipating its most marvellous power. This is pure loss. Earth is burning away, wasted on the empty air. How much energy do you think the spirit of the earth loses in a single night?

If only man would turn and see the reality of the universe shining in the spirit and through the flesh. He would then discover the reason for what has hitherto deceived and perverted his powers of love. Woman stands before him as the lure and symbol of the world. He cannot embrace her except by himself growing, in his turn, to a world scale. And because the world is always growing and always unfinished and always ahead of us, to achieve his love man is engaged in a limitless conquest of the universe and himself. In this sense, man can only attain woman by consummating a union with the universe. Love is a sacred reserve of energy; it is like the blood of spiritual evolution. This is the first revelation we receive from the sense of the earth.

("The Spirit of the Earth" in HE, 32-34)

[Amorized Universe]

Now, what is an *amorized* universe but a universe stimulated, *activated,* to the limit of its vital powers? We have known for a long time that, in virtue of its nature, love alone in the world was capable of indefinitely maintaining and realizing to their limit the potentialities of our action: but that this mysterious power could really operate (by which I mean, quite literally operate) no longer merely on the scale of the pair of lovers or of the family but on that of the whole of mankind or even of the entire universe—that was something that we could not seriously imagine or hope for, so long as in our eyes the cosmos was not transformed into cosmogenesis—and a cosmogenesis of union in which everything, by structure, became inflexibly lovable and loving.

Formerly we had no suspicion even that the world could move as one whole, in relation to itself. Now that we see that it is in motion, we realize that this movement cannot develop fully (that is, that it would lose its momentum) if we were not in the fortunate position of being able, and being obliged, to experience it, outside and beyond any anthropomorphism, as a supreme *Someone.*

Love of evolution: a phrase that was meaningless a mere fifty years ago: and yet an expression of the only psychic factor capable, it would seem,[1] of carrying to its term the effort of planetary self-arrangement on which depends the cosmic success of mankind.

("From Cosmos to Cosmogenesis" in AE, 266-267)

[Love and Unification]

It is clear that the forces of love occupy a dominant position in a world whose formula is 'towards personalization through union'—since love is precisely the bond that brings persons together and unites them.

This, indeed, is confirmed by observation.

Strictly speaking, love does not as yet exist in the zones of the pre-living and the non-reflective, since the centres are either not yet linked together or are only imperfectly centred. Nevertheless there can be no doubt that it is something in the way of love that is adumbrated and grows as a result of the mutual affinity which causes the particles to adhere to one another and maintains their unity during their convergent advance. In any case, the least one can say is that, through the critical threshold of reflection, the transformation undergone by this vague inter-sympathy between the first atoms or the first living beings, as it becomes hominized, is a transformation into love. In the case of sexuality, of the family, and of the race, the transition is apparent. For a careful observer, however, the phenomenon extends much further. For the last two thousand years there has been much talk (though it often raises a smile) about a love of human kind. Is it not finally such a love that, logically and in fact, is now rising and taking distinct shape on our horizon? As soon as men have woken to explicit consciousness of the evolution that carries them along, and begin as one man to fix their eyes on one and the same thing ahead of them, are they not, by that very fact, beginning to love one another?

In truth, the rise in warmth on the surface of the contracting noosphere is not confined to a small group of specially favoured associations, but extends to the whole of inter-human relationships. And, with that, we find love emerging into the fullness of its cosmic function. To the psychologist and the moralist love is simply a 'passion'. To those who, following Plato, look in the very structure of beings for the explanation of its ubiquity, its intensity, and its mobility, love appears as the higher and purified form of a universal interior attractive power.

In a universe whose structure is centro-complex, love is essentially nothing other than the energy proper to cosmogenesis.

That is why, alone of all the world's energies, love displays the power of carrying cosmic personalization, the fruit of centrogenesis, right to its term. Union, we were saying, personalizes. We must never forget, however, that this is on one condition: that the centres it associates must come together not in some indeterminate way (whether by compulsion or indirectly) but spontaneously, centre-to-centre: in other words, *by mutual love.*

In short, only love, by virtue of its specific and unique power of 'personalizing complexes', can achieve the miracle of super-humanizing man through and by means of the forces of collectivization; and, in a still more decisive phase, only love can open for man the door to Omega.

("Centrology" in AE, 118-120)

Only union *through* love and *in* love (using the word 'love' in its widest and most real sense of 'mutual internal affinity'), because it brings individuals together, not superficially and tangentially but centre to centre, can physically possess the property of not merely differentiating but also personalising the elements which comprise it. This amounts to saying that even under the irresistible compulsion of the pressures causing it to unite, Mankind will only find and shape itself if men can learn to love one another in the very act of drawing closer.

("The Directions and Conditions of the Future"
in FM, 244-245)

Despite the compulsions, both geographical and psychic, which oblige men to live and think in an ever closer community, they do not necessarily love each other the more on that account—far from it. The two greatest scientists in the world, being preoccupied with the same problem, may none the less detest each other. This is a strange and sad fact of which we are all aware, and because of this separation of head and heart we are bound to conclude that, however social necessity and logic may impel it from behind, the human mass will only become thoroughly unified under the influence of some form of *affective* energy which will place the human particles in the fortunate position of being unable to love and fulfil themselves individually except by contributing in some degree to the love and fulfilment of all: to the extent that is to say, that all are equal and integral parts of a single universe that is vitally converging. . . .

. . . But in the Christian view only the eventual appearance, at the summit and in the heart of the unified world, of an autonomous centre of congregation is structurally and functionally capable of inspiring, preserving and fully releasing, within a human mass still, spiritually dispersed, the looked-for forces of unanimisation. According to the supporters of this hypothesis only a veritable *super-love,* the attractive power of a veritable 'super-being', can of psychological necessity dominate, possess and synthesize the host of other earthly loves. Failing such a centre of universal convergence, not metaphorical or potential but *real,* there can be no true coherence among totalised Mankind, and therefore no true consistence. A world culminating in the Impersonal can bring us neither the warmth of attraction nor the hope of irreversibility (immortality) without which individual egotism will always have the last word. A veritable *Ego* at the summit of the world is needed for the consummation, without confounding them, of all the elemental *egos* of Earth . . . I have talked of the 'Christian view', but this idea is gaining ground in other circles. Was it not Camus who wrote in *Sisyphe,* 'If Man found that the Universe could love he would be reconciled?' And did not Wells, through his exponent the humanitarian biologist Steele in *The Anatomy of Frustration,* express his need to find, above and beyond humanity, a 'universal lover'?

("Human Unanimisation" in FM, 298-299, 301)

Instinctively and in principle, man normally keeps his distance from man. But on the other hand, how his powers increase if, in research or competition, he feels the breath of affection or comradeship! What fulfilment when, at certain moments of enthusiasm or danger, he finds himself suddenly admitted to the *miracle of a common soul.* These pale or brief illuminations should give us a glimmering of the mighty power of joy and action that is still within the human layer. Far from suspecting it, men suffer and vegetate in their isolation; they need the intervention of a higher impulse, to force them beyond the dead point at which they are halted and propel them into the region of their deep affinity. The sense of the earth is the irresistible pressure which comes at a given moment to unite them in a common enthusiasm. Still lost in a crowd of their kind, men turn away from a plurality which disturbs them. They cannot love millions of strangers. By revealing to each one that a part of himself exists in all the rest, the sense of the earth is now bringing into sight a new principle of universal affection among the mass of living beings: the devoted liking of one element for another within a single world *in progress*.

In love, as we have already said, the attraction of the centre for all convergent beings takes shape and is felt. We are now discovering the possibility and glimpsing the outline of *a second fundamental affective component of the world*: the love of mutual linkage above the love of attraction, elements drawing together to achieve union. We already know a little about the second of these two passions. But who can express the still almost unknown qualitative fulfilment—the vast intoxication of brotherly friendship—which would accompany the victory over internal, residual multiplicity? Consciousness of human unity would at last be achieved. And what a force would accrue to the noosphere, not only for pity and mercy, but *for attack*!

("The Spirit of the Earth" in HE, 35-36)

In its most general form and from the point of view of physics, love is the internal, affectively apprehended, aspect of the affinity which links and draws together the elements of the world, *centre to centre*. This is how it has been understood by the great philosophers from Plato, the poet, to Nicolas of Cusa and other representatives of frigid scholasticism.

Once this definition has been accepted, it gives rise to a series of important consequences.

Love is power of producing inter-centric relationship. It is present, therefore (at least in a rudimentary state), in all the natural centres, living and pre-living, which make up the world; and it represents, too, the most profound, most direct, and most creative form of inter-action that it is possible to conceive between those centres. Love, in fact, is the expression and the agent of universal synthesis.

Love, again, is centric power. Thus, like a light whose spectrum is continually enriched by new, more brilliant and warmer lines, it constantly varies with the perfection of the centres from which it emanates. Man is the only known element of the universe in which noogenesis has advanced far enough to allow the appearance of a closed centre, reflected upon itself; and in him, therefore, we can appreciate that the synthesizing properties of love operate under exceptional conditions and with exceptional effectiveness and clarity. While infra-human beings can converge and associate only in a diffuse common action, at the level of thought it is the psychic nuclei themselves that come out into the open and begin to unite. Organization of imperfectly centred elements gives way to direct synthesis of centres. From this results the extraordinary totality and fullness of vital contact—and from this, in consequence, in conformity with the synthesizing mechanism of the rise of consciousness, the extraordinary growth of personality that can any day be observed in the particular and limited case of a great human affection.

In virtue of his extreme power of loving, combined with his extreme 'centricity' (or, which comes to the same thing, his extreme complexity), man, in so far as he actually loves, is the most magnificently synthesizable of all the elements ever constructed by nature.

If we understand this situation correctly, we can see, as I said earlier, how and why the appearance of a universal human love would be a sure indication that the totalization of mankind in a super-organism, super-personal in nature, is biologically to be anticipated and can be realized in practice.

If men could love one another, if they could reach the pitch of loving, not with the love of husband for wife, of brother for sister, of countryman for fellow-countryman, but of element for element of a world *in process of convergence,* then the great evolutionary law that ever since the beginning of the earth has continually caused more spirit to appear upon more complexity, would operate again with new vigour. It would even be true to say (as our theory enables us to foresee) that it would never operate more vigorously than in this supreme phase of noogenesis, in which the play of vital combinations (until that phase primarily 'functional') would at last have become directly inter-centric. In that case, we could dismiss the bogey of the termitary: there would never have been such colonies if termites had really been capable of mutual love.

("The Rise of the Other" in AE, 70-72)

[Christian Love]

Christian love is incomprehensible to those who have not experienced it. That the infinite and the intangible can be lovable, or that the human heart can beat with genuine charity for a fellow-being, seems impossible to many people I know—in fact almost monstrous. But whether it be founded on an illusion or not, how can we doubt that such a sentiment exists, and even in great intensity? We have only to note crudely the results it produces unceasingly all round us. Is it not a positive fact that thousands of mystics, for twenty centuries, have drawn from its flame a passionate fervour that outstrips by far in brightness and purity the urge and devotion of any human love? Is it not also a fact that, having once experienced it, further thousands of men and women are daily renouncing every other ambition and every other joy save that of abandoning themselves to it and labouring within it more and more completely? Lastly, is it not a fact, as I can warrant, that if the love of God were extinguished in the souls of the faithful, the enormous edifice of rites, of hierarchy and of doctrines that comprise the Church would instantly revert to the dust from which it rose?

It is a phenomenon of capital importance for the science of man that, over an appreciable region of the earth, a zone of thought has appeared and grown in which a genuine universal, love has not only been conceived and preached, but has also been shown to be psychologically possible and operative in practice. It is all the more capital inasmuch as, far from decreasing, the movement seems to wish to gain still greater speed and intensity.

(PM, 295-296)

Followed from its deepest roots in biology, the problem of races, their appearance, awakening and future, thus leads us to the point of recognizing that the only climate in which man can continue to grow is that of devotion and renunciation in the fraternal sense. Indeed, at the rate that consciousness and its ambitions are increasing, the world will explode if it does not learn to love. The future thinking of the earth is organically bound up with the transformation of the forces of hatred into forces of Christian love.

Now, in virtue of the hypothesis we are following, what is the one power capable of working this transformation? From what source will the branches, and human individuals as well, ultimately draw the desire to accept one another and draw one another towards joyful unity? There is only one conceivable source: a growing attraction to the centre of consciousness in which their fibres and their bundle must complete themselves by reuniting. If we study its most profound features, those of liberty, humanity seems certainly to have reached the stage of its evolution in which it cannot from any viewpoint face the problems presented to it by the growth of its inner energy without defining for itself a centre of love and adoration.

Many of my scientific colleagues will, I know, recoil from this conclusion. But I do not see how they can escape it any more than I can, once they make up their minds to look honestly before them. Just as man (as I have already explained elsewhere) will lose the courage to construct and go on seeking, so he will have no more strength to conquer the inner antipathies which separate him from the joys of unity unless he finally becomes conscious that he is drawing near, together with the universe, not only to some thing but to Someone.

("The Natural Units of Humanity" in VP, 214-215)

. . . Since the Christian universe consists structurally in the unification of elemental persons in a supreme personality (the personality of God), the dominating and ultimate energy of the whole system can only be a person-to-person attraction: in other words, a love-attraction. God's love for the world and for each of its elements, and the elements' love, too, for one another and for God, are not, therefore, merely a secondary effect added to the creative process; they are an expression both of its operative factor and of its fundamental dynamism.

. . . Under the unifying influence of divine love, the spiritual elements of the world ('souls') are raised up to a higher state of life. They are 'super-humanized'. The state of union with God is accordingly much more than a mere juridical justification, associated with an extrinsic increase of divine benevolence. From the Christian, Catholic and realist point of view, grace represents a physical super-creation. It raises us a further rung on the ladder of cosmic evolution. In other words, the stuff of which grace is made is strictly biological. This, we shall be seeing later, has a bearing on the theory of the eucharist, and, more generally, on that of all the sacraments.

("Introduction to the Christian Life" in CE, 152-153)

To say that Christ is the term and motive force of evolution, to say that he manifests himself as 'evolver', is implicitly to recognise that he becomes attainable in and through the whole process of evolution. Let us examine the consequences for our interior life of this amazing situation.

There are three, and they may be expressed as follows: 'Under the influence of the Super-Christ, our charity is universalised, becomes dynamic and is synthesised.'

Let us look at each of the terms of this threefold transformation in turn.

1. *First, our charity is universalised.* By definition, the Christian is, and always has been, the man who loves God, and his neighbour as himself. But has not this love necessarily remained hitherto particularist and extrinsic in its explicit realisation? For many who believe, Christ is still the mysterious personage who after having passed through history two thousand years ago now reigns in a Heaven that is divorced from earth; and our neighbour is still a swarm of human individuals, multiplied with no recognisable rule nor reason, and associated together by the arbitrary force of laws and conventions. In such a view there is little or even no place for the immensities of sidereal or living matter, for the multitude of the world's natural elements and events, for the impressive unfolding of cosmic processes.

Now, it is precisely this pluralism, emotionally so confusing, which vanishes under the rays of the Super-Christ, to make way for a warm and resplendent unity.

Since, in fact, everything in the universe ultimately proceeds towards Christ-Omega; since the whole of cosmogenesis is ultimately, through anthropogenesis, expressed in a Christogenesis; it follows that, in the integral totality of its tangible strata, the real is charged with a divine Presence. As the mystics felt instinctively, everything becomes physically and literally lovable in God; and God, in return, becomes intelligible and lovable in everything around us. In the breadth and depth of its cosmic stuff, in the bewildering number of the elements and events that make it up, and in the wide sweep, too, of the overall currents that dominate it and carry it along as one single great river, the world, filled by God, appears to our enlightened eyes as simply a setting in which universal communion can be attained, and a concrete expression of that communion.

2. Secondly, our charity becoutes dynamic. Hitherto, to love God and one's neighbour might have seemed no more than an attitude of contemplation and compassion. Was not to love God to rise above human distractions and passions in order to find rest in the light and unvarying warmth of the divine Sun? And was not to love one's neighbour primarily to bind up the wounds of one's fellow men and alleviate their suffering? Detachment and pity—escape from the world and mitigation of evil—in the eyes of the Gentiles could not those two notes be legitimately regarded as the Christian characteristics of charity?

Here again we find a complete change: our whole outlook widens and is vitalised to the scale of the universalised Christ.

If, let me repeat, the whole progress of the world does indeed conform to a Christogenesis (or, which comes to the same thing, if Christ can be fully attained only at the term and peak of cosmic evolution), then it is abundantly clear that we can make our way towards him and apprehend him only in the effort to complete and synthesise everything in him. In consequence, it is the general ascent of life towards fuller consciousness, it is man's effort in its entirety, that are now organically and with full justification once more included among the things with which charity is concerned and which it hopes to achieve. If we are to love the Super-Christ we must at all costs see to it that the universe and mankind push ahead, in us and in each of our co-elements—in particular in the other 'grains of thought', our fellow-men.

To co-operate in total cosmic evolution is the only deliberate act that can adequately express our devotion to an evolutive and universal Christ.

3. By that very fact, our charity is synthesised. At first that expression may seem obscure, and it should be explained.

In the detail, and on the scale of 'ordinary' life, much that we do is independent of love. To love (between 'persons') is to be drawn together and brought closer *centre-to-centre*. In our lives, this 'centric' condition is seldom achieved. It may be that we are dealing with objects (material, infra-living, or intellectual) which are by their nature non-centred and impersonal; it may be that in our human inter-relationships we come into contact with our fellows only 'tangentially,' through our interests, through our functions, or for business dealings—in either case, we are generally working, or seeking, enjoying ourselves or suffering, without loving—without even suspecting that it is possible for us to love—the thing or person with which we are concerned. Thus our interior life remains fragmented and pluralised.

Consider, on the other hand, what happens if above (or rather at the heart of) this plurality there rises the central reality of Christ the evolver. In virtue of his position as the Omega of the world, Christ, we have seen, represents the focus point towards which and in which all things *converge*. In other words, he appears as a Person with whom all reality (provided we understand that in the appropriate positive sense) effects an approach and a contact in the only direction that is possible: *the line in which their centres lie.*

This can mean but one thing, that every operation, once it is directed towards him, assumes, without any change of its own nature, the psychical character of a centre-to-centre relationship, in other words, of an act of love.

Eating, drinking, working, seeking; creating truth or beauty or happiness; all these things could, until now, have seemed to us heterogeneous, disparate, activities, incapable of being reduced to terms of one another—loving being no more than one of a number of branches in this divergent psychical efflorescence.

Now, however, that it is directed towards the Super-Christ, the fascicle draws itself together. Like the countless shades that combine in nature to produce a single white light, so the infinite modalities of action are fused, without being confused, in one single colour under the mighty power of the universal Christ; and it is love that heads this movement: love, not simply the common factor through which the multiplicity of human activities attains its cohesion, but love, *the higher, universal, and synthesised form of spiritual energy,* in which all the other energies of the soul are transformed and sublimated, once they fall within 'the field of Omega'.

Originally, the Christian had no desire except to be able to love, at all times and whatever he was doing, *at the same time as he was acting.* Now he sees that he can love *by his activity,* in other words he can directly be united to the divine centre by his every action, no matter what form it may take.

In that centre every activity, if I may use the phrase, is 'amorised'.

How could it be otherwise, if the universe is to maintain its equilibrium?

A Super-mankind calls for a Super-Christ.

A Super-Christ calls for a *Super-charity.*

(*"Super-Humanity, Super-Christ, Super-Charity" in SC, 167-171*)

["Love One Another"]

Since the preaching of the Gospel it was possible to believe that man had at last found a definitive and exhaustive expression of inner rectitude, and in consequence of salvation. 'Love one another': it seemed as though all that was finest in morality must have reached its peak and be summed up in that precept once and for all. Today, however, after twenty centuries of experience, it would seem that we have acquired nothing from the Gospel formula. As the years go by not only does mankind seem to be as divided against itself as ever; but, what is more, *a new ideal,* the ideal of conquering force, has continually, for the last two generations, been increasing in strength and mesmeric power, in opposition to doctrines of gentleness and humanity.

We cannot help wondering whether, perhaps, we are witnessing the bankruptcy of charity.

It is this anxiety, I believe, that is allayed, both in theory and in practice, by the fact that the human person is rising up to consciousness of his 'dignity as an atom'.

From the point of view of noogenesis, in the first place, it is perfectly clear that if, all together, our cosmic destiny is to become *one,* then the fundamental and operative law of our activity is to encourage this synthesis by associating more closely. The 'Lord's precept' does not disappear under the harsh light of modern criticism: rather does it leave the domain of sentiment, to become the leading instrument of evolution. 'It leaves the world of dreams, to enter into the system of universal energies and essential laws'. We saw, did we not, that a love is the only milieu in which the stuff of the universe can find equilibrium and consistence at the peak of its complication and centration.

This, however, is not all. While charity is today cheapened in our eyes by the factual setback it has encountered, it undoubtedly suffers much more from its futility and its apparent impotence to justify and inspire our impassioned demand for discovery and conquest. The morality we look for can no longer be based on inter-personal considerations, it must be based on progress. What we need is not lubrication but fuel. As preached to us, charity is static and resigned, and that is why Nietzsche's super-man is now eclipsing the loving-kindness of the Gospel. For all the beauty of the Sermon on the Mount, modern man cannot refrain from listening to the words of Zarathustra:

'Charity—resigned and static . . .'

That expresses the fatal preconception which we have to shake off, and the spectacle of a world in process of concentration is at hand precisely to make us do so.

Among fixed and extrinsically associated monads, it may well be that the supreme virtue consists in easing mutual friction. It is a completely different story in the case of incomplete elements that cannot exist fully except by drawing closer together. For such particles, sympathy becomes the driving impulse to force all obstacles and open up every issue that can lead to unity. From the moment man discovers that, as an atom, he has a responsibility towards a mankind and is in solidarity with a mankind in which he is personally fulfilled, he possesses more than a motive and a driving force for loving 'his neighbour'. There is something much more: there opens out wide before him an unlimited domain of tangible operation into which he *can introduce* the things he feels. He has *the whole vast battlefield of the earth* in which to release, to expend and continually to rejuvenate the passion that animates him. To have to fight, *to be able to fight,* throughout our life, in order to create what we love! An astonishing fulfilment indeed, in which force, purified of violence, emerges from gentleness and loving-kindness, as their climax.

Contrary to the current belief, charity is not out of date, not a thing of the past, in this feverishly expanding world of ours. Rather does it reappear, at the head of the most modern, most scientifically satisfying of moral systems, once, having been transposed into a universe that is being spiritually drawn closer together, it automatically *becomes dynamic.*

("The Atomism of Spirit" in AE, 51-53)

One might at first suppose that all that is needed to ensure the formation of the noosphere, to make it 'set', is the action of planetary compression, which forcibly draws together the reflective particles up to the point where it makes them leave their area of increasing mutual repulsion and ultimately causes them to fall within the radius of their mutual attraction. Here again, however (as in the case of 'falling into complexity'), we must beware of over-simple physical analogies drawn from the other extreme of the world, from the domain of the infinitely simple. However compressed the human particles may be, they must ultimately, if they are to group themselves 'centrically', love one another—with a love that includes all individuals simultaneously and all as one whole.[2] Yet there is no true love in an atmosphere, however warm it be, of the collective; for the collective is the impersonal. If love is to be born and to become firmly established it must find *an* individualized heart, *an* individualized face. The more closely one examines this essential psychic mechanism of union, the more convinced one becomes that the only possible way in which cosmic involution can culminate is to reach its term not simply on a centred *system* of centres, but on *a centre* of centres—that alone, and only that, will suffice.

("My Fundamental Vision" in TF, 187)

'Love one another.' Those words were pronounced two thousand years ago. But today they sound again in our ears in a very different tone. For centuries charity and fraternity could only be presented as a code of moral perfection, or perhaps as a practical method of diminishing the pains or frictions of earthly life. Now since the existence of the noosphere, on the one hand, and the vital necessity we are under of preserving it, on the other, have been revealed to our minds, the voice which speaks takes on a more imperious tone. It no longer says only: 'Love one another in order to be perfect', but adds, 'Love one another or you perish'. 'Realistic' minds are welcome to smile at dreamers who speak of a humanity cemented and armoured no longer with brutality but with love. They are welcome to deny that a maximum of physical power may coincide with a maximum of gentleness and goodness. Their critical scepticism cannot prevent the theory and experience of spiritual energy from combining to warn us that *we have reached a decisive point in human evolution,* at which the only way forward is in the direction of a common passion, a 'conspiration'.

To go on putting our hopes in a social order obtained by external violence would simply mean to abandon all hope of carrying the spirit of the earth to its limits.

Now human energy, being the expression of a movement as irresistible and infallible as the universe itself, cannot possibly be prevented by any obstacle from freely reaching the natural goal of its evolution.

Therefore, despite all checks and all improbabilities, we are inevitably approaching a new age, in which the world will throw off its chains and at last give itself up to the power of its inner affinities.

Either we must doubt the value of everything around us, or we must utterly believe in the possibility, and I should now add in the inevitable consequences, of universal love.

("Human Energy" in HE, 153)

It is not a *tête-à-tête* or a *corps-à-corps* that we need; it is a heart-to-heart.

This being so, the more I consider the fundamental question of the future of the earth, the more it appears to me that the generative principle of its unification is finally to be sought, not in the sole contemplation of a single Truth or in the sole desire for a single Thing, but in the common attraction exercised by a single *Being.* For on the one hand, if the synthesis of the Spirit is to be brought about in its entirety (and this is the only possible definition of progress) it can only be done, in the last resort, through the meeting, *centre to centre,* of human units, such as can only be realised in a universal, mutual love. And on the other hand there is but one possible way in which human elements, innumerably diverse by nature, can love one another: it is by knowing themselves all to be centred upon a single 'supercentre' common to all, to which they can only attain, each at the extreme of himself, through their unity.

'Love one another, recognising in the heart of each of you the same God who is being born.' Those words, first spoken two thousand years ago, now begin to reveal themselves as the essential structural law of what we call progress and evolution. They enter the scientific field of cosmic energy and its necessary laws.

Indeed, the more I strive, in love and wonder, to measure the huge movements of past Life in the light of paleontology, the more I am convinced that this majestic process, which nothing can arrest, can achieve its consummation only in becoming Christianised.

("Some Reflections on Progress" in FM, 78-79)

What the modern mind finds disconcerting in Christian charity is its negative or at least static aspect, and also the 'detached' quality of this great virtue. 'Love one another . . .' Hitherto the gospel precept has seemed simply to mean, 'Do not harm one another', or, 'Seek with all possible care and devotion to diminish injustice, heal wounds and soften enmities in the world around you.' Hitherto, also, the 'supernatural' gift of ourselves which we were required to make to God and to our neighbour appeared to be something opposed to and destructive of the bonds of feeling attaching us to the things of this world.

But if Charity is transplanted into the cone of Time nothing remains of these apparent limitations and restrictions. Within a Universe of convergent structure the only possible way in which an element can draw closer to its neighbouring elements is by *tightening the cone*—that is to say, by causing the whole layer of the world of which it is a part to move towards the apex. In such an order of things no man can love his neighbour without drawing nearer to God—and, of course, reciprocally (but this we knew already). But it is also impossible (this is newer to us) to love either God or our neighbour without assisting the progress, in its physical entirety, of the terrestrial synthesis of the spirit: since it is precisely the progress of this synthesis which enables us to draw closer together among ourselves, while at the same time it raises us towards God. Because we love, and in order that we may love even more, we find ourselves happily and especially compelled to participate in all the endeavours, all the anxieties, all the aspirations and also all the affections of the earth—*in so far as these embody a principle of ascension and synthesis.*

Christian detachment subsists wholly in this wider attitude of mind; but instead of 'leaving behind' it leads on; instead of cutting off, it raises. It is no longer a break-away but a way through; no longer a withdrawal but an act of emerging. Without ceasing to be itself, Charity spreads like an ascending force, like a common essence at the heart of all forms of human activity, whose diversity is finally synthesized in the rich totality of a single operation. Like Christ Himself, and in His image, it is universalised, it acquires a dynamic and is humanised by the fact of doing so.

("The New Spirit" in FM, 98-99)

'Love one another'. This gentle precept, which two thousand years ago came like a soothing oil humbly poured on human suffering, offers itself to our modern spirit as the most powerful, and in fact the only imaginable, principle of the earth's future equilibrium. Shall we at last make up our minds to admit that it is neither weakness nor harmless fad—but that it points out a formal condition for the achievement of life's most organic and most technically advanced progress?

If we did so decide, what awaits us would be the true victory and the only true peace.

In its own heart, force would be constrained to disarm, because we should at last have laid our hands on a stronger weapon with which to replace it.

And man, grown to his full stature, would have found the right road.

("The Moment of Choice" in AE, 20)

Notes

1. By reason of its unitive virtues, which, in a convergent universe, give it the quality of being ultimately the supremely effective and perfectly complete *evolutionary activity*.

2. For by nature (or even, one might say, by definition) sympathy is the only energy that can bring beings together centre to centre (which is, incidentally, the only way of ultra-personalizing them).

Synthesis

[Synthesis of Centers]

As early as in St. Paul and St. John we read that to create, to fulfil and to purify the world is, for God, to unify it by uniting it organically with himself.[1] How does he unify it? By partially immersing himself in things, by becoming 'element,' and then, from this point of vantage in the heart of matter, assuming the control and leadership of what we now call evolution. Christ, principle of universal vitality because sprung up as man among men, put himself in the position (maintained ever since) to subdue under himself, to purify, to direct and superanimate the general ascent of consciousnesses into which he inserted himself. By a perennial act of communion and sublimation, he aggregates to himself the total psychism of the earth. And when he has gathered everything together and transformed everything, he will close in upon himself and his conquests, thereby rejoining, in a final gesture, the divine focus he has never left. Then, as St. Paul tells us, *God shall be all in all.* This is indeed a superior form of 'pantheism'[2] without trace of the poison of adulteration or annihilation: the expectation of perfect unity, steeped in which each element will reach its consummation at the same time as the universe.

The universe fulfilling itself in a synthesis of centres in perfect conformity with the laws of union. God, the Centre of centres. In that final vision the Christian dogma culminates. And so exactly, so perfectly does this coincide with the Omega Point that doubtless I should never have ventured to envisage the latter or formulate the hypothesis rationally if, in my consciousness as a believer, I had not found not only its speculative model but also its living reality.

The very first time we meet it, the idea of a super-human organism seems fantastic. We are so thoroughly used to refusing to admit that anything could exist in nature higher than ourselves! Nevertheless, if, instead of rejecting *a priori* what upsets the accustomed routine of our thinking (and in particular the dimensional limits within which we think), we are willing to entertain it, and then begin to examine it more deeply, it is surprising what order and clarity is introduced into our outlook on the universe by a hypothesis that at first seemed crazy.

The first thing we find is that the actual flow of evolution, which, against all probability, was assumed to have come to a halt on earth with the appearance of man, resumes its normal course. If the terrestrial grains of thought can still combine among themselves, man is no longer an inexplicable dead-end in the cosmic process of noogenesis: in him, and through him, the rise of consciousness is continuing beyond man himself.

Secondly, the rise of number all around us loses its disquieting and senseless appearance. Crushed together on the earth's restricted surface, we were looking anxiously for a field in which to expand. We can now see that that field does not lie in the direction of an escape in space, but can be found in the form of an internal harmonizing in which the multiplication of the other ceases to be a threat and becomes a support, a solace, and a hope for the fulfilment of each individual. By divergence, the multitude can only become a greater evil; on the other hand, by unification upon itself it is effortlessly and limitlessly resolved. We were trying to escape through the circumference: it is only through the axis (by convergence, that is) that we can be released from tension.

The third thing to be transfigured is the spectre of rising collectivization. Judging the future of man from the example of the insects and from certain modern experiments on totalitarian lines, we had grounds for believing that we were caught up in an irresistible mechanism of depersonalization. But if it is indeed the law of 'centration by synthesis' that continues to operate in us through the advances and under the cloak of human socialization, then we should be reassured. Assuming that an ultra-human synthesis is really being produced, then (provided it be properly carried out—and I shall show how that can be done) it can only end, from physical and biological necessity, in causing the appearance of a further degree of organization, and therefore of consciousness, and therefore, again, of freedom. Whatever may have been the short-comings or deviations of our first attempts at association, we are hazarding nothing in surrendering ourselves actively and intelligently to the invasion of the forces of collectivization. They are not, in fact, working to mechanize us but to super-centre and so super-personalize us.

("The Rise of the Other" in AE, 68-69)

[Synthesis of the Earth]

If we are to find a meaning—though it would be better to say *the* meaning—of the ever more intense paroxysm to which the present war (taken as one whole) corresponds, one condition, I believe, is essential and at the same time sufficient in itself. It is that when we look at the world we understand and accept the particular stand-point that is more and more imperatively dictated to observers such as ourselves by the scientific theory—or, to put it more exactly, the scientific fact—of noogenesis.

Let me explain briefly what that means.

Until recent years a marked dualism, or even conflict, ranged physics and biology in opposite camps. On the one hand lay the world of matter, on the other the world of life; and science could not contrive to see how one and the same coherent explanation could cover these two fields of experience, each equally objective. Now, however, as a result of investigations and tentative probings into all directions of the real simultaneously, two points are emerging which would distinctly seem to indicate a way towards a solution of the problem.

The first is the definite relationship of concomitance which is progressively becoming more evident as existing between *conscious spontaneity* and *organic complexity*. So long as a natural particle (a molecule, for example) contains in its structure no more than a small number (some tens, or some hundreds, or even some thousands) of organized atoms, no external trace can be distinguished of what we call life. If, however, the number of atoms incorporated rises to several tens of millions (as would seem to be the case with the organic 'viruses', vegetal animals) then the chemical characteristics develop a fringe of biological properties in the element concerned. Under extreme magnification (approaching 100,000 diameters) the virus particles can be seen as minute rods; and even if these rods do not reproduce themselves in the strict sense of the word, they already have at least the remarkable power of multiplying themselves. Are they infra-bacteria, or are they super-molecules? This is something we cannot decide. Raise the number still higher, and we meet the cell (though when I say the number, we still lack precise numerical data—already, however, such data arc less important, since *structure is* beginning to take precedence over number). And starting with that point, from the unicellular protozoon up to man (man with the million million cells of his body, and the thirty thousand million cells of his brain) the sheer figures become astronomical, without even so being able to give any idea of the fantastic complexity of the super-imposed physico-chemical mechanisms.

In consequence of this, and independently of any consideration or interpretation that is philosophical in order, life appears to us more and more objectively as a specific property of matter that has been taken to an extremely high degree of ordered complexity—or, *which comes to the same thing, of complexity centred upon itself.* Speaking empirically, it is a combined effect of complication and centration.

To arrange beings, as we have just done, according to their analytic degree of centred-complexity is a purely 'spatial' operation. What happens, however, when we try to distribute the same beings in time, in accordance with the presumed date of their formation? A second cardinal fact now emerges, which is sufficiently well established by and large for us to have no hesitation in relying on it. We may express this as follows: *if the chemical and vital elements of the universe are spaced out in astronomical and geological duration, they do not present a random pattern of dispersion: they form a natural series in which their order of appearance coincides essentially with their order of complication.* The phenomenon is particularly easy to follow in the domain of higher life, provided always that we take as the *index* of animal complexity the degree of enrichment and concentration of the *nervous system* in the cranium. Finally, the i is dotted (if I may put it so) by the fascinating case of man—evolution's *latest arrival,* in whom extreme cerebralization (or 'cephalization') of the organism is accompanied by a staggering increase in psychic faculties.

Thus we find a gradual and simultaneous rise of complexity and consciousness.

For my part, I can see only one possible intellectual attitude to this vast fact which a general convergence of all branches of science is gradually forcing us to accept. This is to recognize that the universe is literally *twice* what we thought it was. Until now we used to look on the mass of the cosmos as being animated by a single global movement, the movement that produced the slow dispersal and dissipation of its energies down the gradient of the more probable and of the less demanding of effort. Now a second current is appearing, running in the opposite direction from this first descending current (and yet generated by it): this, too, is cosmic, but in this case it is directed upwards, in the direction of the less probable and the more demanding. It is from this that there gradually emerge, with the passage of time, progressively richer forms of association, forms that are in consequence progressively more organically centred—and, concomitantly, more vitalized.

That is what I mean by noogenesis.

To return from that digression and get back to our subject, let us take a further look at the broiling atmosphere in which the war is today enveloping the earth. Is it an explosion? or a conflagration? or some malignant fever devouring the structure of man? These various diagnoses which, in our trepidation, we suggest to one another, are quite certainly valueless: for, if the temperature around us is rising, it is only doing so, we have seen, in step with an increase in organization.

'An increase in human totalization *and* in human psychic charge'—there we have the two *linked* phenomena whose simultaneous appearance and growth in the course of the crisis we have to explain.

Perhaps you are still undecided?

But, after what we have just said about the existence of the second cosmic current, can you not see that the solution of the problem is contained in the very terms in which it is expressed?

When we speak of 'a progress of organization, duplicated by an intensification of consciousness' what are we expressing? A particular effect of the war which calls for explanation? or is it rather the general law in which the genesis of spirit is historically recorded? In either case, the two factors are identically the same.

This can mean only one thing, that if today's intense crisis is restored, as it must be, to the solid, experiential, framework of modern space-time, it assumes, in two successive steps, both meaning and form.

First, in a general and approximate way, confined to its overall effects of spiritual synthesis, it is evidence of a positive bound in the terrestrial development of noogenesis.

What is much more, however, if we consider closely its strange universalist character, it seems to herald the coming of an important critical point in this noogenesis. Until now mankind, both economically and psychically, constituted no more than scattered, or at any rate loosely associated, fragments on the surface of the earth. The time seems to have come when these fragments are going to fuse and coalesce under the irresistible pressure of geographical, biological, political and social determinisms which have reached an accumulation planetary in order: this global operation coinciding with the awakening of a true 'spirit of the earth', which transcends the spirit of the nation which was all we used to know.

A new order of consciousness emerging from a new order of organic complexity: a hyper-synthesis upon itself of mankind.

Taking a completely objective view—looking at it as coolly as a physicist confronted with the worlds beyond measurement that implacably emerge from his calculations—and whatever protest may be raised by a certain sort of common sense—I cannot see that it is possible to interpret the present progress of the phenomenon of man, in line as it is with the general progress of the world, without arriving at a prospect as fantastic as I have just suggested.

("Universalization and Union" in AE, 86-90)

[Synthesis of the Whole]

The coalescence of elements and the coalescence of stems, the spherical geometry of the earth and psychical curvature of the mind harmonising to counterbalance the individual and collective forces of dispersion in the world and to impose unification—here at last we find the spring and secret of hominisation.

But why should there be unification in the world and what purpose does it serve?

To see the answer to this ultimate question, we have only to put side by side the two equations which have been gradually formulating themselves from the moment we began trying to situate the phenomenon of man in the world.

Evolution = Rise of consciousness,

Rise of consciousness = Union effected.

The general gathering together in which, by correlated actions of the *without* and the *within* of the earth, the totality of thinking units and thinking forces are engaged—the aggregation in a single block of a mankind whose fragments weld together and interpenetrate before our eyes in spite of (indeed in proportion to) their efforts to separate—all this becomes intelligible from top to bottom as soon as we perceive it as the natural culmination of a cosmic processus of organisation which has never varied since those remote ages when our planet was young.

First the molecules of carbon compounds with their thousands of atoms symmetrically grouped; next the cell which, within a very small volume, contains thousands of molecules linked in a complicated system; then the metazoa in which the cell is no more than an almost infinitesimal element; and later the manifold attempts made sporadically by the metazoa to enter into symbiosis and raise themselves to a higher biological condition.

And now, as a germination of planetary dimensions, comes the thinking layer which over its full extent develops and intertwines its fibres, not to confuse and neutralise them but to reinforce them in the living unity of a single tissue.

Really I can see no coherent, and therefore scientific way of grouping this immense succession of facts but as a gigantic psycho-biological operation, a sort of *mega-synthesis,* the 'super-arrangement' to which all the thinking elements of the earth find themselves today individually and collectively subject.

Mega-synthesis in the tangential, and therefore and thereby a leap forward of the radial energies along the principal axis of evolution: ever more complexity and thus ever more consciousness. If that is what really happens, what more do we need to convince ourselves of the vital error hidden in the depths of any doctrine of isolation? The egocentric ideal of a future reserved for those who have managed to attain egoistically the extremity of 'everyone for him-self' is false and against nature. No element could move and grow except with and by all the others with itself.

Also false and against nature is the racial ideal of one branch draining off for itself alone all the sap of the tree and rising over the death of other branches. To reach the sun nothing less is required than the combined growth of the entire foliage.

The outcome of the world, the gates of the future, the entry into the super-human—these are not thrown open to a few of the privi-leged nor to one chosen people to the exclusion of all others. They will open only to an advance of *all together,* in a direction in which *all together*[3] can join and find completion in a renovation of the earth, a renovation whose physical degree of reality we must now consider and whose outline we must make clearer.

(PM, 243-245)

An infallible synthesis of the whole, operated by combined internal and external influences; such, in brief, would appear to be (apart from the exceptional amplifications we meet in miracles) the most general and most perfected form of God's action upon the world: respecting all, 'forced into' many roundabout ways and obliged to tolerate many things which shock us at first—but ultimately inte-grating and transforming all.

("The Modes of Divine Action in the Universe" in CE, 35)

[Christianity and Unification]

Christianity is essentially the religion of personality. And it is so to such a degree that it is at present in danger of losing its influence on the human soul by the kind of inability it shows of understand-ing the organic links of which the universe is composed. For ninety per cent of those who view Him from outside, the Christian God looks like a great landowner administering his estates, the world. Now this conventional picture, which is too well justified by appear-ances, corresponds in no way to the dogmatic basis or point of view of the Gospels. And for this reason. The essence of Christianity is neither more nor less than a belief in the unification of the world in

God by the Incarnation. All the rest is only secondary explanation or illustration. In view of this, so long as human society had not emerged from the 'neolithic', family phase of its development (that is to say until the dawn of the modern scientific-industrial phase) clearly the Incarnation could only find symbols of a juridical nature to express it. But since our modern discovery of the great unities and vast energies of the cosmos, the ancient words begin to assume a new and more satisfying meaning. To be the alpha and omega, Christ must, without losing his precise humanity, become co-extensive with the physical expanse of time and space. In order to reign on earth, He must 'super-animate' the world. In Him henceforth, by the whole logic of Christianity, personality expands (or rather centres itself) till it becomes universal. Is this not exactly the God we are waiting for?

I will not go so far as to say that this religious renaissance is yet self-conscious. In all realms, the old framework resists hardest when it is at breaking-point. But my experience of Christianity allows me to affirm this: whatever formalisms may still persist, the transformation of which I speak has already taken place in the most living parts of the Christian organism. Beneath a surface pessimism, individualism or juridicism, Christ the King is *already worshipped today as the God of progress and evolution.*

Earlier, when I was analysing the conditions that a centre of the universe must satisfy, I spoke of a love stronger than sexual attraction, of a love which would embrace the whole earth, of a love which would find the heart of the universe. It might seem that I was speculating on a utopia. But all I was doing in reality was to develop the potentialities contained in the factual reality of Christianity. In the actual simplicity of his worship, the believer perceives and performs all that I seemed to be dreaming of.

With this coincidence as evidence, I begin to think in the most critical and positivistic parts of my being that the Christian phenomenon might well be what it claims to be, and what every theory of a personal universe appeals to as a final test of its truth: the reflection of the supreme consciousness on the elements of consciousness it has collected—in fact a revelation.

("Sketch of a Personalistic Universe" in HE, 91-92)

To confirm the presence at the summit of the world of what we have called the Omega Point,[4] do we not find here the very cross-check we were waiting for? Here surely is the ray of sunshine striking through the clouds, the reflection onto what is ascending of that which is already on high, the rupture of our solitude. The palpable influence on our world of *an other* and supreme Someone . . . Is not the Christian phenomenon, which rises upwards at the heart of the social phenomenon, precisely that?

In the presence of such perfection in coincidence, even if I were not a Christian but only a man of science, I think I would ask myself this question.

(PM, 298-299)

For the last forty years my attitude and my activities have been based on the threefold, ever stronger, conviction:

a. First, that (for many irresistible reasons) we have just entered historically a period of neo-humanism (characterized by the surmise, or even the acceptance as proved, that Man is far from having completed the biological curve of his growth—which means that he has not only a future in time, but also 'a future' to look forward to).

b. Secondly, that the conflict—only an apparent conflict—between this neo-humanism and the 'classic' formulation of Christianity is the underlying source of all today's religious disquiet.

c. Finally, that the synthesis 'in Christo Jesu' between the ascensional force of traditional Christianity and the propulsive force of modern neo-humanism is what our world, albeit confusedly, looks to for its salvation (and the Society of Jesus, incidentally, has once again exactly the same role in this situation, but at a higher stage, as it had 400 years ago when it was confronted by the Humanism of the Renaissance).

("The Basis of My Attitude" in HM, 147)

Christianity indeed contributes a common spirit and a common form: it makes souls cleave together by charity; it makes them adhere to the will of God; it spiritualizes them in desire and affection. But what positive, progressive, precise end are we to assign to human efforts? In what natural direction are we to advance? To what tangible end should we unite, *all of us?*

I can't believe that the world was given to man simply to *keep him busy*, as if it were a wheel to turn. There must be a precise effort to be made, a definite result to be obtained, and this must be the *axis* of human work and of the human lineage, serving as the *support* or matter of our fidelity to God, acting as the *dynamic bond* of our charity. Obviously, it's God [our Lord] who, ultimately, is all this. But under what human form, adapted to human becoming, does God offer himself, to be served, to be won? Detachment is purely negative and disintegrating (if it is not qualified); love of the divine will is a simple form that needs a support; charity is unifying, but, in itself, 'static' . . . It's evidently in the *natural perfecting* of souls, *achieved by the combined effort of all science, all aesthetic, all morality* that we must seek a way to coordinate the dispersed effort of human beings.

(MM, 181-182)

Notes

1. Following Greek thought—following all thought in fact—are not 'to be' and 'to be one' identical?

2. 'En pasi panta Theos.'

3. Even if they do so only under the influence of a few, an *élite*.

4. To be more exact, 'to confirm the presence at the summit of the world of something in line with, but still more elevated than, the Omega point.' This is in deference to the theological concept of the 'supernatural' according to which the binding contact between God and the world, *hic et nunc* inchoate, attains to a super-intimacy (hence also a super-gratuitousness) of which man can have no inkling and to which he can lay no claim by virtue of his 'nature' alone.

Reconciliation in Christ

[Christ, Center of All Things]

Let us pray

Lord Jesus Christ, you truly contain within your gentleness, within your humanity, all the unyielding immensity and grandeur of the world. And it is because of this, it is because there exists in you this ineffable synthesis of what our human thought and experience would never have dared join together in order to adore them—element and totality, the one and the many, mind and matter, the infinite and the personal; it is because of the indefinable contours which this complexity gives to your appearance and to your activity, that my heart, enamoured of cosmic reality, gives itself passionately to you.

I love you, Lord Jesus, because of the multitude who shelter within you and whom, if one clings closely to you, one can hear with all the other beings murmuring, praying, weeping. . . .

I love you because of the transcendent and inexorable fixity of your purposes, which causes your sweet friendship to be coloured by an intransigent determinism and to gather us all ruthlessly into the folds of its will.

I love you as the source, the activating and life-giving ambience, the term and consummation, of the world, even of the natural world, and of its process of becoming.

You the Centre at which all things meet and which stretches out over all things so as to draw them back into itself: I love you for the extensions of your body and soul to the farthest corners of creation through grace, through life, and through matter.

Lord Jesus, you who are as gentle as the human heart, as fiery as the forces of nature, as intimate as life itself, you in whom I can melt away and with whom I must have mastery and freedom: I love you as a world, as *this* world which has captivated my heart; and it is you, I now realize, that my brother-men, even those who do not believe, sense and seek throughout the magic immensities of the cosmos.

Lord Jesus, you are the centre towards which all things are moving: if it be possible, make a place for us all in the company of those elect and holy ones whom your loving care has liberated one by one from the chaos of our present existence and who now are being slowly incorporated into you in the unity of the new earth.

("Cosmic Life" in WTW, 69-70)

Because, Lord, by every innate impulse and through all the hazards of my life I have been driven ceaselessly to search for you and to set you in the heart of the universe of matter, I shall have the joy, when death comes, of closing my eyes amidst the splendour of a universal transparency aglow with fire . . .

It is as if the fact of bringing together and connecting the two poles, tangible and intangible, external and internal, of the world which bears us onwards had caused everything to burst into flames and set everything free.

In the guise of a tiny baby in its mother's arms, obeying the great laws of birth and infancy, you came, Lord Jesus, to dwell in my infant-soul; and then, as you re-enacted in me—and in so doing extended the range of—your growth through the Church, that same humanity which once was born and dwelt in Palestine began now to spread out gradually everywhere like an iridescence of unnumbered hues through which, without destroying anything, your presence penetrated—and endued with supervitality—every other presence about me.

And all this took place because, in a universe which was disclosing itself to me as structurally convergent, you, by right of your resurrection, had assumed the dominating position of all-inclusive Centre in which everything is gathered together.

(HU, 150-151; "The Heart of Matter" in HM, 55-56)

Nothing, Lord Jesus, can subsist outside of your flesh; so that even those who have been cast out from your love are still, unhappily for them, the beneficiaries of your presence upholding them in existence. All of us, inescapably, exist in you, the universal *milieu* in which and through which all things live and have their being.

(*"The Mass on the World" in HM, 132*)

[Christ and Unitive Transformation]

We can say as a first approximation that the *milieu* whose rich and mobile homogeneity has revealed itself all around us as a condition and a consequence of the most Christian attitudes (such as right intention and resignation) is formed by the divine omnipresence. The immensity of God is the essential attribute which allows us to seize him everywhere, within us and around us.

This answer begins to satisfy our minds in that it circumscribes the problem. However, it does not give to the power *in quo vivimus et sumus* the sharp lines with which we should wish to trace the features of the one thing needful. Under what form, proper to our creation and adapted to our universe, does the divine immensity manifest itself to, and become relevant to, mankind? We feel it charged with that sanctifying grace which the Catholic faith causes to circulate everywhere as the true sap of the world; which, in its attributes, is very like that charity *(manete in dilectione mea)* which will one day, the Scriptures tell us, be the only stable principle of natures and powers; which, too, is fundamentally similar to the wonderful and substantial divine will, whose marrow is everywhere present and constitutes the true food of our lives, *omne delectamentum in se habentem*. What is, when all is said and done, the concrete link which binds all these universal entities together and confers on them a final power of gaining hold of us?

The essence of Christianity consists in asking oneself that question, and in answering: 'The Word incarnate, our Lord Jesus Christ.'

Let us examine step by step how we can validate to ourselves this prodigious identification of the Son of Man and the divine *milieu*.

A first step, unquestionably, is to see the divine omnipresence in which we find ourselves plunged as *an omnipresence of action*. God enfolds us and penetrates us by creating and preserving us.

Now let us go a little further. Under what form, and with what end in view, has the Creator given us, and still preserves in us, the gift of participated being? Under the form of an essential aspiration towards him—and with a view to the unhoped-for cleaving which is to make us one and the same complex thing with him. The action by which God maintains us in the field of his presence is *a unitive transformation.*

Let us go further still. What is the supreme and complex reality for which the divine operation moulds us? It is revealed to us by St. Paul and St. John. It is the quantitative repletion and the qualitative consummation of all things: it is the mysterious Pleroma, in which the substantial *one* and the created *many* fuse without confusion in a *whole* which, without adding anything essential to God, will nevertheless be a sort of triumph and generalisation of being.

At last we are nearing our goal. What is the active centre, the living link, the organising soul of the Pleroma? St. Paul, again, proclaims it with all his resounding voice: it is he in whom everything is reunited, and in whom all things are consummated—through whom the whole created edifice receives its consistency—Christ dead and risen *qui replet omnia, in quo omnia constant.*

And now let us link the first and last terms of this long series of identities. We shall then see with a wave of joy that *the divine omnipresence* translates itself within our universe by the network of the organising forces of the total Christ. God exerts pressure, in us and upon us—through the intermediary of all the powers of heaven, earth and hell—only in the act of forming and consummating Christ who saves and sur-animates the world. And since, in the course of this operation, Christ himself does not act as a dead or passive point of convergence, but as a centre of radiation for the energies which lead the universe back to God through his humanity, the layers of divine action finally come to us impregnated with his organic energies.

The divine *milieu* henceforward assumes for us the savour and the specific features which we desire. In it we recognise an omnipresence which acts upon us by assimilating us in it, *in unitate corporis Christi.* As a consequence of the Incarnation, the divine immensity has transformed itself for us into *the omnipresence of christification.* All the good that I can do *opus et operatio* is physically gathered in, by something of itself, into the reality of the consummated Christ. Everything I endure, with faith and love, by way of diminishment or death, makes me a little more closely an integral part of his mystical body. Quite specifically it is *Christ whom we make or whom we undergo in all things.* Not only *diligentibus omnia convertuntur in bonum* but, more clearly still, *convertuntur in Deum* and, quite explicitly, *concertuntur in Christum.*

(DM, 121-123)

Christ, as we know, fulfils Himself gradually, through the ages in the sum of our individual endeavours. Why should we treat this fulfilment as though it possessed none but a metaphorical significance, confining it entirely within the abstract domain of purely supernatural action? Without the process of biological evolution, which produced the human brain, there would be no sanctified souls; and similarly, without the evolution of collective thought, through which alone the plenitude of human consciousness can be attained on earth, how can there be a consummated Christ? In other words, without the constant striving of every human cell to unite with all the others, would the Parousia be physically possible? I doubt it.

That is why I believe that this coming together, from all four corners of the intellectual world, of a great mass of naturally religious spirits, does not portend the building of a new temple on the ruins of all others but the laying of new foundations to which the old Church is gradually being moved.

Little by little the idea is coming to light in Christian consciousness that the 'phylogenesis' of the whole man, and not merely the 'ontogenesis' of his moral virtues, is hallowed, in the sense that the charity of the believer may more resemble an impulse of constructive energy and his self-detachment be more in the nature of a positive effort.

In response to the cry of a world trembling with the desire for unity, and already equipped, through the workings of material progress, with the external links of this unity, Christ is already revealing himself, in the depths of men's hearts, as the Shepherd (the Animator) of the Universe. We may indeed believe that the time is approaching when many men, old and new believers, having understood that from the depths of Matter to the highest peak of the Spirit there is only *one evolution,* will seek the fullness of their strength and their peace in the assured certainty that the whole of the world's industrial, aesthetic, scientific and moral endeavour serves physically to complete the Body of Christ, whose charity animates and recreates all things.

Fulfilling the profound need for unity which pervades the world, and crowning it with renewed faith in Christ the Physical Centre of Creation; finding in this need the natural energy required for the renewal of the world's life; thus do I see the New Jerusalem, descending from Heaven and rising from the Earth.

("A Note on Progress" in FM, 23-24)

The higher organic unity—the higher spirituality—towards which souls essentially tend, does not seem to be inaugurated in any of the specifically terrestrial associations we see taking shape around us. If we are to understand the true term of cosmic concentration (spiritualization), we must—as we would naturally anticipate—look for the answer in that same Religion whose moral teaching we saw to be so admirably in harmony with the laws that govern the development of the universe. Christianity answers that the term of the world is Christ.

Christ, it is true, is not the centre whom all things here below could *naturally* aspire to be one with. To be destined for Christ is a gratuitous favour of the Creator we have no right to count upon. Nevertheless it remains true that the Incarnation so completely *recast* the universe in the supernatural that, *in concrete fact*, we can no longer ask, or imagine, towards what Centre the elements of this world, had they not been raised up by grace, would have gravitated. Physically speaking, there is only one dynamism in the present world, that which gathers all things to Christ. Christ is the centre to which all the successfully realized, living, *elect* portions of the cosmos make their way, in whom each finds its being. In him, 'the plenitude of the universe,' *omnia creatur* because *omnia uniuntur*—things are created because all things are made one—and there we meet again the precise formula of creative union.

Simply to consider the human soul, analysed as a structure that is composite in origin . . ., may well be sufficient in itself to induce our minds to build up the ontological system put forward in this essay. *Without* knowledge of Christ, this exposition would be extremely vulnerable and hypothetical, particularly in the extrapolation that led us to anticipate a spirituality, still to be realized, that is to be born from the sum of our souls. *With* knowledge of Christ, this almost delirious dream becomes to some degree a Reality known by faith. As the reader must have seen for some time, the philosophy of creative union is simply the development—generalization, extension to the universe—of what the Church teaches us about the growth of Christ. *It is the philosophy of the universe expressed in terms of the notion of the mystical body.* It was primarily as such that I myself came to grasp it, and it is only so that it can be understood: by striving to love and hold Christ in all things.

For the believer who has understood—in their full force and with no qualification—the words of St John and St Paul, Christ reveals himself at the heart of *every* being that progresses, as a Centre that is at once very near and very distant: very near, because he is, and it is his will to be, at the source of every affection; very distant, because the being cannot unite himself to Christ except at the term of a long process of perfection.

Precisely because there exists in all beings a common centre, scattered and separable though they are in appearance, they meet together at a deeper level. The more they perfect themselves naturally and sanctify themselves in grace, the more they come together and fuse into one, within the single, unifying Centre to which they aspire: and we may call that Centre equally well the *point* upon which they converge, or the *ambience* in which they float.

("Creative Union" in WTW, 173-175)

Christ could, no doubt, be content, exercising no more than a collective spiritual influence, thus to give life to the human cells that prolong him, mystically, through the universe: but he does more. By means of sacramental communion he consummates the union of the faithful in Himself through an individual and integral contact of soul with soul, flesh with flesh; he instils even into the matter of their being, side by side with the imperative need to adhere to the mystical Body, a seed of resurrection. Christ, as does all life, anticipates our desires and efforts: in the first place through the incarnation, and then through the Eucharist, he organizes us for himself and implants himself in us. But, again as all life does, he demands the co-operation of our good will and our actions.

We give him this essential collaboration by exerting an effort actively to become assimilated, by lovingly submitting our own autonomy to His: this assimilation lies in loving-kindness and humility, in community of suffering, by which the Passion of Calvary is continued and completed, but above all in charity, that wonderful virtue which makes us see and cherish Christ in every man and so enables us to forward, in the 'immediacy' of a single act, the unification of all in One.

We may be tempted to believe, and may perhaps be told, that in the course of this painfully acquired communion, all we are doing is simply to bring about moral beauties in our souls and a superficial resemblance to God, similar to those improvements through which, in social life, men who attach importance to their personal cultural development, are accustomed to better their natural personality. Nothing could be more mistaken. Our efforts have an impact that is far more permanent and profound. When our activity is animated by grace it is as effective and 'creative' as life, the Mother of Organisms, and it builds up a Body in the true sense of the word. This is the Body of Christ, which seeks to be realized in each one of us.

The mystical Body of Christ should, in fact, be conceived as a physical Reality, *in the strongest sense the words can bear.* Only so can the great mysteries and the great virtues of religion; only so can Christ's role as mediator, the importance of Communion, and the immense value of charity, *assume their full significance;* only so can the Person of the Saviour retain its full hold on our minds and continue to provide the driving force our destinies demand.

("Cosmic Life" in WTW, 50-51)

[Christ and the Universe]

Let me describe how I picture to myself, for the moment, the relationship between Christ and the Universe.

In a general way I think that the co-extension of Christ and the World must be understood primarily in the sense of a physical, organic, influence exerted by Christ on the essential movement (or the sum total of the essential movements) that causes the Universe to grow (= *creative or transforming action*).

That being so, let us, to simplify matters, say that: o = the natural term (x) of human (and cosmic) advances; and , = the supernatural term (plenitude of Christ) of the Kingdom of God.

I conceive three principal relations between o and ,:

1. Either o and , are two disparate (independent) terms developing on two different planes within the same created activity (for example, , is the product of human actions regarded as moral and 'effected for God'; and o is the fruit, with no value for the supernatural world, of those same actions in so far as they achieve their end in this world of time).

2. Or o and , *are two antagonistic terms*, each tending to eliminate the other, so that every point at which created activity comes in is a place where there is a choice between, and a separation between, o and , (= the doctrine of renunciation, pure and simple).

3. Or, finally, o and, *are two hierarchically ordered terms*, , being a magnification of o, which it has taken to itself and sublimated, 'along its initial axis.' (For example, we can conceive how natural human effort and grace work together, each for an essential part, in the development of Spirit: Spirit *continues to produce itself in its natural substance* at the same time as God elevates it to the supernatural order. In such conditions, the World is not merely an exercise-ground: it is *a work* to be carried through.)

The first of these hypotheses seems to me to be dualist and spurious, neither one thing nor the other. (I have criticized it at length in *Cosmic Life*.)

I find the second theoretically attractive; but in practice it seems to me inhuman and impossible to reconcile:

1. either with the practice of the Church, which has always openly encouraged human work and given it her blessing;

2. or with the most elementary religious psychology, which discloses a strict connection between the natural expansion of human faculties and their capacity for love of God. The Universe stimulates the 'zest for being,' and provides the nourishment which are transformed into love of God. To my mind, at least, this process is extremely clear: Heaven cannot dispense with Earth.

Until further orders, therefore, I hold to the third solution, which has the advantage of being directly suited to my double instinctive need:

1. to feel God underlying all natural energy, and

2. to find a universal, absolute, value in all human action *(non solum quoad operationem, sed etiam quoad opus).*

In a real and literal sense we may say, if we accept the hypothesis of Christ's adopting and supernaturalising of the natural evolution of the World, *quidquid patimur, Christus agit* and *quidquid agimus, Christus agitur*—whatever is done to us, it is Christ who does it, and, whatever we do, it is to Christ we do it.

This way of looking at human activity and passivity as integrally sanctified and divinized has become so familiar to me that it is no effort to me to live with it. I find in it an ease and breadth of movement, a clarity of judgement and decision, which make me earnestly wish that many others besides myself should understand and adopt the same position.

It is most important to note that this concept of the World's *conjoined ends* (natural and supernatural) has nothing in common with a theory of hedonism or 'hold fast to all you have.'

Its aim is, no doubt, to channel towards God, to harness for Heaven, *the whole* of the World's drive towards the Beautiful and the Good. But it maintains (as does every theory of true transformation):

1. that natural progress, as well as supernatural, underlies individual work and renunciation.

2. that natural development is subordinated to the kingdom of God.

3. that the centre of gravity of human effort gradually shifts towards the concerns of heaven as certain fields of lower activity are left behind or exhausted (it is thus that virginity tends to replace the marital state).

("My Universe" in HM, 202-204)

For me, my God, all joy and all achievement, the very purpose of my being and all my love of life, all depend on this one basic vision of the union between yourself and the universe. Let others, fulfilling a function more august than mine, proclaim your splendours as pure Spirit; as for me, dominated as I am by a vocation which springs from the inmost fibres of my being, I have no desire, I have no ability, to proclaim anything except the innumerable prolongations of your incarnate Being in the world of matter; I can preach only the mystery of your flesh, you the Soul shining forth through all that surrounds us.

("The Mass on the World" in HM, 133)

[Christ, Synthesis of the Uncreated and the Created]

'Nova et vetera'—'New things and old.' It is part of the normal economy of the Christian life that certain elements, long dormant in revealed truth, suddenly develop into powerful branches; and this happens commensurately with new times and needs, and in answer to their demands.

In our own day, this, it seems to me, is the part reserved for the grand and essentially dogmatic idea of the Christian *pleroma*: the mysterious synthesis of the uncreated and the created—the grand completion (at once quantitative and qualitative) of the universe in God. It is impossible to read St Paul without being astounded by three things simultaneously: first, the fundamental importance attached by the apostle to this idea, interpreted with the utmost realism; secondly, the relative obscurity to which it has hitherto been relegated by preachers and theologians; and thirdly, its astonishing appropriateness to the religious needs of the present day. Here we have the concept of God gathering to himself not merely a diffuse multiplicity of souls, but the solid, organic, reality of a universe, taken from top to bottom in the complete extent and unity of its energies—and do we not find in that precisely what we were feeling our way towards?

It would, indeed, seem that under the guidance of a divine instinct, and parallel with the rise of modern humanist aspirations, the sap of Christianity is even now flowing into the bud that has been dormant so long, and will soon make it burst into flower. We can now clearly distinguish a fundamental movement in the Church, which also started just two hundred years ago, in the cult based on devotion to the heart of Jesus, and which is now clearly directed towards worship of Christ—of Christ considered in the ways in which he influences the whole mystical body, and in consequence, the whole human social organism; the love of Christ being seen as the energy in which all the chosen elements of creation are fused together without thereby being confused. Rome has recently made a gesture which marks a decisive stage in the development of dogma, expressing and sanctioning in the figure of Christ the King this irresistible advance of Christian consciousness towards a more universalist and more realist appreciation of the Incarnation.

What I have in mind, and what I dream about, is that the Church should follow up the logical extension of this movement, and so make plain and actual to the world, as St Paul did to his converts, the great figure of him in whom the *pleroma* finds its physical principle, its expression, and its consistence: Christ-Omega, the Universal-Christ. 'Descendit, ascendit, *ut repleret onnia*'—'He descended, and he ascended, that he might fill all things.'[1] St Paul's imagery made rather a vague impression, no doubt, on the Romans, the Corinthians, the Ephesians, or the Colossians, because in those days the 'world', the 'whole' (with all that those words now imply for us of the organically defined), had not yet come to exist in man's consciousness; but for us, fascinated by the newly discovered magnitude of the universe, it expresses exactly that aspect of God which is needed to satisfy our capacity for worship. Between Christ the King and the Universal Christ, there is perhaps no more than a slight difference of emphasis, but it is nevertheless all-important. It is the whole difference between an external power, which can only be juridical and static, and an internal domination which, inchoate in matter and culminating in grace, operates upon us by and through all the organic linkages of the progressing world.

This figure of the Universal Christ, the prime mover, the saviour, the master and the term of what our age calls evolution, entails no risk, we should note, of the disappearance of the man-Christ, or of a deviation of mysticism into some pantheistic and impersonal form of worship.

The Universal Christ, born from an expansion of the heart of Jesus, requires the historical reality of his human nature if he is not to disappear; and at the same time, as a function of the mechanism specific to love, he does not absorb but completes the personality of the elements which he gathers together at the term of union. Nor, again, is there any danger that the faithful who are drawn to the Universal Christ will forget heaven and allow themselves to succumb to a pagan naturalism and be drawn into a materialist conquest of the earth: for does not the Universal Christ, in his full glory, always emerge from the Cross?

So, there is no danger: on the other hand, what advantages are to be reaped, and how alluring the prospect!

This (and I speak from experience) is something of which I am deeply convinced. The religious consciousness of today, now finally won over to the idea of some 'super-mankind' to be born from our efforts, but unable to find any concrete image or rule of action that will answer its aspirations—this modern consciousness *could never resist* a Christianity which presented itself as the saviour of the earth's most real and living hopes. This would mean a complete and radical conversion of neo-paganism; and it would mean also a new infusion of the lifeblood of mankind into the heart, too often starved of that human energy, of those who believe.

It is only the Christian (and he *only in so far as* he absorbs into himself the humano-divine properties of the Universal Christ) who is in a position today to answer the complex demands of nature and grace by an incredibly rich and simple act, by *a completely synthetic act,* in which the spirit of detachment and the spirit of conquest combine, correct and elevate one another—the spirit of tradition and the spirit of adventurous enquiry, the spirit of the earth and the spirit of God.

May we not say that if the Church wishes to guide the convulsions of the modern world to a fruitful issue, all she needs to do is to summon us to the discovery and the exercise of this completely modern form of charity?

After two thousand years, the affirmation of a Christian optimism in the nativity of the Universal Christ: is not that the message and the rallying cry we need?

("The Awaited Word" in TF, 97-100)

[Incarnation and Convergence]

Completely to adjust the idea of Redemption to the demands of evolution is an arduous task, even though it brings freedom with it. The figure of Christ emerges from the attempt with added grandeur and beauty; but not without meeting resistance.

In the case of the idea of the Incarnation, things work out quite differently. When the face of Christ is projected, along the axis of this mystery, upon a universe that is evolutive in structure, it expands and fills out effortlessly. Within this organic and moving framework, the features of the God-man spread out and are amplified with surprising ease. There they assume their true proportions, as in their own natural context.

If we are to grasp the reason for this affinity and this successful projection, we must clearly understand what is meant by an evolutive world. It is one in which the consistence of the elements and their stability of balance lie in the direction not of matter but of spirit; in such a universe, we must remember, the fundamental property of the cosmic mass is to concentrate upon itself, within an ever-growing consciousness, as a result of attraction or synthesis. In spite of the appearance, so impressive as a factor in physics, of secondary phenomena of progressive dispersion (such as entropy), there is only one real evolution, *the evolution of convergence,* because it alone is positive and creative. There is no need for me to discuss this point again, for I have already dealt with it on several occasions elsewhere; but it has a consequence, of great importance for the Incarnation, to which I must return. It is this: quite apart from any religious consideration, we are obliged, by the very process of thought and experience, to assume the existence in the universe of a centre of universal confluence. As a structural necessity, if the cosmos is to hold together and progress, there must be in it a specially important place in which, as though at a universal crossroads, everything can be seen, can be felt, can be controlled, can be vitalized, can *be in touch* with everything else. Is not that an admirable place at which to position (or rather to recognize) Christ?

If we assume Christ to be established by his incarnation at this remarkable cosmic point of all convergence, he then immediately becomes co-extensive with the vastness of space. There is no longer any danger that his personality or his sovereignty may vanish, submerged in too enormous a universe. The dizzy immensities of the heavens no longer have any significance for our faith and our hope, if the countless beings which fill the ideal spheres are all embraced, through their centre, in a common infinity.

In such a position, again, Christ is commensurate with the abyss of time into which the roots of space are driven. We might have thought that his frail humanity would be lost in that abyss, taking our beliefs with it. But what value is, in fact, measured by the appearance in history of a life in a universe where the existence of the least monad is seen to be tied up with, and synchronous with, the whole evolution of things? The fact that Christ emerged into the field of human experience for just one moment, two thousand years ago, cannot prevent him from being the axis and the peak of a universal maturing.

In such a position, finally, Christ, wholly 'supernatural' though his domain may ultimately be, gradually radiates his influence throughout the whole mass of nature. Since, in concrete fact, only one single process of synthesis is going on *from top to bottom* of the whole universe, no element, and no movement, can exist at any level of the world outside the 'informing' action of the principal centre of things. Already co-extensive with space and co-extensive with duration, Christ is also automatically, in virtue of his position at the central point of the world, co-extensive with the scale of values which are spaced out between the peaks of spirit and the depths of matter.

Projected, then, on the screen of evolution, Christ, in an exact, physical, unvarnished sense, is seen to possess those most awesome properties which St Paul lavishly attributes to him. He is the First, and he is the Head. In him all things received their first impulse, in him all things hold together and all things are consummated. Once again, we might have feared that by immeasurably enlarging the limits of the world, science would make it more and more impossible to believe literally in that magnificent Pauline paean. And now we find that the contrary is true: it provides it with a perfect confirmation, so fine that we hardly dare to accept it. The greater the universe grows in our eyes, the more we see that it is made ready for unity. No, there is no danger that either 'height, breadth, or depth' can ever interpose between us and worship of Christ Jesus—provided that we have complete and final confidence in those immensities.

("Christology and Evolution" in CE, 88-89)

By definition and in essence Christianity is the religion of the Incarnation: God uniting Himself with the world which He created, to unify it and in some sort incorporate it in Himself. To the worshipper of Christ this act expresses the history of the universe.

But how does it operate, this gradual conquest and assimilation of Earth by Heaven? In the first place quantitatively, by the addition to the Mystical Body of an increasing multitude of human souls, 'until the number shall be complete'. But also qualitatively, by the steady growth, within the bosom of the Church, of a certain Christological perspective. Through the living *tradition* of a faith and a mystique the Christian organism diffuses or expresses in itself an ever more awakened sense of Christ present and active in the fulfilments of the world. We cannot continue to love Christ without discovering Him more and more. The maturing of a collective consciousness accompanied by numerical expansion: these are two aspects inseparably linked in the historical unfolding of the Incarnation. . . .

. . . To the Christian humanist—faithful in this to the most sure theology of the Incarnation—there is neither separation nor discordance, but coherent subordination, between the genesis of Mankind in the World and the genesis of Christ in Mankind through His Church. The two processes are inevitably linked in their structure, the second requiring the first as the matter upon which it descends in order to super-animate it. This view entirely respects the progressive, and experientially known, concentration of human thought in an increasingly acute consciousness of its unitary destiny. But instead of the vague centre of convergence envisaged as the ultimate end of this process of evolution, the personal and defined reality of the Word Incarnate, in which everything acquires consistence, appears and takes its place.

Life for Man. Man for Christ. Christ for God.

("Social Heredity and Progress" in FM, 34-36)

[Convergence of Religions Upon a Universal Christ]

If we Christians wish to *retain* in Christ the very qualities on which his power and our worship are based, we have no better way—no other way, even—of doing so than fully to accept the most modern concepts of evolution. Under the combined pressure of science and philosophy, we are being forced, experientially and intellectually, to accept the world as a coordinated system of activity which is gradually rising up towards freedom and consciousness. The only satisfactory way of interpreting this process (as I added earlier) is to regard it as irreversible and convergent. Thus, ahead of us, a *universal cosmic centre* is taking on definition, in which everything reaches its term, in which everything is explained, is felt, and is ordered. It is, then, in this physical pole of universal evolution that we must, in my view, locate and recognize the plenitude of Christ. For *in no other type of cosmos,* and *in no other place,* can any being, *no matter how divine he be,* carry out the function of universal consolidation and universal animation which Christian dogma attributes to Christ.[2] By disclosing a world-peak, evolution makes Christ possible, just as Christ, by giving meaning and direction to the world, makes evolution possible.

I am only too well aware how staggering is this idea of a being capable of gathering up all the fibres of the developing cosmos into his own activity and individual experience. But, in conceiving such a marvel, all I am doing (let me repeat) is to transpose into terms of physical reality the juridical expressions in which the Church has clothed her faith. In just the same way, the humblest Catholic unwittingly, through his creed, imposes a particular structure on the universe. It is a fantastic but a coherent story: for, as I pointed out earlier, is it not a mere quantitative illusion which makes us regard the personal and the universal as incompatible?

For my own part, I set out resolutely in the only direction in which it seemed to me possible to carry my faith further, and so retain it. I tried to place at the head of the universe which I adored from birth, the risen Christ whom others had taught me to know. And the result of that attempt has been that I have never for the last twenty-five years ceased to marvel at the infinite possibilities which the 'universalization' of Christ opens up for religious thought.

Judging from first appearances, Catholicism disappointed me by its narrow representations of the world and its failure to understand the part played by matter. Now I realize that, on the model of the incarnate God whom Christianity reveals to me, I can be saved only by becoming one with the universe. Thereby, too, my deepest 'pantheist' aspirations are satisfied, guided, and reassured. The world around me becomes divine. And yet the flames do not consume me, nor do the floods dissolve me. For, unlike the false monisms which urge one through passivity into unconsciousness, the 'pan-Christism' which I am discovering places union at the term of an arduous process of differentiation. I shall become the Other only by being utterly myself. I shall attain spirit only by bringing out the complete range of the forces of matter. The total Christ is consummated and may be attained, only at the term of universal evolution. In him I have found what my being dreamed of: a personalized universe, whose domination personalizes me. And I hold this 'world-soul' no longer simply as a fragile creation of my individual thought, but as the product of a long historical revelation, in which even those whose faith is weakest must inevitably recognize one of the principal lines of human progress.

For (and this is perhaps the most wonderful part of the whole story) the universal Christ in whom my personal faith finds satisfaction, is none other than the authentic expression of the Christ of the gospel. Christ renewed, it is true, by contact with the modern world, but at the same time Christ become *even greater in order* still to remain the same Christ. I have been reproached as being an innovator. In truth, the more I have thought about the magnificent cosmic attributes lavished by St Paul on the risen Christ, and the more I have considered the masterful significance of the Christian virtues, the more clearly have I realized that Christianity takes on its full value only when extended (as I find it rewarding to do) to cosmic dimensions. Inexhaustibly fructified by one another, my individual faith in the world and my Christian faith in Christ have never ceased to develop and grow more profound. *By this sign,* which argues a continual agreement between what is most determinedly emergent in me and what is most alive in the Christian religion, I have finally and permanently recognized that in the latter I have found the complement I sought to my own self, and to that I have surrendered.[3]

But, if I have thus surrendered myself, why should not others, all others, also do the same? I began by saying that what I am now writing is a personal confession. Deep in my mind, however, as I have proceeded, I have felt that something greater than myself was making its way into me. The passion for the world from which my faith springs; the dissatisfaction, too, which I experience at first when I am confronted by any of the ancient forms of religion—are not both these traces in my heart of the uneasiness and expectancy which characterize the religious state of the world today?

In the great river of mankind, the three currents (Eastern, human and Christian) are still at cross-purposes. Nevertheless there are sure indications which make it clear that they are coming to run together. The East seems already almost to have forgotten the original passivity of its pantheism. The cult of progress is continually opening up its cosmogonies ever more widely to the forces of spirit and emancipation. Christianity is beginning to accept man's effort. In these three branches the same spirit which made me what I am is obscurely at work.

In that case, surely the solution for which modern mankind is seeking must essentially be exactly the solution which I have come upon. I believe that this is so, and it is in this vision that my hopes are fulfilled. A general convergence of religions upon a universal Christ who fundamentally satisfies them all: that seems to me the only possible conversion of the world, and the only form in which a religion of the Future can be conceived.

("How I Believe" in CE, 127-130)

[Reconciled in Christ]

We can see, then, that what characterizes the Universal Element as we find it realized in Christ, is not that it is a quasi-matter, a plastic or informable element, an agent of absorption, but a quasi-soul, a plasmatic or informing element, a force of determination.[4]

The unique, universal, *necessariurn,* so defined, possesses the twofold power

(i) of dominating us, as a power that assimilates us.

(ii) and at the same time, of completing us individually to the degree that it fuses us into itself.

The transcendence of God, and the persistence of human personality—necessary conditions

of Christian orthodoxy

and of the complete satisfaction of our cosmic desire . . . —are thus completely safeguarded.

Through the totality of its properties, the Christian Universal Element is seen to be capable of uniting upon itself the most diametrically opposed tendencies of both human thought and act.

(i) Fundamentally, it effects within itself the union *of God and the world.* The two supreme loves, the natural and the supernatural, that, seen from one angle, appear to draw our hearts in contrary directions—towards the kingdom of heaven or towards mastery of the earth—are reconciled in the impassioned quest for the cosmic Christ.

The two stars, whose attractive forces seem to conflict with one another, are seen to be in reality each an extension of the other: it is *through the fulfilment of the world* that we reach Christ.

(ii) In our own particular destiny, this conjunction manifests itself in the reconciliation (already pointed out) *of the One and the Multiple.* Through the extreme perfection of its action, the Form of Christ allows the determinations of the element it integrates in itself to subsist, and even accentuates them. It unites us to itself to the degree that each one of us, according to our vocation, is more fully differentiated.

(iii) We can thus, in our effort to enter into Christ, make *equal* use (according to circumstances) of either of the two extremes to which our will may be directed: we may both *surrender ourselves and resist, accept and fight.* On the one hand, *if we have faith,* the irresistible forces of life and matter become for us, in very reality, the organizing activity of Christ assimilating us to himself. On the other hand, since all well-ordered activity here below is directed *towards Spirit,* and Spirit *towards Christ,* our *total* human effort *(the more* it is undertaken with *good intention)* collaborates in the plenitude of the Incarnation. All Christian imperturbability in the face of earthly vicissitudes, and all human enthusiasm in the face of a world to be conquered, are reconciled in those who have built their lives in the 'mystical milieu' constituted by the Universal Element.

(iv) The more, following every human line of development, we seek to win the unique *necessarium* in the fulfilment of our own personality and of the world, the more it leads us, through its universal embrace, to reject our self-centred interests for ever more immense ends. Moreover, *as a result of its tendency to isolate itself* (in the pure state) from the particular forms in which we apprehend it . . ., it gradually causes us to enter into a close and direct relationship with itself: when we contemplate it, when we make it the object of our prayer, we are transported to the vital point to which all things flow together and become open to influence in the depth of their spiritual being. The effort we make within that element to realize ourselves according to the fulness of our powers, thus ends *in making us renounce ourselves,* and become stabilized in an inflexible tension—and that is the most effective form of action.

= The Universal Element makes *the transcendent immediate; it unifies, by differentiating, the Multiple;* it allows us *to complete what already exists and to win full possession of what we already hold; it detaches us from the world by attaching us to it.*

In that element, the apparently most incompatible attitudes of monism and pluralism—of (moral) pragmatism and self-surrender—of contempt for the world and the cult of the earth—are effortlessly combined.

Through that element, it becomes possible to use *all life's forces to produce one and the same real thing.*

If, in conclusion, I had to sum up in one word the 'spirit' and course of life of the man who has seen the smile of the universal Christ at the term of all things, I would choose the word that narrow usage has made offensive: *Integrism.*

Integrism in purity—that goes without saying; and it means, *in the first place,* the authentic Christ, Christ in his truth and supernaturality. Simply in flat form, without further qualification, Christ has the power to conquer the world and incorporate it in himself.

But *integrism,* too, *in universality*—not a single element of created energy, not one iota of the redeemable world, must be lacking to the plenitude of Christ.

Around every distinct truth there spreads a *penumbra,* and at the root of every disciplined energy there lies a *disorder,* which absolute-minded men fear and wish to suppress, in their anxiety to include in their inflexible systems nothing that is not *certain* and *crystal clear.* They forget that the area of uncertain illumination and ill-defined aspirations that they reject from *their* universe is not a by-product or waste product, but the *living surface* of the Spirit of man: they are trying to cut away the sap-wood and yet keep alive, the heart of the oak.

Not only so that no chosen particle may be omitted from the *pleroma* (nothing is so small as to be inessential to its totality) but so that the universe *may be given its* true *form under the influence* of Christ, *we must* bring about the reign of Christ even—indeed, above all—*in the continually nascent fringe of the world.*

The first privilege of the incarnate Word—and the most powerful appeal he makes to our generation—is that he is the Principle in whom the universe develops.

Above all, then, seek Christ *in his integrity.*
("The Universal Element" in WTW, 299-302)

The principle of unity which saves our guilty world, wherein all is in process of returning to dust, is Christ. Through the force of his magnetism, the light of his ethical teaching, the unitive power of his very being, Jesus establishes again at the heart of the world the harmony of all endeavours and the convergence of all beings. Let us read the gospel boldly and we shall see that no idea can better convey to our minds the *redemptive function of the World* than that of a unification of all flesh in one and the same Spirit.[4]

1. *The Divine Magnetism.* Christ's primordial role is to draw to himself all that, before him, moved at random. For lack of an influence powerful enough to guide their wayward paths into a uniform direction, intelligent creatures, we have seen, hesitated and parted company. For the universe to subsist, *even in its natural evolution*, it was necessary above all that the dynamic soul of one and the same vigorous impetus should again be instilled into men. God chose the love of his incarnate Son as the *prime mover of the restored universe.*

Christ, then, clothed his person in the most sensible and most intimate charms of human individuality. He adorned that humanity with the most entrancing and most masterful splendours of the universe. And he came among us as the synthesis, surpassing all hope, of all perfection, such that every man was necessarily obliged to see and feel his presence, either to hate him or to love him.

As soon as he had appeared, a thrill passed through the seething mass of mankind that made it tremble in every fibre. It vibrated as one whole—since a Multitude of the elect was already isolating itself in the midst of the Multitude that still persisted, in spite of everything, in wandering aimlessly. In serried ranks, those who had freely chosen fidelity gathered around the Shepherd whose voice, like an assurance of life, echoed deep in their hearts. And they answered him, 'Wheresoever you go, we shall follow in your footsteps.'

On that day *ignorance was conquered by* the Incarnation, and the universe was given back its eagerness for its unparalleled development: on the day when Christ, to save the world that was withering away even in its natural roots, took his place at the head of Creation.

Moreover, the road our Saviour followed and man was called on to follow with him, was *that very road* that being had always taken in order to leave non-being far behind. The reflective, heavenly, task to which Christ summoned and drew us, united in a common urge, was an exact continuation of the unconscious, terrestrial work of former ages: for, under an outward appearance of kindly and humble moral teaching, *the law of purity and Christian charity* hides an operation that is pure fire, in which the original plurality of being is recast and fused until its unity is consummated. . . .

. . . 3. *New joy and New Suffering*. As Christ becomes incarnate in the universe and expels the guilty plurality of the world, so, step by step, the other evil effect of the Multitude—suffering—retreats and decreases. In its most external and sensible forms, no doubt, pain has not yet ceased to threaten us and disorganize us. The earth is still a plane of blood and tears. Already, however, the blood flows less freely and the tears are not so bitter. Above the torn flesh and the agonized hearts, into that deep zone in which the soul is moulded for eternal life, *peace has entered*, a peace such as the evil world has no knowledge of and cannot give—mastering peace, which conquers, and flows back to cover even the outermost layers of sensibility—*the peace that is the awareness of Unity*.

The human heart finds first in Jesus Christ the answer to its prayers, so manifold and so impatient that it seemed as though nothing could ever satisfy them all at one and the same time. The insoluble problem of our desires is solved without difficulty by the adorable divino-human reality who comes effortlessly, as it were, *to fill exactly to the brim their deep and complex void*. Passions cease to trample on one another and tear one another apart; the flesh bows meekly before spirit and is tamed. The riddle of our growth is explained in one word. Since Christ has been at hand, *our whole being* is expanding and is *delectably made one*.

At the same time, since Christ has been at hand, *communication has been established between the souls* that, before his coming, knew the misery of feeling isolated, shut in, impenetrable to one another. At last, crossing the fallen barrier of their temporary envelope, they are meeting and making contact in the unity of Christ.

Christ consumes with his glance my entire being. And with that same glance, that same presence, he enters into those who are around me and whom I love. Thanks to him therefore I am united with them, as in a divine *milieu*, through their inmost selves, and I can act upon them with all the resources of my being.

Christ *binds* us and *reveals* us to one another.

What my lips fail to convey to my brother or my sister he will tell them better than I. What my heart desires for them with anxious, helpless ardour he will grant them if it be good. What men cannot hear because of the feebleness of my voice, what they shut their ears against so as not to hear it, this I can confide to Christ who will one day tell it again, to their hearts. And if all this is so I can indeed die with my ideal, I can be buried with the vision I wanted to share with others. Christ gathers up for the life of tomorrow our stifled ambitions, our inadequate understandings, our uncompleted or clumsy but sincere endeavours. *Nunc dimittis, Domine, servum tuum in pace. . . .*

It happens sometimes that a man who is pure of heart will discern in himself, besides the happiness which brings peace to his own individual desires and affections, a quite *special joy, springing from a source outside himself,* which enfolds him in an *immeasurable sense of well-being.* This is the flowing back into his own diminutive personality of the new glow of health which Christ through his Incarnation has infused into humanity as a whole: in him, souls are gladdened with a feeling of warmth, for now they can live in communion with one another.

They see with amazement that the monstrous multitude of humankind forms but one heart and one soul, indistinguishable from the Heart and Soul of Christ.

But if they are to share in this joy and this vision they must first of all have had the courage *to break through the narrow confines of their individuality, depersonalize themselves, so to speak,* in order to become centred in Christ. For this is Christ's law, and it is categorical: *Si quis vult post me venire, abneget semetipsum.*

("The Struggle against the Multitude" in WTW, 106-107, 110-111)

Notes

1. Ephesians 4:9-10.

2. In other words, Christ needs to find a world-peak for his consummation, just as he needed to find a woman for his conception.

3. The more I think about it, the less I can see any criterion for truth other than the establishment of a growing maximum of universal coherence. Such an achievement has something *objective* about it, going beyond the effects of temperament.

4. Any reader who may be surprised by this forthright statement should remember what St John says in his Gospel (11:51-2): 'He [Caiaphas] did not say this of his own accord, but being high priest that year he prophesied that Jesus should die for the nation, and not for the nation only, but to gather into one the children of God who are scattered abroad.' (Note by French E.)

Communion

[Communion with God through the World]

It used to appear that there were only two attitudes mathematically possible for man: to love heaven or to love earth. With a new view of space, a third road is opening up: to make our way to heaven *through* earth. There is a communion (the true communion) with God through the world; and to surrender oneself to it is not to take the impossible step of trying to serve two masters.

Such a Christianity is still in reality the true gospel teaching, since it represents the same force applied to the elevation of mankind above to tangible, in a common love.

("Christology and Evolution" in CE, 93)

There is a communion with God, and a communion with earth, and a communion with God through earth.

("Cosmic Life" in WTW, 14)

In itself, *detachment by passing through* is in perfect harmony with the idea of the Incarnation in which Christianity is summed up. The movement carried out by the man who plunges into the world, in order first to share in things and then to carry them along with him—this movement, let me emphasize, is an exact replica of the baptismal act: 'He who descended', says St Paul, 'is he also who ascended . . . that he might fill all things.' It is quite natural, accordingly, that, under the pressure of the sense of man for which she serves as a channel, the Church of God should correct anything rather too 'oriental' (or negative) that might be found in her theory of renunciation. This comparatively new proposition, that Christian

perfection consists not so much in purifying oneself from the refuse
of the earth as in divinizing creation, is a forward step. In the most
conservative quarters, it is beginning to be recognized that there is a
communion with God through earth—a sacrament of the
world—spreading like a halo round the Eucharist; but there is still a
grudging reserve in allotting the share that has at last been accorded
to terrestrial sources of nourishment.

("The Evolution of Chastity" in TF, 73)

Thus, in a communion with God through the world, is fulfilled
the final longing that quickens the sense of religion: *to worship in ourselves something that is 'us.'* God with us! God does not give himself to
the soul as some superadded good, some outside supplement. He
does more, and better. He comes to us through the inner road of the
world; he comes down into us through that zone in which our
incomplete being is mingled with the universal substance. In that
day-spring of ourselves, our consciousness grows bright with God,
through a sort of internal metamorphosis of the created being,
which allows us to attain the transcendent without having to
emerge from ourselves. Without this divinization *by transmutation* of
our being it would be impossible to explain why our faith attaches
such inestimable value to every sanctified soul. Thus the Absolute of
experience is *the beginning of God in us.* We have both the right and the
duty to give our allegiance to the soul of the world and to surrender
ourselves to it. The contact we shall try to make with it is ordained
for leading us to Christ: moreover, it cannot be fully realized objectively except in Christ.

("The Soul of the World" in WTW, 187-188)

Rich with the sap of the world, I rise up towards the Spirit whose
vesture is the magnificence of the material universe but who smiles
at me from far beyond all victories; and, lost in the mystery of the
flesh of God, I cannot tell which is the more radiant bliss: to have
found the Word and so be able to achieve the mastery of matter, or to
have mastered matter and so be able to attain and submit to the light
of God.

Grant, Lord, that your descent into the universal Species may not
be for me just something loved and cherished, like the fruit of some

philosophical speculation, but may become for me truly a real Presence. Whether we like it or not by power and by right you are incarnate in the world and we are all of us dependent upon you. But in fact you are far, and how far, from being equally close to us all. We are all of us together carried in the one world-womb; yet each of us is our own little microcosm in which the Incarnation is wrought independently with degrees of intensity, and shades that are incommunicable. And that is why, in our prayer at the altar, we ask that the consecration may be brought about *for us*: *Ut nobis Corpus et Sanguis fiat . . .* If I firmly believe that everything around me is the body and blood of the Word, then for me (and in one sense for me alone) is brought about that marvellous 'diaphany' which causes the luminous warmth of a single life to be objectively discernible in and to shine forth from the depths of every event, every element: whereas if, unhappily, my faith should flag, at once the light is quenched and everything becomes darkened, everything disintegrates.

You have come down, Lord, into this day which is now beginning. But alas, how infinitely different in degree is your presence for one and another of us in the events which are now preparing and which all of us together will experience! In the very same circumstances which are soon to surround me and my fellow men you may be present in small measure, in great measure, more and more or not at all.

Therefore, Lord, that no poison may harm me this day, no death destroy me, no wine befuddle me, that in every creature I may discover and sense you, I beg you: give me faith.

("The Mass on the World" in HM, 126-127)

[Contemplation-Action Communion]

Action and acceptance: these two halves of our life—this inhaling and exhaling of our nature—are transfigured and clarified for us in the rays of creative union. Whatever we do, it is to Christ we do it. Whatever is done to us, it is Christ who does it. Christian piety has always drawn strength from these words of universal and constant union; but has it, I wonder, always been able, or been bold enough, to give to that union the forceful realism that, since St Paul first wrote these words, we have been entitled to expect?

Once we make up our minds to take the words of Revelation liter-ally—and to do so is the ideal of all true religion—then the whole mass of the universe is gradually bathed in light. And just as science shows us, at the lower limits of matter, an ethereal fluid in which everything is immersed and from which everything emerges, so at the upper limits of Spirit a mystical ambience appears in which everything floats and everything converges.

And in this rich and living ambience, the attributes, seemingly the most contradictory, of attachment and detachment, of action and contemplation, of the one and the multiple, of spirit and matter, are reconciled without difficulty in conformity with the designs of creative union: everything becomes one by becoming self.

When I am working for the progress of the universe, so to prepare for Christ a body less unworthy of him, I am attaching myself to the world and to myself—but at the same time I am detaching myself from it, because this world itself, divorced from Christ and his light, seems to me full of darkness and has no power to attract me. The light ahead eludes me as I move from zone to zone, and if I am to fol-low it I must reach those regions where activity is the most far-reaching in its ambitions, the least self-centred in its outlook, the most chaste in its dreams of union.

During this ascending progress, things are still sharply defined for me. It is through them, in fact, that Christ becomes tangible to me—it is through them that he reaches me and has contact with me. I cannot, therefore, dispense with them; and, logically, I shall be in the forefront of the realists, since I cannot apprehend God except by completing the world. Nevertheless, if I am still untiring in my pur-suit of created beings and my attempt to perfect them, it is solely in the hope that in them I may find the divine Fire which plays in them as though in the purest crystal. Is it not in the heavenly Jerusalem that the elements of the new earth will be so transparent, reflecting so brilliantly, that nothing, seemingly, will subsist but the rays, materialised in us, of God's glory?[1]

Mystical writers disagree as to whether action must precede con-templation as a preparation for it, or whether it springs from con-templation, as a superabundant gift from God. I must confess that such problems mean nothing to me. Whether I am acting or praying, whether I am painfully opening up my soul by work, or whether God takes possession of it through the passivities that come from within or without, I am equally conscious of finding unity. It is in this consciousness that the mystical activity 'formally' resides. Whether I am actively impelled towards development by the sensibly perceptible aspirations of my nature, or painfully mastered by material contacts, or visited by the graces of prayer, in each case I am equally moving in the mystical Milieu. *First and foremost,* I am in Christo Jesu; it is only *afterwards* that I am acting, or suffering, or contemplating.

If we had to give a more exact name to the mystical Milieu we would say that it is a Flesh—for it has all the properties the flesh has of palpable domination and limitless embrace. When given life by the universal Christ, the world is so active and has such warmth, that not one of the impressions I receive from it fails to 'inform' me a little more with God. Like a powerful organism, the world transforms me into him who animates it. 'The bread of the Eucharist,' says St Gregory of Nyssa, 'is stronger than our flesh; that is why it is the bread that assimilates us, and not we the bread, when we receive it.' At the same time, however, this transformed world, this universal flesh, so close at hand and so tangible, can only, it seems to us, be apprehended in the far distance of sublimity. When passion is lofty and noble, the man and woman who come together meet only at the term of their spiritual growth. This law of human union is the law of our cosmic union. Christ holds us by the most material fibres of nature. Nevertheless, we shall possess him perfectly only when our personal being, and the world with it, have step by step reached the full limit of their unification.

("My Universe" in SC, 73-76)

[Holy Communion]

Just as, when I turn my mind and reason to things that lie outside me, I have no right to dissociate myself from their destiny—so I cannot, in my personal being, escape from the Divine, whose dominating power I can see growing ever more supreme wherever I look.

Even had I ever imagined that it was I who held the consecrated Bread and gave myself its nourishment, I now see with blinding clarity that it is the Bread that takes hold of me and draws me to itself.

That small, seemingly lifeless, Host has become for me as vast as the world, as insatiable as a furnace. I am encircled by its power. It seeks to close around me.

An inexhaustible and universal communion is the term of the universal consecration.

I cannot, Lord, evade such massive power: I can only yield to it in blissful surrender.

And first, my God, I entrust myself to the generalized forces of matter, of life, of grace. The ocean of energies that our weakness cannot control: upon which we drift—hardly conscious of our heading, hardly able to change our course—this has now become for me the comforting mantle of your creative action. That part of us which is *in nobis sine nobis*—in me, so large a part that my freedom seems to be lost in it—I can feel warm, animated, charged with the organizing virtue of your body, Jesus.

In everything in me that has subsistence and resonance, in everything that enlarges me from within, that arouses me, attracts me, or wounds me from without, it is you, Lord, who are at work upon me—it is you who mould and spiritualize my formless clay—you that change me into yourself.

To take possession of me, my God, you who are more remote than all and deeper than all, you take to yourself and unite together the immensity of the world and the intimate depths of myself.

I can feel that all the strain and struggle of the universe reaches down into the most hidden places of my being.

But, Lord I do not passively give way to these blessed passivities: I offer myself to them, actively, and do all I can to promote them.

I know how the life-giving power of the host can be blocked by our freedom of will. If I seal up the entry into my heart I must dwell in darkness—and not only I—my individual soul—but the whole universe in so far as its activity sustains my organism and awakens my consciousness, and in so far also as I act upon it in my turn to draw forth from it the materials of sensation, of ideas, of moral goodness, of holiness of life. But if, on the other hand, my *heart is open to you*, then at once through the pure intent of my will the divine must flood into the universe, in so far as the universe is centred on me. Since, by virtue of my consent, I shall have become a living particle of the Body of Christ, all that affects me must in the end help on the growth of the total Christ. Christ will flood into and over me, me and *my* cosmos.

How I long, Lord Christ, for this to be!
May my acceptance be ever more complete, more comprehensive, more intense!
May my being, in its self-offering to you, become ever more open and more transparent to your influence!
And may I thus feel your activity coming ever closer, your presence growing ever more intense, everywhere around me.
Fiat, fiat.

In order to assist your action in me through all things, I shall do more than make myself receptive and offer myself to the passivities of life. I shall faithfully associate myself with the work you effect in my body and my soul. I shall strive to obey and anticipate your least promptings. My dearest wish, Master, is that I might offer so little resistance to you that you could no longer distinguish me from yourself—so perfectly would we be united, in a communion of will.

And yet, Lord, you look to me for even more than this perfect docility. It would not, you see, exhaust the positive richness of my activity. It would affect only the *formal*—not the *material*—aspect of my work: and it is the whole of my being, Lord Jesus, that you would have me give you, tree and fruit alike, the finished work as well as the harnessed power, the *opus* together with the *operatio*. To allay your hunger and quench your thirst, to nourish your body and bring it to its full stature, you need to find in us a substance which will be truly food for you. And this food ready to be transformed into you, this nourishment for your flesh, I will prepare for you by liberating the *spirit* in myself and in everything:
Through an effort (even a purely natural effort) to learn the truth, to live the good, to create the beautiful;
Through cutting away all inferior and evil energies;
Through practising that charity towards men which alone can gather up the multitude into a single soul. . . .
To promote, in however small a degree, *the awakening of spirit* in the world, is to *offer to the* incarnate *Word an increase of reality and consistence:* it is to allow his influence to increase in intensity around us.

And this means but one thing, Lord: that through the whole width and breadth of the Real, through all its past and through all that it will become, through all that I undergo and all that I do, through all that I am bound by, through every enterprise, through my whole life's work, I can make my way to you, be one with you, and progress endlessly in that union.

With a fulness no man has conceived you realized, through your Incarnation, love's threefold dream: to be so enveloped in the object of love as to be absorbed in it—endlessly to intensify its presence—and, without ever knowing surfeit, to be lost in it.

I pray that Christ's influence, spiritually substantial, physically mortifying, may ever spread wider among all beings, and that thence it may pour down upon me and bring me life.

I pray that this brief and limited contact with the sacramental species may introduce me to a universal and eternal communion with Christ, with his omni-operant will and his boundless mystical Body.

Corpus, sanguis Domini nostri Jesu Christi custodiant animam meam in vitam aeternam. Amen.

("The Priest" in WTW, 214-218)

. . . From the beginning of the Messianic preparation, up till the Parousia, passing through the historic manifestation of Jesus and the phases of growth of his Church, a single event has been developing in the world: the Incarnation, realised, in each individual, through the Eucharist.

All the communions of a life-time are one communion.

All the communions of all men now living are one communion.

All the communions of all men, present, past and future, are one communion.

Have we ever sufficiently considered the physical immensity of man, and his extraordinary relations with the universe, in order to realise in our minds the formidable implications of this elementary truth?

Let us conjure up in our minds, as best we can, the vast multitudes of men in every epoch and in every land. According to the catechism we believe that this fearful anonymous throng is, by right, subject to the physical and overmastering contact of him whose appanage it is to be able *omnia sibi subicere* (by right, and to a certain extent in fact; for who can tell where the diffusion of Christ, with the influence of grace, stops, as it spreads outward from the faithful at the heart of the human family?). Yes, the human layer of the earth is wholly and continuously under the organising influx of the incarnate Christ. This we all believe, as one of the most certain points of our faith. . . .

. . . *Grant, O God, that when I draw near to the altar to communicate, I may henceforth discern the infinite perspectives hidden beneath the smallness and the nearness of the Host in which you art concealed. I have already accustomed myself to seeing, beneath the stillness of that piece of bread, a devouring power which, in the words of the greatest doctors of your Church, far from being consumed by me, consumes me. Give me the strength to rise above the remaining illusions which tend to make me think of your touch as circumscribed and momentary.*

I am beginning to understand: under the sacramental Species it is primarily through the 'accidents' of matter that you touch me, but, as a consequence, it is also through the whole universe in proportion as this ebbs and flows over me under your primary influence. In a true sense the arms and the heart which you open to me are nothing less than all the united Powers of the world which, penetrated and permeated to their depths by your will, your tastes and your temperament, converge upon my being to form it, nourish it and bear it along towards the centre of your fire. In the Host it is my life that you are offering me, O Jesus.

What can I do to gather up and answer that universal and enveloping embrace? Quomodo comprehendam ut comprehensus sim? *To the total offer that is made me, I can only answer by a total acceptance. I shall therefore react to the eucharistic contact with the entire effort of my life—of my life of today and of my life of tomorrow, of my personal life and of my life as linked to all other lives. Periodically, the sacred Species may perhaps fade away in me. But each time they will leave me a little more deeply engulfed in the layers of your omnipresence: living and dying, I shall never at any moment cease to move forward in you. Thus the precept implicit in your Church, that we must communicate everywhere and always, is justified with extraordinary force and precision. The Eucharist must invade my life. My life must become, as a result of the sacrament, an unlimited and endless contact with you—that life which seemed, a few moments ago, like a baptism with you in the waters of the world, now reveals itself to me as communion with you through the world. It is the sacrament of life. The sacrament of my life—of my life received, of my life lived, of my life surrendered. . . .*

Because you ascended into heaven after having descended into hell, you have so filled the universe in every direction, Jesus, that henceforth it is blessedly impossible for us to escape you. Quo ibo a spiritu tuo, et quo a facie tua fugiam. *Now I know that for certain. Neither life, whose advance increases your hold upon me; nor death, which throws me into your hands; nor the good or evil spiritual powers which are your living instruments; nor the energies of matter into which you have plunged; nor the irreversible stream of duration whose rhythm and flow you control without appeal; nor the unfathomable abysses of space which are the measure of your greatness,* neque mors, neque vita, neque angeli, neque principatus, neque potestates, neque virtutes, neque instantia, neque futura, neque fortitudo, neque altitudo, neque profundum, neque ulla creatura[2]—*none of these things will be able to separate me from your substantial love, because they are all only the veil, the 'species', under which you take hold of me in order that I may take hold of you.*

Once again, Lord, I ask which is the most precious of these two beatitudes: that all things for me should be a contact with you? or that you should be so 'universal' that I can undergo you and grasp you in every creature?

Sometimes people think that they can increase your attraction in my eyes by stressing almost exclusively the charm and goodness of your human life in the past. But truly, O Lord, if I wanted to cherish only a man, then I would surely turn to those whom you have given me in the allurement of their present flowering. Are there not, with our mothers, brothers, friends and sisters, enough irresistibly lovable people around us? Why should we turn to Judea two thousand years ago? No, what I cry out for, like every being, with my whole life and all my earthly passion, is something very different from an equal to cherish: it is a God to adore.

To adore . . . That means to lose oneself in the unfathomable, to plunge into the inexhaustible, to find peace in the incorruptible, to be absorbed in defined immensity, to offer oneself to the fire and the transparency, to annihilate oneself in proportion as one becomes more deliberately conscious of oneself, and to give of one's deepest to that whose depth has no end. Whom, then, can we adore?

The more man becomes man, the more will he become prey to a need, a need that is always more explicit, more subtle and more magnificent, the need to adore.

Disperse, O Jesus, the clouds with your lightning! Show yourself to us as the Mighty, the Radiant, the Risen! Come to us once again as the Pantocrator who filled the solitude of the cupolas in the ancient basilicas! Nothing less than this

*Parousia is needed to counter-balance and dominate in our hearts the glory of
the world that is coming into view. And so that we should triumph over the
world with you, come to us clothed in the glory of the world.*

(DM, 124, 126,-128)

Receive, O Lord, this all-embracing host which your whole creation, moved by your magnetism, offers you at this dawn of a new
day.

This bread, our toil, is of itself, I know, but an immense fragmentation; this wine, our pain, is no more, I know, than a draught that
dissolves. Yet in the very depths of this formless mass you have
implanted—and this I am sure of, for I sense it—a desire, irresistible, hallowing, which makes us cry out, believer and unbeliever
alike: 'Lord, make us *one.*'

("The Mass on the World" in HM, 121)

Notes

1. 'Et civitas non eget sole neque luna . . . nam claritas Dei illuminaavit eam, et
lucerna eius est Agnus'—'and the city has no need of sun or moon . . . for the glory of
God is its light, and its lamp is the lamb' (Apoc. 21:23).

2. Rom. VIII, 38.

Chronology

1881	Pierre Teilhard de Chardin is born on May 1 at Sarcenat, France. He was the fourth child of eleven brothers and sisters.
1892–1897	He is student at the Jesuit Collège of Notre-Dame de Mongré.
1897	He receives a *baccalauréat de philosophie*.
1898	He receives a *baccalauréat de mathématiques*.
1899	On March 20, he enters the Jesuit noviciate at Aix-en-Provence.
1901	On March 25, he pronounces his first vows at Laval.
1902	He receives his *licence ès lettres*.
1902–1905	He studies philosophy at la maison Saint-Louis (Jersey).
1905–1908	He is appointed professor of chemistry and physics at le collège secondaire Jésuite de la Sainte-Famille, in Cairo. He makes several scientific excursions.
1908–1912	He studies theology at ore Place (Hastings, Sussex, England).
1911	On August 24, he is ordained priest.
1912	He starts working with the celebrated paleontologist, Marcellin Boule, in Paris.
1913	He makes a scientific excursion in Spain with l'abbé Breuil.
1914	He is mobilized to the thirteenth section of infirmary of the army.
1915–1917	He is a stretcher-bearer. He receives the military medal and the Legion of Honor.
1918	He pronounces his solemn vows at Sainte-Foy-lès-Lyon.
1919	He is demobilized.
1919–1920	He receives his certificates in Geology, Botany, and Zoology.
1922	He defends his doctoral *dissertation ès sciences,* and is appointed to a teaching position in Geology at L'Institut Catholique de Paris.
1923	He travels to China.
1924	He returns to France. He loses his teaching position at L'Institut Catholique de Paris.
1925	Beginning of an exile that lasted about 20 years.
1926	Departure to China.

1927–1928	Stay in France.
1929–1933	He takes several trips and scientific expeditions to Central Asia, the U.S.A., Hawaii, Japan, The Gobi Desert, and London. In February 1932, his father dies. In September 1932, he returns to France for four months.
1933	He travels to China and the U.S.A.
1934–1936	He travels to Tibetan border. He returns to France. He travels again to India, the Red Sea, Cashmir, and Bandung. In February 1936, his mother dies, and in August, his sister Marguerite-Marie dies.
1937–1939	He takes trips to the U.S.A., France, China, Burma, Java, and Vancouver.
1939–1946	He has a long stay in China because of World War II.
1940	He co-founds, with Father Pierre Leroy, the Geo-biologic Institute of Peking.
1943	He creates, with Father Pierre Leroy, the Geo-biology magazine, *Geobiologia.*
1946	He returns to France.
1947	He is called to Rome and is refused a position at Le College de France. On June 1, he has a heart attack.
1948	He travels to the U.S.A., then returns to France.
1949	He has pleurisy. He travels to Rome.
1950	He is elected member of L'Institut de France (Académie des sciences).
1951	He takes a trip to South Africa, then he returns to the U.S.A. where he continues to work with the Wenner Foundation in New York.
1952–1953	He takes trips to southern U.S.A. and to south Africa.
1954	He returns to France for two months. This was his last trip to his home land.
1955	On April 10, Easter Sunday in New York, Teilhard dies suddenly at the age of 74. He is buried in the Jesuit Novitiate Cemetery in Hyde Park, New York, some fifty miles away from New York City.

Bibliography

Works by Pierre Teilhard de Chardin

A. *Oeuvres de Pierre Teilhard de Chardin.* Paris: Editions du Seuil. A series of thirteen volumes which are listed below with translation information.

I.–*Le Phénomène Humain.* 1955. Eng. trans. *The Phenomenon of Man* by Bernard Wall. New York: Harper & Row, 1959.

II.–*L'Apparition de l'Homme.* 1956. Eng. trans. *The Appearance of Man* by J.M. Cohen. New York: Harper & Row, 1965.

III.–*La Vision du Passé.* 1957. Eng. trans. *The Vision of the Past* by J.M. Cohen. New York: Harper & Row, 1966.

IV.–*Le Milieu Divin.* 1957. Eng. trans. *The Divine Milieu.* New York: Harper & Row, 1960.

V.–*L'Avenir de l'Homme,* 1959. Eng. trans. *The Future of Man* by Norman Denny. New York: Haper Colophon Books, Harper & Row, 1964.

VI.–*L'Energie Humaine,* 1962. Eng. trans. *Human Energy* by J.M. Cohen. New York and London: Harcourt Brace Jovanovich, 1969.

VII.–*L'Activation de l'Energie.* 1963. Eng. trans. *Activation of Energy* by René Hague. New York and London: Harcourt Brace Jovanovich, 1970.

VIII.–*La Place de l'Homme dans la Nature.* 1965. Eng. trans. *Man's Place in Nature* by René Hague. New York: Harper & Row, 1966.

IX.–*Science et Christ.* 1965. Eng. trans. *Science and Christ* by René Hague. New York: Harper & Row, 1968.

X.–*Comment Je Crois.* 1969. Eng. trans. *Christianity and Evolution* by René Hague. New York and London: Harcourt Brace Jovanovich, 1971.

XI.–*Les Directions de l'Avenir.* 1973. Eng. trans. *Towards the Future* by René Hague. New York and London: Harcourt Brace Jovanovich, 1975.

XII.–*Ecrits du Temps de la Guerre.* 1976. (Also by Editions Bernard Grasset, 1965.) Eng. trans. *Writings in Time of War* by René Hague. London and New York: Collins and Harper & Row, 1968.

XIII.–*Le Coeur de la Matière.* 1976. Eng. trans. *The Heart of Matter* by René Hague. New York and London: Harcourt Brace Jovanovich, 1978. It contains also 5 essays first appeared in the French edition of *Ecrits du Temps de la Guerre.*

Hymne de l'Univers. Paris: Editions du Seuil, 1961. English trans. *Hymn of the Universe* by Gerald Vann, O.P.. London and New York: Collins and Harper & Row, 1965.

B. Chronology of Teilhard de Chardin's Works[*]

1913

La préhistoire et ses Progrès, II—The Progress of Prehistory, AM.

1916

La Vie cosmique, XII—Cosmic Life, WTW.

La Maîtrise du Monde et le Règne de Dieu, XII—Mastery of the World and the Kingdom of God, WTW.

Le Christ dans la Matière. Trois Histoires comme Benson, XII—Christ in the World of Matter. Three stories in the Style of Benson, HU.

1917

La Lutte contre la Multitude. Interprétation possible de la figure du Monde, XII—The Struggle against the Multitude. A Possible Interpretation of the Form of the World, WTW.

Le Milieu mystique, XII—The Mystical Milieu, WTW.

La Nostalgie du Front, XII—Nostalgia of the Front, HM.

L'Union créatrice, XII—Creative Union, WTW.

1918

L'Ame du Monde, XII—The Soul of the World, WTW.

La Grande Monade (Manuscrit trouvé dans une tranchée),XII—The Great Monad (A Manuscript Found in a Trench), HM.

L'Eternel Féminin, XII—The Eternal Feminine, WTW.

Mon Univers, XII—My Universe, HM.

Le Prêtre, XII—The Priest, WTW.

La Foi qui opère, XII—Operative Faith, WTW.

Forma Christi, XII—Forma Christi, WTW.

Note sur "L'Elément Universel" du Monde, XII—Note on the 'Universal Element' of the World, WTW.

1919

Sur la notion de Transformation créatrice, X—On the Notion of Creative Transformation, CE.

Note sur l'union physique entre l'Humanité du Christ et les fidèles au cours de la sanctification, X—Note on the Physical Union between the Humanity of Christ and the Faithful in the Course of Their Sanctification, CE.

Note pour servir à l'Evangelisation des Temps nouveaux, XII—Note on the Presentation of the Gospel in a New Age, HM.

Terre Promise, XII—The Promised Land, WTW.

L'Elément universel, XII—The Universal Element, WTW.

Les Noms de la Matière, XII—The Names of Matter, HM.

La Puissance spirituelle de la Matière, XII—The Spiritual Power of Matter, HU.

1920

Note sur l'essence du Transformisme, XIII—Note on the Essence of Transformism, HM.

Note sur le Christ-universel, IX—Note on the Universal Christ, SC.

Note sur les Modes de l'Action Divine dans l'Univers., X—Note on the Modes of Divine Action in the Universe, CE.

Chute, Rédemption et Géocentrie, X—Fall, Redemption, and Geocentrism, CE.

Note sur le Progrès, V—A Note on Progress, FM.

1921

Sur mon attitude vis-à-vis de l'Eglise officielle, XIII—On My Attitude to the Official Church, HM.

Science et Christ (ou Analyse et Synthèse). Remarques sur la manière dont l'étude scientifique de la Matière peut et doit servir à remonter jusqu'au Centre Divin, IX—Science and Christ or Analysis and Synthesis. Remarks on the way in which the scientific study of matter can and must help to lead us up to the divine centre, SC.

Les Hommes Fossiles. A propos d'un livre récent, II—Fossil Men. Reflections on a Recent Book, AM.

Comment se pose aujourd'hui la question du transformisme, III—How the Transformist Question Presents Itself Today, VP.

La Face de la Terre, III—The Face of the Earth, VP.

1922

Note sur quelques représentations historiques possibles du péché originel, X—Note on Some Possible Historical Representations of Original Sin, CE.

1923

La Messe sur le Monde, XIII—The Mass on the World, HM and HU.

Panthéisme et Christianisme, X—Pantheism and Christianity, CE.

La paléontologie et l'Apparition de l'Homme, II—Paleontology and the Appearance of Man, AM.

La Loi d'irréversibilité en évolution, III—On the Law of Irreversibility in Evolution, VP.

1924

Mon Univers, IX—My Universe, SC.

Texte sur la fin du monde, V—The End of the World, FM.

1925

L'Histore naturelle du Monde. Réflexions sur la valeur et l'avenir de la systématique, III—The Natural History of the World. Reflections on the Value and Future of Systematics, VP.

Le Paradoxe transformiste. A propos de la dernière critique du transformisme par M. Vialleton,

---

[*] Limited only to the 13 volumes of the "Oeuvres" and the *Hymne de l'Univers,* published by Editions du Seuil. Roman numbers indicate the volume of the "Oeuvres" where the essay can be found, and capital letters indicate the title of the book in its English translation.

III—The Transformist Paradox. On the Latest Criticism by M. Vialleton, VP.

L'Hominisation. Introduction à une étude scientifique du Phénomène humain, III—Hominization. Introduction to a Scientific Study of the Phenomenon of Man, VP.

1926

Sur l'Apparence nécessairement discontinue de toute série évolutive, III—On the Necessarily Discontinuous Appearance of Every Evolutionary Series, VP.

Les Fondements et le Fond de l'idée d'évolution, III—The Basis and Foundations of the Idea of Evolution, VP.

1926-27

(révisé en 1932) Le Milieu Divin, IV (en entier)—The Divine Milieu, DM.

1928

Les Mouvements de la Vie, III—The Movements of Life, VP.

Allocution pour le mariage d'Odette Bacot et jean Teilhard d'Evry, XIII—At the Wedding of Odette Bacot and Jean Teilhard d'Evry, HM.

Le Phénomène humain, IX—The Phenomenon of Man, SC.

1929

Le Sens humain, XI—The Sense of Man, TF.

1930

Que faut-il penser du Transformisme? III—What Should We Think of Transformism?, VP.

Une importante découverte de paléontologie humaine: Le Sinanthropus Pekinensis, II—Sinanthropus Pekinensis. An Important Discovery in Human Paleontology, AM.

Le Phénomène humain, III—The Phenomenon of Man, VP.

1931

L'Esprit de la Terre, VI—The Spirit of the Earth, HE.

1932

La Place de l'Homme dans la Nature, III—Man's Place in Nature, VP.

La Route de l'ouest. Vers une mystique nouvelle, XI—The Road of the West: To a New Mysticism, TF.

1933

La Signification de la Valeur contructrice de la Souffrance, VI—The Significance and Positive Value of Suffering, HE.

Le Christianisme dans le Monde, IX—Christianity in the World, SC.

L'Incroyance moderne. Cause profonde et Remède, IX Modern Unbelief. Its Underlying Cause and Remedy, SC.

Christologie et Evolution, X—Christology and Evolution, CE.

1934

L'Evolution de la Chasteté, XI—The Evolution of Chastity, TF.

Les Fouilles préhistoriques de Peking, II—The Prehistoric Excavations of Peking, AM.

Comment je crois, X—How I Believe, CE.

1935

La Faune pléistocène et l'Ancienneté de l'Homme en Amerique du Nord, II—The Pleistocene Fauna and the Age of Man in North America, AM.

Allocution pour le mariage d'Eliane Basse et d'Hervé de la Goublaye de Ménorval, XIII—At the Wedding of M. and Mme de la Goublaye de Ménorval, HM.

La Découverte du Passé, III—The Discovery of the Past, VP.

1936

Esquisse d'un Univers personnel, VI—Sketch of a Personalistic Universe, HE.

Quelques réflexions sur la conversion du Monde. A l'Usage d'un Prince de l'Eglise, IX—Some Reflections on the Conversion of the World, SC.

Sauvons l'Humanité. Réflexion sur la crise présente, IX—The Salvation of Mankind. Thoughts on the Present Crisis, SC.

1937

Le Phénomène spirituel, VI—The Phenomenon of Spirituality, HE.

La Découverte du Sinanthrope, II—The Discovery of Sinanthropus, AM.

L'Energie Humaine, VI — Human Energy, HE.

1938

Hérédité sociale et Education. Notes sur la valeur humano-chrétienne de l'enseignement, V—Social Heredity and Progress. Notes on the Human-Christian Value of Education, FM.

1938-40

(Remanié et complété en 1947 et 1948) Le Phénomène Humain, I (en entier)—The Phenomenon of Man, PM.

1939

La Grande Option, V—The Grand Option, FM.

Comment comprendre et utiliser l'Art dans la ligne de l'Energie humaine, XI—The Function of Art as an Expression of Human Energy, TF.

La Mystique de la Science, VI—The Mystic of Science, HE.

Quelques Vues générales sur l'essence du Christianisme, X—Some General Views on the Essence of Christianity, CE.

Les Unités humaines naturelles. Essai d'une Biologie et d'une Morale des races, III—The Natural Units of Humanity. An Attempt to outline a Racial Biology and Morality, VP.

L'Heure de choisir. Un sens possible de la guerre, VII—The Moment of Choice. A Possible Interpretation of War, AE.

1940

La Parole attendue, XI—The Awaited Word, TF.

1941

Réflexions sur le Progrès, V—Some Reflections on Progress, FM.

L'Atomisme de l'Esprit. Un essai pour comprendre la structure de l'étoffe de l'Univers, VII—The Atomism of Spirit. An Attempt to Understand the Structure of the Stuff of the Universe, AE.

1942

Note sur la notion de Perfection chrétienne, XI—A Note on the Concept of Christian Perfection, TF.

La Montée de l'Autre, VII—The Rise of the Other, AE.

L'Esprit nouveau. I. Le Cône du Temps. II. La Transposition "Conique" de l'Action, V—The New Spirit, FM.

Universalisation et Union: Un effort pour voir clair, VII—Universalization and Union. An Attempt at Clarifications, AE.

Le Christ évoluteur ou un développement logique de la notion de Redemption. Réflexions sur la nature de "l'Action formelle" du Christ dans le Monde, X—Christ the Evolver, or a Logical Development of the Idea of Redemption, CE.

La Place de l'Homme dans l'Univers. Réflexions sur la complexité, III—Man's Place in the Universe. Reflections on Complexity, VP.

1943

Super-Humanité, Super-Christ, Super-Charité. De Nouvelles dimensions pour l'Avenir, IX—Super-Humanity, Super Christ, Super-Charity. Some New Dimensions for the Future, SC.

La Question de l'Homme Fossile. Découvertes Récentes et Problèmes actuels, II—The Question of Fossil Man. Recent Discoveries and Present-Day Problems, AM.

Réflexions sur le Bonheur, XI—Reflections on Happiness, TF.

1944

Introduction à la Vie chrétienne. Introduction au Christianisme, X—Introduction to the Christian Life. Introduction to Christianity, CE.

La Centrologie. Essai d'une dialectique de l'Union, VII—Centrology. An Essay in a Dialectic of Union, AE.

1945

Vie et Planètes. Que se passe-t-il en ce moment sur la Terre? V—Life and the Planets. What is happening at this moment on Earth, FM.

La Morale peut-elle se passer de soubassements métaphysiques avoués ou inavoués? XI—Can Moral Science Dispense with a Metaphysical Foundation? TF.

L'Analyse de la Vie, VII—The Analysis of Life, AE.

Action et Activation, IX—Action and Activation, SC.

Christianisme et Evolution. Suggestions pour servir à une Théologie nouvelle, X—Christianity and Evolution: Suggestions for a New Theology, CE.

Un Grand événement qui se dessine: La Planétisation humaine, V—A Great Event Foreshadowed: The Planetisation of Mankind, FM.

1946

Catholicisme et Science, IX—Catholicism and Science, SC.

Quelques réflexions sur le retentissement spirituel de la bombe atomique, V—Some Reflections on the Spiritual Repercussions of the Atom Bomb, FM.

Sur les degrés de certitude scientifique de l'idée d'Evolution, IX—Degrees of Scientific Certainty in the Idea of Evolution, SC.

Esquisse d'une dialectique de l'Esprit, VII—Outline of a Dialectic of Spirit, AE.

Oecumenisme, IX—Ecumenism, SC.

1947

La Foi en la Paix, V—Faith in Peace, FM.

Une Interprétation biologique plausible de l'Histoire humaine. La Formation de la "Noosphère", V—The Formation of the Noosphere. A Plausible Biological Interpretation of Human History, FM.

Place de la technique dans une Biologie générale de l'Humanité, VII—The Place of Technology in a General Biology of Mankind, VII, AE.

La Foi en l'Homme, V—Faith in Man, FM.

L'Apport spirituel de l'Extrême-Orient. Quelques Réflexions personnelles, XI—The Spiritual Contribution of the Far East: Some Personal Reflections, TF.

Quelques Réflexions sur les Droits de l'Homme, V—Some Reflections on the Rights of Man, FM.

Evolution zoologique et Invention, III—Zoological. Evolution and Invention, VP.

Sur la valeur religieuse de la Recherche, IX—The Religious Value of Research, SC.

Le Rebondissement humain de l'Evolution et ses Conséquences, V—The Human Rebound of Evolution and its Consequences, FM.

Lettre à Emmanuel Mounier, IX—Letter to Emmanuel Mounier, SC.

Réflexions sur le péché originel, X—Reflections on Original Sin, CE.

Agitation ou Genèse? Y a-t-il dans l'Univers un axe principal d'évolution? (Un effort pour voir clair), V—Turmoil or Genesis? Is there in the Universe a Main Axis of Evolution? (An Attempt to see Clearly), FM.

1948

Trois Choses que je vois (ou: Une Weltanschauung en trois points, XI—Two Principles and a Corollary (or a Weltanschauung in Three Stages), TF.

Ma position intellectuelle, XIII — My Intellectual Position, HM.

Sur la nature du Phénomène social humain et sur ses relations cachées avec la Gravité, VII—On the Nature of the Phenomenon of Human Society, and Its Hidden Relationship with Gravity, AE.

Les Directions et les Conditions de l'Avenir, V—The Directions and Conditions of the Future, FM.

Note-mémento sur la structure biologique de l'Hmanité, IX—Note on the Biological Structure of Mankind, SC.

Comment je vois, XI—My Fundamental Vision, TF.

Titres et Travaux de Pierre Teilhard de Chardin, XIII—Qualifications, Career, Field-Work and Writings of Pierre Teilhard de Chardin, HM.

Observations sur l'Enseignement de la Préhistoire, XIII—Note on the Teaching of Prehistory, HM.

A la Base de Mon Attitude (incipit), XIII—The Basis of My Attitude, HM.

Remarque essentielle à propos du "Phénomène Humain", XIII—My 'Phenomenon of Man': An Essential Observation, HM.

Quelques Remarques sur la place et la part du Mal dans un Monde en évolution. Appendice de "Le Phénomène Humain", I—Appendix: Some Remarks on the Place and Part of Evil in a World in Evolution, PM.

Allocution pour le Mariage de Christine Dresch et Claude-Marie Haardt, XIII—At the Wedding of Christine Dresch and Claude-Marie Haardt, HM.

1949

Les Conditions psychologiques de l'Unification humaine, VII—The Psychological Conditions of the Unification of Man, AE.

Un Phénomène de contre-évolution en Biologie humaine ou la peur de l'existence, VII—A Phenomenon of Counter-Evolution in Human Biology or the Existential Fear, AE.

L'Essence de l'Idée de Démocratie. Approche biologique du problème, V—The Essence of the Democratic Idea. A Biological Approach to the Problem, FM.

Une Nouvelle Question de Galilée: oui ou non l'Humanité se meut-elle biologiquement sur elle-même? V—Does Mankind Move Biologically upon Itself? Galileo's Question Re-Stated, FM.

Le Sens de l'espèce chez l'Homme, VII—The Sense of the Species in Man, AE.

La Place de l'homme dans la Nature. Le groupe zoologique Humain, VIII (en entier)—Man's Place in Nature. The Human Zoological Group. Le Coeur du problème, V—The Heart of the Problem, FM.

La Vision du Passé. Ce qu'elle apporte à la Science et ce qu'elle lui ôte, III—The Vision of the Past. What It Brings to and Takes away from Science, VP.

1950

Sur l'existence probable, en avant de nous, d'un "Ultra-Humain" (Réflexions d'un biologiste), V—On the Probable Existence ahead of Us of an "Ultra-Human" (Reflections of a Biologist), FM.

L'Energie spirituelle de la Souffrance, VII—The Spiritual Energy of Suffering, AE.

Comment concevoir et espérer que se réalise sur Terre l'unanimisation humaine? V—How May We Conceive and Hope That Human Unanimisation Will Be Realised on Earth? FM.

Quest-ce que la Vie? IX—What Is Life? SC.

Du Préhumain à l'Ultra-Humain ou "Les Phases d'une planète vivante", V—From the Pre-Human to the Ultra-Human: The Phases of a Living Planet, FM.

Le Phénomène chrétien, X—The Christian Phenomenon, CE.

Evolution de l'idée d'évolution, III—Evolution of the Idea of Evolution, VP.

Les Australopithèques et le Chaînon manquant ou "Missing Link" de l'évolution, II—The Australopithecines and the 'Missing Link' in Evolution, AM.

L'Evolution de la responsabilité dans le Monde, VII—The Evolution of the Responsibility in the World, AE.

La Carrière Scientifique du P. Teilhard de Chardin, XIII—The Scientific Career of Pierre Teilhard de Chardin, HM.

Pour y voir clair. Réflexions sur deux formes inverses d'esprit. VII—A Clarification. Reflections on Two Converse Forms of Spirit, AE.

Le Coeur de l,a Matière, XIII—The Heart of Matter, HM.

Monogénisme et Monophylétisme. Une distinction essentielle à faire, X—Monogenism and Monophyletism: An Essential Distinction, CE.

Le Goût de vivre, VII—The Zest for Living, AE.

1951

La Structure phylétique du Groupe humain, II—The Phyletic Structure of the Human Group, AM.

Un Seuil mental sous nos pas: du Cosmos à la Cosmogénèse, VII—A Mental Threshold across Our Path: From Cosmos to Cosmogenesis, AE.

Réflexions sur la probabilité scientifique et les conséquences religieuses d'un Ultra-Humain, VII—Reflections on the Scientific Probability and the Religious Consequences of an Ultra-Human, AE.

Note sur la réalité actuelle et la signification évolutive d'une Orthogénèse humaine, III—Note on the Present Reality and Evolutionary Significance of a Human Orthogenesis, VP.

La Biologie, poussée à fond, peut-elle nous conduire à émerger dans le Transcendant? IX—Can Biology, Taken to its Extreme Limit, Enable Us to Emerge into the Transcendent, SC.

La Convergence de l'Univers, VII—The Convergence of the Universe, AE.

Quelques Remarques "Pour y voir clair" sur l'essence du sentiment mystique, XI—Some Notes on the Mystical Sense: An Attempt at Clarification, TF.

Notes de Préhistoire Sud-Africaine, II—Notes on South African Prehistory, AM.

Transformation et Prolongements en l'Homme du Mécanisme de l'Evolution, VII—The Transformation and Continuation in Man of the Mechanism of Evolution, AE.

Un Problème Majeur pour l'Anthropologie: Y a-t-il, oui ou non, chez l'Homme, prolongation et transformation du processus biologique de l'Evolution? VII—A Major Problem for Anthropology: Is there or is there not, in Man, a Continuation and Transformation of the Biological Process of Evolution? AE.

1952

Australopithèques, Pithécanthropes et Structure phylétique des Hominiens, II—Australopithecines, Pithecanthropians and the Phyletic Structure of the Hominians, AM.

Observations sur les Australopithécinés, II—Observations on the Australopithecines, AM.

La Réflexion de l'Energie, VII—The Reflection of Energy, AE.

Ce que le monde attend en ce moment de l'Eglise de Dieu: Une généralisation et un approfondissement du sens de la Croix, X—What the World Is Looking for from the Church of God at This Moment: A Generalizing and a Deepening of the Meaning of the Cross, CE.

Hominisation et Spéciation, III—Hominization and Speciation, VP.

La Fin de l'Espèce, V—The End of the Species, FM.

1953

Réflexions sur la compression humaine, VII—Reflections on the Compression of Mankind, AE.

En Regardant un cyclotron. Réflexions sur le reploiement sur soi de l'Energie humaine, VII—Reflections on the Folding-Back upon Itself of Human Energy, AE.

Contingence de l'Univers et goût humain de survivre, ou comment repenser, en conformité avec les Lois de l'Energétique, la notion chrétienne de création? X—The Contingence of the Universe and Man's Zest for Survival, or How Can One Rethink the Christian Notion of Creation to Conform with the Laws of Energetics? CE.

L'Energie d'Evolution, VII—The Energy of Evolution, AE.

Une Suite au Probléme des origines humaines. La Multiplicité des mondes habités, X—A Sequel to the Problem of Human Origins: The Plurality of Inhabited Worlds, CE.

L'Etoffe de l'Univers, VII—The Stuff of the Universe, AE.

Mes Litanies, X—My Litany, CE.

Le Dieu de l'Evolution, X—The God of Evolution, CE.

Sur la probabilité d'une bifurcation précoce du Phylum humain au voisinage immédiat de ses origines, II—On the Probability of an Early Bifurcation of the Human Phylum in the Immediate Neighbourhood of the Origins, AM.

L'Activation de l'Energie humaine, VII—The Activation of Human Energy, AE.

1954

Un Sommaire de ma perspective "Phénoménologique" du monde, XI—A Summary of My 'Phenomenological' View of the World, TF.

Les Singularités de l'Espèce Humaine, suivi d'un Apendice: Remarques complémentaires sur la Nature du Point Oméga ou de la Singularité du phénomène chrétien, II—The Singularities of the Human Species. Appendix: Complementary Remarks on the Nature of the Point Omega, or the Unique Nature of the Christian Phenomenon, AM.

Les Recherches pour la découverte des origines humaines en Afrique au sud du Sahara, II—The Search for the Discovery of Human Origins South of the Sahara, AM.

Le Phénomène Humain (Comment, au-delà d'une "Anthropologie" philosophico-juridicao-litteraire, établir une Science de l'Homme, C'est-à-dire une Anthropodynamique et une Anthropogénése?), XIII—The Phenonmenon of Man. (How Can One Go beyond a Philosophico-Juridico-Literary "Anthropology" and Establish a True Science of Man: An Anthropodynamics and an Anthropogenesis?) HM.

L'Afrique et les origines humaines, II—Africa and Human Origins, AM.

1955

Une Défense de l'Orthogénèse à propos des figures de spéciation, III—A Defense of Orthogenesis in the Matter of Patterns of Speciation, VP.

Barrière de la Mort et Co-Reflexion, ou de l'Eveil imminent de la conscience humaine au sens de son irréversion, VII—The Death-Barrier and Co-Reflection, or the Imminent Awakening of Human Consciousness to the Sense of Its Irreversibility, AE.

Le Christique, XIII—The Christic, HM.

Recherche, Travail et Adoration, IX—Research, Work, and Worship, SC.

Dernière page du journal de Pierre Teilhard de Chardin, V—Last Page of the Journal of Pierre Teilhard de Chardin. FM.

C. Letters

Lettres de Voyage (1923-1955), Paris: Bernard Grasset, 1956. Eng. trans. *Letters from a Traveller*. London and New York: Collins and Harper & Row, 1962.

Genèse d'une Pensée (Lettres, 1914-1919), Paris: Bernard Grasset, 1961. Eng. Trans. *The Making of a Mind. Letters from a Soldier-Priest (1914-1919)* by René Hague. New York: Harper & Row, 1965.

Lettres d'Egypte (1905-1908). Aubier-Montaigne, 1963.

Lettres à Léontine Zanta (1923-1939), Desclée de Brouwer, 1965. Eng. trans. *Letters to Leontine Zanta* by Bernard Wall. New York: Harper & Row, 1969.

Lettres d'Hastings et de Paris (1908-1914), Aubier-Montaigne, 1965. Eng. trans. *Letters from Hastings (1908-1912)* by Judith de Stefano. New York: Herder and Herder, 1968.

Blondel et Teilhard de Chardin (1919), Correspondance commentée par H. de Lubac. Paris: Beauchesne, 1965. Eng. trans. *Pierre Teilhard de Chardin, Maurice Blondel: Correspondence* by William

Whitman. New York: Herder and Herder, 1967.

Accomplir l'Homme: Lettres Inédites (1926-1952), Paris: Bernard Grasset, 1968. Eng. trans. *Letters to two Friends (1926-1952)*. New York: The New American Library, 1968.

Dans le Sillage des Siranthropes. Lettres Inédites de Pierre Teilhard de Chardin et J. Gunnar Anderson présentées par Pierre Leroy (1919-1934) . Fayard, 1971.

Lettres Intimes à Auguste Valensin, Bruno de Solages, Henri de Lubac, André Ravier (1919-1955), Aubier-Montaigne, 1974.

Lettres Familieres de Pierre Teilhard de Chardin Mon Ami (1948-1955), présentées par Pierre Leroy, Le Centurion, 1974.

Lettres à Jeanne Mortier. Paris: Editions du Seuil, 1984.

Lettres Inédites. Lettres à l'Abbé Gaudefroy et a l'Abbé Breuil, Le Rocher, 1988.

The Letters of Teilhard de Chardin & Lucile Swan, edited by Thomas M. Kinq, S.J., and Mary Wood Gilbert. Washington, D.C.: Georgetown University Press, 1993.

Works on the Thought of Teilhard de Chardin

Barthélemy-Madaule, Madeleine. *Bergson et Teilhard de Chardin* Paris: Editions du Seuil, 1966.

_____.*La Personne et le Drame Humain chez Teilhard de Chardin*. Paris: Editions du Seuil, 1967.

Bravo, Francisco. *La Vision de l'Histoire chez Teilhard de Chardin*. Paris: Le Cerf, 1970.

Braybrooke, Neville (ed.). *Teilhard de Chardin: Pilgrim of the Future*. New York: Seabury, 1964.

Bruteau, Beatrice. *Evolution toward Divinity: Teilhard de Chardin and the Hindu Traditions*. Wheaton: The Theosophical Publishing House, 1974.

Corbishley, Thomas.*The Spirituality of Teilhard de Chardin*. Paramus, N.J., and New York: Paulist Press, 1971.

Cousins, E.H. (ed.). *Process Theology*. New York: Newman Press, 1971.

Cuénot, Claude. (ed.). *Science and Faith in Teilhard de Chardin*. Translated by Noel Lindsey with a comment by Roger Garaudy. London: Garnstone Press, 1967.

Faricy, Robert L., S.J. *Teilhard de Chardin's Theology of the Christian in the World*. New York: Sheed and Ward, 1967.

_____. *The Spirituality of Teilhard de Chardin*. Minneapolis, MN: Winston Press, 1981.

Grau, Joseph A.. *Morality and the Human Future in the Thought of Teilhard de Chardin*. Cranbury, N.J., and London: Associated University Press, 1976.

Gray, Donald P.. *The One and the Many: Teilhard de Chardin's Vision of Unity*. New York: Herder and Herder, 1969.

King, Thomas M., S.J. *Teilhard de Chardin*. Wilmington, Delaware: Michael Glazier, 1988.

_____. *Teilhard's Mysticism of Knowing*. New York: The Seabury Press, 1981.

King, Ursula. *Towards a New Mysticism: Teilhard de Chardin & Eastern Religions*. New York: Seabury Press, 1981.

_____. *The Spirit of One Earth: Reflections on Teilhard de Chardin and Global Spirituality*. New York: Paragon House, 1989.

_____. *Christ in All Things*. Maryknoll, N.Y.: Orbis Books, 1997.

de Lubac, Henri. *The Eternal Feminine: Study of the Text of Teilhard de Chardin*. Translated by René Hague. New York: Harper & Row, Publishers, 1970.

_____. *The Religion of Teilhard de Chardin*.

Translated by René Hague. Image Books. Garden City, N.Y.: Doubleday & Co., 1968.

———. *Teilhard de Chardin: The Man and His Meaning*. Translated by René Hague. New York: Burns & Oates Ltd., 1965.

Maalouf, Jean. *Le Mystère du Mal dans l'oeuvre de Teilhard de Chardin*. Cerf, 1986.

———. *Touch a Single Leaf: Teilhard and Peace*. Mulberry Books, 1993.

———. *The Divine Milieu: A Spiritual Classic for Today and Tomorrow*. Teilhard Studies, Fall 1999.

Martin, Sister Maria Gratia, I.H.M.. *The Spirituality of Teilhard de Chardin*. New York: Newman Press, 1968.

Marving, Kessler, S.J., and Brown, Bernard, S.J. *Dimensions of the Future: The Spirituality of Teilhard de Chardin*. Washington: Corpus Books, 1968.

Mathieu, Pierre-Louis. *La Pensée Politique et Economique de Teilhard de Chardin*. Paris: Editions du Seuil, 1969.

McGurn, Sister Margaret, I.H.M.. *Global Spirituality: Planetary Consciousness in the Thought of Teilhard de Chardin and Robert Muller*. Ardsley-on-Hudson, N.Y.: World Happiness and Cooperation, 1981.

Mermod, Denis. *La Morale chez Teilhard de Chardin*. Paris: Editions Universitaires, 1967.

Mooney, Christopher F., S.J.. *Teilhard de Chardin and the Mystery of Christ*. Image Books. Garden City, N.Y.: Doubleday and Co., Inc., 1968.

Muller, Robert. *New Genesis. Shaping a Global Spirituality*. Image Books. Garden City, N.Y.: Doubleday & Co., Inc., 1984.

O'Connor, Sister Catherine R., C.S.J.. *Woman and Cosmos: The Feminine in the Thought of Pierre Teilhard de Chardin*. Englewood Cliffs, N.J.: Prentice-Hall, Inc., 1974.

Rabut, Olivier, O.P.. *Teilhard de Chardin. A Critical Study*. New York: Sheed and Ward, 1961.

Rideau, Emile. *La Pensée du Père Teilhard de Chardin*. Paris: Editions du Seuil, 1965.

Smulders, Pierre. *La Vision de Teilhard de Chardin: Essai de Réflexions Théologiques*. Paris: Desclée de Brouwer, 1965.

Wildiers, N. M.. *An Introduction to Teilhard de Chardin*. Translated by Hubert Hoskins. Fontana Books. London: Collins, 1968.

Acknowledgments

Excerpts from *Toward the Future, The Heart of the Matter, Christianity and Evolution, Activation of Energy* used with permission of Harcourt, Inc. (© 1973, 1976, 1969, 1963 by Editions du Seuil, Paris. English translations by Rene Hague, © 1975, 1978, 1971, 1970 by Harcourt, Inc.).

Excerpts from *The Divine Milieu, The Future of Man, The Phenomenon of Man* used with permission of HarperCollins Publishers, Inc. (© 1957, 1959, 1955 by Editions du Seuil, Paris. English translations ©1960 [renewed 1988], 1964, 1959 by William Collins Sons & Co., London, and Harper & Row Publishers, Inc., New York).

Excerpts from *The Making of a Mind* and *Writings in Time of War* by Pierre Teilhard de Chardin, originally published in French as *Genése d'une Pensée* and *Ecrits du Temps de la Guerre*, ©1961 and 1965 by Editions Bernard Grasset, ©1965 and 1968 in the English translation by William Collins Sons & Company Ltd., London and Harper & Row, Publishers, Inc., New York, are reprinted by permission of Georges Borchardt, Inc., for Editions Bernard Grasset.

Excerpts from *Science and Christ, Human Energy* and *The Vision of the Past* by Pierre Teilhard de Chardin, originally published in French as *Science et Christ, L'Energie Humaine* and *La Vision du Passé* ©1965, 1962, 1957 by Editions du Seuil, ©1968, 1969, 1966 in the English translation by William Collins Sons & Company Ltd., London and Harper & Row, Publishers, Inc., New York, are reprinted by permission of Georges Borchardt, Inc., for Editions du Seuil.